Winamp Hotkeys

Press This Key	To Do This
F1	See the About box
Ctrl+A	Toggle Winamp to always stay on top of the screen
Alt+W	Toggle main window on and off the screen
Alt+T	Toggle Minibrowser
Alt+S	Select skins
Ctrl+P	Go to preferences
Alt+F	Call up the main menu
J	Jump to a new song
Alt+3	Edit the current song's information
Shift+V	Fadeout and stop
C	Toggle pause of playing song
Insert	Open directory to play all its contents
Up arrow	Turn up the volume
Down arrow	Turn down the volume
F1 and click Keyboard Info tab	See more shortcuts

MP3 Compression Rates and Sound Quality

Compressing Sound at Roughly This Rate...	Results in This Quality...	At This Mode...	...And Shrinks the File By This Much
8 kHz *	Telephone sound	Mono	96:1
32 kHz	AM radio	Mono	24:1
64 kHz	FM radio	Stereo	26...24:1
96 kHz	Roughly CD	Stereo	16:1
128 kHz	Nearly indistinguishable from CD	Stereo	14...12:1

For instance, shrinking a file at a 8 kHz rate gives you telephone quality, mono sound. The file's compressed to 96 times smaller than its original size, though, making it very tiny.

Quick Tips

- ✔ To play MP3s in the car, plug a cassette adapter into your car's tape player and plug the adapter's cable into your portable MP3 player's earphone or line out jack.

- ✔ To play MP3 files on home stereos, convert them to WAV files with Winamp's built-in Nullsoft Disk Writer Plug-in. Then use CD burning software to create a music CD.

- ✔ For the latest answers to Frequently Asked Questions, head to www.mp3-faq.org/absmFAQ.txt.

MP3 For Dummies®

Best MP3 Sites for News, Software, and Music

Go Here	To Get This
www.mp3.com	MP3 songs, news, reviews, forum, links
www.rollingstone.com	Songs in all formats, news, artist encyclopedia
www.dailyMP3.com	News, files, search engines, low-price hardware searches, forum, links
www.emusic.com	News, MP3 song purchases, software, lots of Independent label connections
www.rioport.com	Songs, software, and Rio connections
www.mpeg.org	News, beginners information, lists of MP3 players, product reviews, search engines, links

MP3-Related Newsgroups

These newsgroups, discussed in Chapters 3 and 4, carry MP3 files or information about them. Not every Internet Service Provider carries every newsgroup, however, so don't be surprised if you don't find all of these in your listing.

This Newsgroup	Carries This Information
alt.binaries.sounds.mp3.1940s	Music from the 1940s
alt.binaries.sounds.mp3.1950s	Music from the 1950s
alt.binaries.sounds.mp3.1960s	Music from the 1960s
alt.binaries.sounds.mp3.1970s	Music from the 1970s
alt.binaries.sounds.mp3.1980s	Music from the 1980s
alt.binaries.sounds.mp3.1990s	Music from the 1990s
alt.binaries.sounds.mp3	One large collection of all music posted in the newsgroups from 1950s through 1990s
alt.binaries.sounds.mp3.beatles	Beatles songs
alt.binaries.sounds.mp3.bootlegs	Usually recordings of live shows
alt.binaries.sounds.mp3.brazilian	Brazilian music
alt.binaries.sounds.mp3.d	Discussion of mp3 sound files
alt.binaries.sounds.mp3.indie	Music from Independent labels
alt.binaries.sounds.mp3.novelty recordings	Comedy and novelty songs
alt.binaries.sounds.mp3.requests	Requests for MP3 songs go here
alt.binaries.sounds.mp3.video-games	Videogame-related MP3s
alt.binaries.sounds.mp3.zappa	Frank Zappa music
alt.binaries.remixes.mp3	Usually famous songs remixed by somebody else

...For Dummies®: Bestselling Book Series for Beginners

™

BESTSELLING BOOK SERIES

References for the Rest of Us! ®

Are you intimidated and confused by computers? Do you find that traditional manuals are overloaded with technical details you'll never use? Do your friends and family always call you to fix simple problems on their PCs? Then the *...For Dummies*® computer book series from IDG Books Worldwide is for you.

...For Dummies books are written for those frustrated computer users who know they aren't really dumb but find that PC hardware, software, and indeed the unique vocabulary of computing make them feel helpless. *...For Dummies* books use a lighthearted approach, a down-to-earth style, and even cartoons and humorous icons to dispel computer novices' fears and build their confidence. Lighthearted but not lightweight, these books are a perfect survival guide for anyone forced to use a computer.

> *"I like my copy so much I told friends; now they bought copies."*
>
> — Irene C., Orwell, Ohio

> *"Quick, concise, nontechnical, and humorous."*
>
> — Jay A., Elburn, Illinois

> *"Thanks, I needed this book. Now I can sleep at night."*
>
> — Robin F., British Columbia, Canada

Already, millions of satisfied readers agree. They have made *...For Dummies* books the #1 introductory level computer book series and have written asking for more. So, if you're looking for the most fun and easy way to learn about computers, look to *...For Dummies* books to give you a helping hand.

by Andy Rathbone

IDG BOOKS WORLDWIDE

IDG Books Worldwide, Inc.
An International Data Group Company

Foster City, CA ◆ Chicago, IL ◆ Indianapolis, IN ◆ New York, NY

MP3 For Dummies®

Published by
IDG Books Worldwide, Inc.
An International Data Group Company
919 E. Hillsdale Blvd.
Suite 400
Foster City, CA 94404
www.idgbooks.com (IDG Books Worldwide Web site)
www.dummies.com (Dummies Press Web site)

Library of Congress Catalog Card No.: 99-65871

ISBN: 0-7645-0585-8

Printed in the United States of America

10 9 8 7 6 5 4 3 2

1O/RS/RQ/ZZ/IN

Distributed in the United States by IDG Books Worldwide, Inc.

Distributed by CDG Books Canada Inc. for Canada; by Transworld Publishers Limited in the United Kingdom; by IDG Norge Books for Norway; by IDG Sweden Books for Sweden; by IDG Books Australia Publishing Corporation Pty. Ltd. for Australia and New Zealand; by TransQuest Publishers Pte Ltd. for Singapore, Malaysia, Thailand, Indonesia, and Hong Kong; by Gotop Information Inc. for Taiwan; by ICG Muse, Inc. for Japan; by Intersoft for South Africa; by Eyrolles for France; by International Thomson Publishing for Germany, Austria and Switzerland; by Distribuidora Cuspide for Argentina; by LR International for Brazil; by Galileo Libros for Chile; by Ediciones ZETA S.C.R. Ltda. for Peru; by WS Computer Publishing Corporation, Inc., for the Philippines; by Contemporanea de Ediciones for Venezuela; by Express Computer Distributors for the Caribbean and West Indies; by Micronesia Media Distributor, Inc. for Micronesia; by Chips Computadoras S.A. de C.V. for Mexico; by Editorial Norma de Panama S.A. for Panama; by American Bookshops for Finland.

For general information on IDG Books Worldwide's books in the U.S., please call our Consumer Customer Service department at 800-762-2974. For reseller information, including discounts and premium sales, please call our Reseller Customer Service department at 800-434-3422.

For information on where to purchase IDG Books Worldwide's books outside the U.S., please contact our International Sales department at 317-596-5530 or fax 317-596-5692.

For consumer information on foreign language translations, please contact our Customer Service department at 1-800-434-3422, fax 317-596-5692, or e-mail rights@idgbooks.com.

For information on licensing foreign or domestic rights, please phone +1-650-655-3109.

For sales inquiries and special prices for bulk quantities, please contact our Sales department at 650-655-3200 or write to the address above.

For information on using IDG Books Worldwide's books in the classroom or for ordering examination copies, please contact our Educational Sales department at 800-434-2086 or fax 317-596-5499.

For press review copies, author interviews, or other publicity information, please contact our Public Relations department at 650-655-3000 or fax 650-655-3299.

For authorization to photocopy items for corporate, personal, or educational use, please contact Copyright Clearance Center, 222 Rosewood Drive, Danvers, MA 01923, or fax 978-750-4470.

is a registered trademark under exclusive license to IDG Books Worldwide, Inc. from International Data Group, Inc.

About the Author

Andy Rathbone started geeking around with computers in 1985 when he bought a boxy CP/M Kaypro 2X with lime-green letters. Like other budding nerds, he soon began playing with null-modem adaptors, dialing up computer bulletin boards, and working part-time at Radio Shack.

In between playing computer games, he served as editor of the *Daily Aztec* newspaper at San Diego State University. After graduating with a comparative literature degree, he went to work for a bizarre underground coffee-table magazine that sort of disappeared.

Andy began combining his two interests, words and computers, by selling articles to a local computing magazine. During the next few years, Andy started ghostwriting computer books for more famous computer authors, as well as writing several hundred articles about computers for technoid publications like Supercomputing Review, CompuServe magazine, ID Systems, DataPro, and Shareware.

In 1992, *DOS For Dummies* author/legend Dan Gookin invited Andy to team up on *PCs For Dummies*. Andy then branched off on his own, writing the award-winning *Windows For Dummies* series and dozens of other *For Dummies* books, including *Upgrading & Fixing PCs For Dummies*, *Multimedia and CD-ROMs For Dummies*, *OS/2 For Dummies*, *MORE Windows For Dummies*, *Dummies 101: Windows 98*, and *Windows NT For Dummies* with Sharon Crawford.

He currently has more than 11 million copies of his books in print, which have been translated into more than 30 languages.

Andy lives with his most-excellent wife, Tina, and their cat in San Diego, California. When not writing, he fiddles with his MIDI synthesizer and tries to keep the cat off both keyboards.

ABOUT IDG BOOKS WORLDWIDE

Welcome to the world of IDG Books Worldwide.

IDG Books Worldwide, Inc., is a subsidiary of International Data Group, the world's largest publisher of computer-related information and the leading global provider of information services on information technology. IDG was founded more than 30 years ago by Patrick J. McGovern and now employs more than 9,000 people worldwide. IDG publishes more than 290 computer publications in over 75 countries. More than 90 million people read one or more IDG publications each month.

Launched in 1990, IDG Books Worldwide is today the #1 publisher of best-selling computer books in the United States. We are proud to have received eight awards from the Computer Press Association in recognition of editorial excellence and three from Computer Currents' First Annual Readers' Choice Awards. Our best-selling *...For Dummies*® series has more than 50 million copies in print with translations in 31 languages. IDG Books Worldwide, through a joint venture with IDG's Hi-Tech Beijing, became the first U.S. publisher to publish a computer book in the People's Republic of China. In record time, IDG Books Worldwide has become the first choice for millions of readers around the world who want to learn how to better manage their businesses.

Our mission is simple: Every one of our books is designed to bring extra value and skill-building instructions to the reader. Our books are written by experts who understand and care about our readers. The knowledge base of our editorial staff comes from years of experience in publishing, education, and journalism — experience we use to produce books to carry us into the new millennium. In short, we care about books, so we attract the best people. We devote special attention to details such as audience, interior design, use of icons, and illustrations. And because we use an efficient process of authoring, editing, and desktop publishing our books electronically, we can spend more time ensuring superior content and less time on the technicalities of making books.

You can count on our commitment to deliver high-quality books at competitive prices on topics you want to read about. At IDG Books Worldwide, we continue in the IDG tradition of delivering quality for more than 30 years. You'll find no better book on a subject than one from IDG Books Worldwide.

John Kilcullen
Chairman and CEO
IDG Books Worldwide, Inc.

Steven Berkowitz
President and Publisher
IDG Books Worldwide, Inc.

VIII WINNER

Eighth Annual Computer Press Awards ≥1992

IX WINNER

Ninth Annual Computer Press Awards ≥1993

X WINNER

Tenth Annual Computer Press Awards ≥1994

XI WINNER

Eleventh Annual Computer Press Awards ≥1995

IDG is the world's leading IT media, research and exposition company. Founded in 1964, IDG had 1997 revenues of $2.05 billion and has more than 9,000 employees worldwide. IDG offers the widest range of media options that reach IT buyers in 75 countries representing 95% of worldwide IT spending. IDG's diverse product and services portfolio spans six key areas including print publishing, online publishing, expositions and conferences, market research, education and training, and global marketing services. More than 90 million people read one or more of IDG's 290 magazines and newspapers, including IDG's leading global brands — Computerworld, PC World, Network World, Macworld and the Channel World family of publications. IDG Books Worldwide is one of the fastest-growing computer book publishers in the world, with more than 700 titles in 36 languages. The "...For Dummies®" series alone has more than 50 million copies in print. IDG offers online users the largest network of technology-specific Web sites around the world through IDG.net (http://www.idg.net), which comprises more than 225 targeted Web sites in 55 countries worldwide. International Data Corporation (IDC) is the world's largest provider of information technology data, analysis and consulting, with research centers in over 41 countries and more than 400 research analysts worldwide. IDG World Expo is a leading producer of more than 168 globally branded conferences and expositions in 35 countries including E3 (Electronic Entertainment Expo), Macworld Expo, ComNet, Windows World Expo, ICE (Internet Commerce Expo), Agenda, DEMO, and Spotlight. IDG's training subsidiary, ExecuTrain, is the world's largest computer training company, with more than 230 locations worldwide and 785 training courses. IDG Marketing Services helps industry-leading IT companies build international brand recognition by developing global integrated marketing programs via IDG's print, online and exposition products worldwide. Further information about the company can be found at www.idg.com.
1/24/99

Dedication

To the free spirit of MP3. Go get 'em.

Author's Acknowledgments

Thanks to Dan Gookin and his wife, Sandy; Matt Wagner; Tina Rathbone; Colleen Totz; Steve Hayes; Paula Lowell; Derek Sivers; Justin Frankel (I registered Winamp!); my Cassiopeia E-105; the cool people at Creative Labs, Diamond Multimedia, Sensory Science and MP3.com; and everybody who sent me artwork.

Publisher's Acknowledgments

We're proud of this book; please register your comments through our IDG Books Worldwide Online Registration Form located at http://my2cents.dummies.com.

Some of the people who helped bring this book to market include the following:

Acquisitions, Editorial, and Media Development

Project Editor: Colleen Totz

Acquisitions Editor: Steven H. Hayes

Copy Editor: Paula Lowell

Technical Editor: Derek Sivers

Media Development Editor: Marita Ellixson

Associate Permissions Editor: Carmen Krikorian

Editorial Manager: Mary C. Corder

Media Development Coordinator: Megan Roney

Media Development Manager: Heather Heath Dismore

Production

Project Coordinator: Maridee V. Ennis

Layout and Graphics: Amy M. Adrian, Angela F. Hunckler, Barry Offringa, Jill Piscitelli, Doug Rollison, Brent Savage, Janet Seib, Michael A. Sullivan, Brian Torwelle, Maggie Ubertini, Mary Jo Weis, Dan Whetstine

Proofreaders: Laura Albert, John Greenough, Betty Kish, Marianne Santy, Rebecca Senninger

Indexer: Liz Cunningham

Special Help
Constance Carlisle; Beth Parlon

General and Administrative

IDG Books Worldwide, Inc.: John Kilcullen, CEO; Steven Berkowitz, President and Publisher

IDG Books Technology Publishing Group: Richard Swadley, Senior Vice President and Publisher; Walter Bruce III, Vice President and Associate Publisher; Joseph Wikert, Associate Publisher; Mary Bednarek, Branded Product Development Director; Mary Corder, Editorial Director; Barry Pruett, Publishing Manager; Michelle Baxter, Publishing Manager

IDG Books Consumer Publishing Group: Roland Elgey, Senior Vice President and Publisher; Kathleen A. Welton, Vice President and Publisher; Kevin Thornton, Acquisitions Manager; Kristin A. Cocks, Editorial Director

IDG Books Internet Publishing Group: Brenda McLaughlin, Senior Vice President and Publisher; Diane Graves Steele, Vice President and Associate Publisher; Sofia Marchant, Online Marketing Manager

IDG Books Production for Dummies Press: Debbie Stailey, Associate Director of Production; Cindy L. Phipps, Manager of Project Coordination, Production Proofreading, and Indexing; Tony Augsburger, Manager of Prepress, Reprints, and Systems; Laura Carpenter, Production Control Manager; Shelley Lea, Supervisor of Graphics and Design; Debbie J. Gates, Production Systems Specialist; Robert Springer, Supervisor of Proofreading; Kathie Schutte, Production Supervisor

Dummies Packaging and Book Design: Patty Page, Manager, Promotions Marketing

◆

The publisher would like to give special thanks to Patrick J. McGovern, without whom this book would not have been possible.

◆

Contents at a Glance

Table of Contents

· ·

Introduction

● ●

*T*his book doesn't aim for digital audio engineers. It doesn't examine the evolution of musical storage from vinyl to 8-track to cassettes to CDs to minidiscs and whatever else lurks around the corner.

No, this book sticks with the fast-moving format that's caught nearly everyone off guard — MP3.

MP3 is simply another boring, compression mechanism — a pair of computerized vice-grips for sound. MP3 squeezes music files down to roughly one-tenth of their size while preserving their near-CD-quality sound.

The exciting part lies with what those MP3 files can do:

- ✔ By converting your CDs into MP3 format, you stuff hundreds of songs into your computer — without losing their sound quality. MP3 easily turns your computer into a 300-disc CD-changer for playing back songs in any order.

- ✔ MP3 technology turns your computer into a personalized radio station, broadcasting MP3 songs over the Internet.

- ✔ Pocket-sized portable MP3 players let you listen to tunes while you hit the trails. MP3 players have no moving parts, so the music doesn't skip or stutter, even if you fall off your horse.

- ✔ Thousands of bands upload free MP3 songs to the Internet. Tom Petty uploaded an MP3 song from his new CD — even before the CD had hit the stores.

- ✔ MP3 turns *you* into a record agent. Thousands of unsigned bands upload MP3 songs to the Internet, hoping you'll lend them an ear. If you like what you hear, the band sells you its CD, usually for half of record store prices.

- ✔ MP3 plays more than music; *The New York Times* releases new MP3 files daily. A narrator reads the front page while you're eating breakfast or driving to work. (Chapter 5 shows how to play MP3 files in your car.)

And the best thing about MP3? Almost every MP3 file on the Internet is free.

About This Book

Don't read this whole book cover to cover. Please pick and choose what you need. When you want to convert your CD collection to MP3 files, head for that particular chapter: Read the steps you need, and start copying the music into your computer.

Just want to set up your own MP3 radio station, and broadcast your collection of MP3 files over the Internet? Another chapter carries that information, as well as tips for finding the best MP3 stations already being broadcast.

Can't decide on a portable MP3 player? Yet another chapter reviews the market, complete with pictures of the biggest contenders and tips for getting the best sound.

Or, in case your current computer isn't beefy enough to handle the heavy demands of MP3 production or playing, you'll find detailed instructions for adding or replacing CD drives, hard drives, and Iomega Jaz drives.

Another chapter contains troubleshooting information for connecting to the Internet and configuring your browser. You'll also find out how to connect your computer to your home stereo, for extra-beefy sound.

In short, this book contains everything you need to know to create MP3s, download them, play them, store them on CDs or other formats, organize them, and even broadcast them on the Internet.

How to Use This Book

For best results, jump into Chapter 1. It explains the basics behind MP3 in easy-to-understand terms. It's perfect for people who hate reading manuals. By skimming Chapter 1, you'll quickly discover what stuff you need to know and which chapters you need to read.

Chapter 1 also lets you gauge your MP3 knowledge and confirm whether you've been hearing rumors or fact on the Internet.

Please Don't Read This!

Many computer books quickly sink into the mire of technical goo. This book wades above the goo-level by telling you everything you need to know about MP3 as quickly and as simply as possible.

Still, you may want to know what a few of those weird audio technology words mean. Complicated, engineering-level material is cordoned off in a section marked "Technical Stuff." Feel free to steer on past it and return when your mood's ready.

And What About You?

Chances are, you're a music lover. You're not necessarily a computer lover, but you know enough to get by. You're fairly new to the terms and concepts surrounding MP3, and you just need something to get you started.

When your computer mumbles something about proxy servers, and you just want to listen to that hot new band, this book shows you how to break down those barriers and get back to the good stuff.

How This Book Is Organized

Whenever we come home from the grocery store, I love packing the refrigerator. I just get a weird, Tetris-like thrill from trying to fit the tortillas, orange juice, asparagus, and everything else into the shelves and hydrators.

So it's no surprise that I've organized this book into five basic sections, each designed to serve a basic need:

Part I: What's MP3, and How Do I Use It?

Start here for the basics. Chapter 1 collects each topic from the book and explains them in simple terms. Consider it an expanded Cheat Sheet; head here when you're looking for a few memory-jogging hints.

When you need more information about that topic, you'll find an entire chapter devoted to it elsewhere in the book.

Chapter 2 shows how to upgrade your computer to MP3 standards. If you're not using a fast Pentium with a huge hard drive, or you're thinking about a CD drive that reads *and* writes, grab that credit card and a screwdriver. You'll find instructions for installing all that gear.

Part II: Downloading and Playing MP3 Files from the Internet

Okay, where *are* all these MP3 songs? This section shows you how to locate the free MP3 songs floating around the Internet (and set up your Internet browser and other utilities to ferret them out automatically). Then you discover how to play the songs on your computer or portable MP3 player.

Sick of your computer's tiny speakers? You'll find out how to connect your computer's sound card to your fancy home stereo — and what to do if that suddenly makes everything sound *worse*.

Big Fun Department: Broadcast your own MP3 Internet radio station for the bopping pleasure of your friends worldwide.

Part III: Creating Your Own MP3 Files

When you're tired of everybody else's MP3s, here's how to make your own — legally — from your own CDs, records, tapes, or even the soundtrack from a TV or VCR.

After you get the MP3-creation bug, and your hard drive begins to swell, this section shows you how to store hundreds of songs onto a single CD using a CD-RW drive.

Part IV: MP3s for the Musician

Do you play guitar in the woods? Do you fiddle around with a home studio? Or are you a band member who's tiring of the bar scene? Shower singer? This part of the book helps musicians create and record compositions, and then transform the recordings into professional-quality MP3s. Plus, it contains interviews with musicians who've used MP3s to further their career — for better or worse.

Part V: The Part of Tens

A tradition in the ...*For Dummies* books, The Part of Tens contains information organized into quick-scan lists of factoids. Here you'll find the ten best places to find MP3 files, ten ways MP3 makes you a better musician, the ten best MP3 utilities, ten MP3 rumors, and other handy tidbits.

Part VI: Appendixes

Two goodies ride back here. First, you'll find a glossary defining some of the uglier terms used by MP3 aficionados. You'll also find explanations behind the freebie CD on this book's back cover. It contains dozens of MP3 songs, and all the MP3 software you need to begin making and playing your own.

Icons Used in This Book

Computer users can't escape icons — little push buttons with pictures. Because this book is a computer book, icons seemed to fall into place. Here's what each of this book's icons mean so you can read them or quickly avoid them.

You'll find some particularly sound advice here. These tips show you how to improve your computer's sound.

If you don't remember the important items marked with this icon, you probably won't remember where to find it again, either.

Feel free to skip over this one. It marks technical stuff you really don't need to know. But if you want to travel a little deeper into the MP3 world, you can find some directions plotted out here.

A stalwart, all-purpose tip lurks here — something to make your computer work better, speed something up, or remove some of the grunt work.

You're heading into dangerous ground here. Be extra careful or something quite unpleasant might happen.

Where to Go from Here

Open Chapter 1 and give it a quick rundown. It'll either confirm what you know or tell you what you need to brush up on. Enjoy!

Part I

What's MP3 and How Do I Use It?

The 5th Wave   By Rich Tennant

GUS, THE OFFICE TINKERER, TRIES LAYING A SCAT-TRACK OVER AN MP3 FILE.

A little harder please, Gus.

In this part . . .

Early last summer, the word "mp3" surpassed "sex" as the most requested search term on the Internet. Rolling Stone and even cooler magazines talk about MP3 as the next big thing. People yak about it over the Internet and in the corners at cocktail parties. But what exactly is it?

MP3 is simply a boring technology that squishes audio files into less than 10 percent of their size while retaining nearly CD-quality sound. And the size and sound quality are the exciting parts: These tiny hi-fi computer files can be quickly copied and sent over the Internet.

Being new, MP3 confuses many people. Are MP3s *really* legal? Which are legal and which aren't? How can you tell the difference? Where are the free MP3 songs, and how can you get them? How can you play them? How can you convert your own CDs to MP3 files? And, if you're a musician, how can you record your songs and convert them to MP3?

This section explains the answers, plus some vital information you didn't know you needed to know. You'll find ways to turn your computer into an MP3 player — and one that sounds as good or better than your home stereo.

Chapter 1

Just Get Me Going!

. . . .

In This Chapter

▶ Joining the pack of MP3 users

▶ Understanding the legalities (and illegalities) of MP3

▶ Finding the best MP3 files

▶ Playing MP3 files

▶ Creating MP3 files off your CDs, records, DVD players, TV, or movie soundtracks

▶ Making your own songs into MP3 files

▶ Turning MP3 songs into normal, audio CD songs

. . . .

*T*his chapter examines the bare-bones basics of MP3 — the breakthrough format for squeezing large audio files into one-tenth their normal size. When you're ready for some meatier information, a chapter later in the book puts the information on your plate.

Dig in.

Joining the Pack of MP3 Users

Technically speaking, zillions of people now rely on MP3 technology. Although many people think MP3 can only copy or "rip" songs from CDs onto computers, the technology lends itself to many tasks.

This section describes the different ways people use MP3. You're probably familiar with many of these; the rest may give you some ideas.

Music lovers

The majority of MP3 users love music. Some MP3 files contain speeches, newspapers, sound effects, or verbal postcards, but most MP3 files are filled with music. Why?

Because musical MP3 files make the following tasks easier:

- **Creating personal radio stations:** MP3 "radio stations" allow people to listen to or create customized radio stations. Anybody with an Internet account can broadcast their MP3 collection to listeners anywhere in the world. (Tune in to Chapter 7.)

- **Finding rare songs:** Can't find an old, out-of-print song that's in the public domain? Chances are, someone has converted it to MP3 and uploaded it to the Internet for free downloading. (Chapter 3 shows how to find MP3 files.)

- **Finding new bands:** Today's record company agents don't seek musical talent as much as they look for music that *sells*, which leads to waves of newly signed bands with the same sound. Using MP3, undiscovered bands can post their songs inexpensively on the Internet, giving the public first chance to hear new talent. (Bands get their own section later in this chapter, as well as Chapters 13 through 15.)

- **Making "Greatest Hits" CDs:** With the latest batch of inexpensive CD-RW drives, computers can read from *and* write to CDs. You can convert MP3 files to a standard format and copy them to a CD for a home stereo to play. Make your own "Greatest Jazz Hits of the '50s" package! (Find out how in Chapter 11.)

- **Organizing songs:** Computers can organize a huge number of songs much better than that tall, black CD rack in the corner. How fast can you find a favorite Beastie Boys single, pull it from the case, put it in the CD player, find the song, and push the Play button? Double-clicking that MP3 file's name and hearing it play is much faster: immediate satisfaction. Plus, a CD holds only around ten songs. Your hard drive can hold thousands.

- **Playing on portable players:** Get out of the way, Sony Discman. Portable MP3 players don't have any moving parts: While wearing a Diamond Rio or Creative Labs Nomad MP3 player, skateboarders won't hear any sound skips or bumps, even when rail-sliding down the stairs at City Hall. (Chapter 6 covers the portable MP3 players.)

- **Trading bootleg recordings:** Some people make copies of their CDs and trade or give them away. If the artist hasn't authorized the distribution of those MP3 copies, these CD copiers are currently breaking the law. In fact, so are the people in possession of illegal copied MP3s. Illegal copying hurts the artist, because they no longer get paid for their work. Besides, do we really want to rip off cool people like Neil Young?

Bands

For every band on the charts, hundreds of thousands of new bands still flail away on their Stratocasters in the garage. Most new bands can barely afford beer. Without large gobs of money, bands can't distribute CDs through the music store chains or pay the marketing and advertising costs to expose people to their music. (Landing a song on *Dawson's Creek,* or any of the dozens of TV and movie soundtracks, costs a lot — and takes many connections.)

With MP3, new bands only pay to record their tunes. A bass player with a Pentium can create an MP3 song from the recording and upload it to dozens of Internet sites that showcase new talent. MP3.com, one of the leading Web sites carrying MP3 files, offers more than 100,000 songs from at least 10,000 musicians worldwide.

Bands now bypass the record labels and record chains and let millions of people hear their songs. But where's the cash? (***Hint:*** It's all described in Chapters 12 through 15.)

> ✔ **Quick "Where's the Cash?" Department:** If listeners like what they hear on MP3, they buy the band's CD through mail order. Chances are that the bass player can already create the band's CDs using his CD Read/Write drive. The band's paycheck hinges on talent and public appeal, not advertising dollar.
>
> ✔ The listeners are happy, because they're hearing fresh, new talent that they've discovered themselves. The band's happy because they can compete on merit, not cash.
>
> ✔ In fact, everybody's happy except the recording industry and music stores.

Record companies

A few savvy record companies finally realized that they can embrace MP3 technology instead of battling it. Some smaller independent labels release a few of their artists' tunes in MP3 format, then offer to sell the entire CD mail order. (Check out www.emusic.com.)

Not many have seen the light, however. The industry still thinks MP3 means they'll lose money. (Maybe they should talk to the companies who stuff free samples into our newspapers, magazines, and mail boxes.)

As more record companies realize how MP3 can be a cost-effective marketing tool, expect to hear more mainstream MP3 songs released legally on the Internet.

Disc jockeys

Toting around turntables, CD players, and boxes of records can be rough on the back of your average disc jockey. That's why many DJs now carry a laptop to work. It's easier to mix MP3 songs on a laptop and pump the results out to the dance floor.

With MP3 technology, several evening's worth of music can be stored onto the computer. The DJ can grab songs instantly, make them blend into each other, play at the same beat, and incorporate other digital tricks unavailable to their turntable predecessors.

- One of the most popular programs for the dance floor, Virtual Turntables (`carrot.prohosting.com`), replaces expensive equipment with an on-screen multichannel mixer board. Cyberknobs include fading, backspin, scratching, balance adjustment, and an automatic pitch-matching system.

- VisioSonic (`www.visiosonic.com`) not only creates MP3 DJ software, it markets a self-contained MP3 player with real control knobs, sliders, and other gizmos that keep DJs happy.

- Designed and used by disc jockeys, T.A.M.S. (Total Advanced Music System) performs similar functions. You can download a demo version of the software at `members.xoom.com/tamsmusic/web.htm`.

- MP3s are moving onto the ballfields and hockey rinks, too. PC Disc Jockey (`www.alhena-design.com/pcdj`), designed by Daniel Lewis, injects sound effects into the PA system at sporting events when the action's ebbing.

New MP3 disc jockey programs pop up all the time. To find the most current, search for the words "disc jockey" and MP3 using one of the search engines described in Chapter 3.

Print media

MP3 files aren't just filled with tunes. Check out `www.audible.com` for the latest of spoken word files. At last look, they gave away the first five chapters of John Grisham's *The Testament* — more than enough to see whether you want to buy the work.

Every day, pick up free MP3 files narrating *The New York Times,* for example, all updated daily.

The Audible site also carries MP3-format *audiobooks* with lectures, readings, and business/technology news. (I cover them in Chapter 3.)

Comedy lovers

Comedians quickly jumped on the MP3 stage. They're converting sets into MP3 format, distributing them on the Net for free, and hoping that chuckling listeners may laugh their way to the music store and buy their latest CD.

At last look, a site showed authorized stand-up comedy MP3s from George Carlin, Red Foxx, Maryellen Hooper, and John Pinette — the large guy from the last episode of *Seinfeld*. (Chapter 3 carries the scoop.)

Students

Other than listening to tunes while running to classes (or sitting in class), students use MP3 technology in another important way: Some portable MP3 players also serve as digital tape recorders, letting you record notes or even classroom lectures (if you have the professor's permission, of course).

Taking a literature class? Audible's Web site (www.audible.com) carries poems by Emily Dickinson and study guides to works like *The Great Gatsby*. Audible.com lets you download hundreds of lectures and courses from Harvard and Stanford. Some are free; others require payments.

Studying Martin Luther King Jr. or Winston Churchill? Download their speeches to hear what they *really* sounded like. You can also find foreign language tutorials.

Understanding the Legalities (And Illegalities) of MP3

The technology behind MP3 is perfectly legal. So are baseball bats, automobiles, and laser pointers. All of these things can be used illegally, however.

Standard disclaimer: Digital music issues are still being tossed around in the courts. But let's start with what's generally assumed to be legal: Downloading MP3 songs from the Internet if the artist has authorized those songs for distribution is legal.

Nobody will press charges if you make MP3 copies of your CDs, albums, and soundtracks for your own personal use.

Now, for the illegal parts. Giving away or selling any of the MP3 copies you've made from your CDs, albums, or video sound tracks is illegal. Some Web sites say downloading a bootleg CD "if you only keep it 24 hours" is okay. That's not true. It's still illegal. Just keep in mind the following points:

✔ In short, MP3 technology *is* legal, and you're encouraged to download, copy, and trade authorized MP3s. *Authorized* means the MP3 files have been approved for distribution by the artist who created them. The last section of this book lists many legitimate Web sites that carry authorized — legal — MP3s.

✔ Feel free to make your own MP3 copies from your own collection of CDs. You can even copy those MP3 songs onto another CD using your computer's CD-RW drive — as long as you don't give away or sell either the original CD or the copy you've made. If you give away the copy, you must destroy the original, or vice versa.

✔ To be perfectly clear, any time you make unauthorized copies and give them away, sell them, or post them on a Web site, you're breaking the law.

✔ Trading unauthorized MP3 songs means the record company doesn't make any money. Many consumers won't cry over that. But illegal MP3s also hurt the artist who created the work.

✔ The Recording Industry Association of America (www.riaa.com) currently says it's against the law to copy a CD to your computer's hard drive — even for your own personal use. The computer hardware industry takes an opposite view, saying it's okay to copy CDs to your hard drive for personal use. The courts are still chewing the issues.

✔ You can find more RIAA views on MP3s in Chapter 18.

Finding the Best MP3 Files

Thousands of MP3 files are scattered around the Internet. The key is to know where to look.

First, a list of Web sites appears in the back of this book; Chapter 3 shows how to locate the Internet's most current MP3 Web sites using search engines. The search engines automatically scour the Internet to locate MP3 sites and songs.

Never been to the Internet's newsgroups? It's a completely separate world from the Web, yet it's one of the easiest places to find MP3 files and information. Chapter 4 covers that area.

FTP (File Transfer Protocol) is one of the fastest and most complicated ways to find MP3 files. You need special software and a detective's cap to figure it all out. But when the switches are set correctly, it's a rocket. FTP is described in Chapters 3 and 4, as well.

Finally, Chapter 4 shows how to turn your computer into an MP3-fetching robot; it'll scour the Internet's FTP sites for MP3 files and return a list, ready to be checked out.

Check out the "Part of Tens" in the back of the book; many Web sites now review authorized MP3s uploaded by bands. By reading the reviews, you can narrow your downloads to the bands you think you'll enjoy the most.

What *is* an MP3 file, anyway?

A German research firm, the Fraunhofer Institute, developed a file compression technique back in 1991 that squeezes songs to roughly one-tenth the size of an audio CD file.

The Motion Picture Experts Group (MPEG) approved the compression technique as an Official Standard, and dubbed it "MP3-1 Audio Layer 3." Everybody else simply calls it "MP3."

Many Internet users embraced MP3 technology as a quick and convenient way to send music files back and forth through e-mail and Web sites.

Contrary to popular belief, MP3 files don't *always* contain CD-quality sound. The more you compress a file, the worse it will sound. But MP3-1 Audio Layer 3 defines a compression rate that preserves near CD-quality for sound files.

The Cheat Sheet at the front of this book compares compression rates and sound quality. The more you compress a sound file, the smaller it becomes, but the worse it sounds. (Hint: Most MP3 songs are compressed at 128Kps to preserve their high sound quality.)

So, how does MP3 technology work? When sounds are digitized, the computer grabs *all* the sound and stores it as numbers. Even if parts of the sound are beyond the range of human hearing, they're digitized anyway. (Your dog may be able to hear them.)

MP3 technology compresses the file by removing any numbers representing sounds beyond the range of human hearing. Technically, MP3 files aren't the same as a CD audio file. Realistically, however, they sound pretty darn close.

Playing and Creating MP3 Songs

You can listen to MP3 files on your computer, provided it has a sound card and speakers. For the best sound, however, connect the computer's sound-card to your home stereo, as described in Chapter 5.

Portable MP3 players, discussed in Chapter 6, are the latest toys. Clip one on your belt and bop through the grocery aisle. Many Windows CE palmtops can play MP3 files, as well.

Creating MP3 files from your own CDs

Referred to as *ripping* in the trade, this term means placing your musical CD — the latest by the Rolling Stones, for example — into your computer's disc drive and telling the software to copy a song or songs onto your hard drive. (I cover ripping in Chapter 8.)

Encoder software then compresses the large, ripped WAV file into the small MP3 format, letting you delete the original recording. (Chapter 8 covers this process.)

Some "all-in-one" software can both rip and encode. Just insert the CD, and your MP3 files appear on the hard drive.

Creating MP3 files off your records, DVDs, TV, or movie soundtracks

Find the wires that normally connect to the home stereo's amplifier and connect them to the computer's sound card. (Chapter 8 describes the adapters you'll need, where to find them, and how to route them.)

Turning your own songs into MP3 files

Musicians need to compose, record, and edit the songs — that's the hard part (see Chapter 12). Step two is recording the songs onto the hard drive and converting them to MP3 format (a process described in Chapter 13).

Copying MP3 files onto CDs

If your computer has a CD-RW drive, you can free up your hard drive by storing your MP3 files onto CDs, a process described in Chapter 11. Whereas a normal audio CD only holds about ten songs, a computer's CD can store hundreds of MP3 files.

Just insert the MP3 disc into your computer, load up your MP3 player, and start listening. Of course, if you want to listen to MP3 songs in your normal, home stereo's CD player, you need to convert them back to normal audio format, a process described in the next paragraph.

Turning MP3 files into CD-player-compatible songs

You can play back MP3 files fine on your computer and portable MP3 player. But you can't play them on your home stereo, even if they're copied to a CD with a computer's CD-RW.

Instead, you need software that reads the MP3 file and decompresses it back into the size that home stereos can recognize. Because the music files return to normal size, you can fit only the normal number of songs — ten or twelve — on the CD. I cover the process in Chapter 11.

TECHNICAL STUFF

How does MP3 differ from other formats?

Computerized sound formats vary widely in their size and sound quality.

The tamest, MIDI files, don't contain music, or any type of audio. Instead, they contain instructions for musical instruments: Which instrument should play which note at what time, and for how long. But when the instruments follow the instructions, they play a song. MIDI files sound wildly different depending on how they're played back. On a cheap sound card, you may hear a toy organ. An expensive synthesizer playing the same MIDI song could sound like ragtime piano with a stand-up bass being slapped in the background. A five-minute song averages about 40K.

The largest of the group, WAV files, contain uncompressed sound recordings. They sound the best, but a five-minute song copied from a CD averages around 50MB.

MP3 shrinks that same song to around 4.5MB, yet preserves the sound quality so that it's nearly indistinguishable from the original.

An older format, MOD, takes loops of compressed sound and repeats them to create songs. You can't record a live performance and store it in MOD format; you just build songs on a computer. Size varies wildly, but a five-minute song rarely consumes more than 40K.

RealAudio earned fame by broadcasting audio over the Internet — a process known as "streaming." RealAudio's compression system works to enhance quick streaming, not quality, so MP3 almost always sounds much better. RealAudio's MP3 contribution is RealAudio Jukebox, which turns CDs into MP3 files.

Microsoft's Audio format typifies the company's business insight. When Microsoft sees something take off, they either buy it or copy it. In this case, they hauled out their own format, got Mick Fleetwood to say it was cool at Los Angeles' House of Blues, and hoped it would kill MP3. However, Microsoft's format doesn't sound as good, and its built-in copyright protection struck a sour note with MP3 fans. Microsoft's latest version of Windows Media Player (Version 6.0 and above) plays its new Audio format and MP3. It's available at www.microsoft.com/windows/mediaplayer/default.asp.

Another format, QuickTime, started as a way for Macintosh computers to play videos, but now IBM-compatibles play the files, as well. Ending in the letters MOV, QuickTime differs from other compression techniques in that it's not proprietary — it uses industry-standard methods of streaming sound and video. That means it can be played back on just about any computer.

Yamaha, a huge music corporation, created the VQF format. Actually, VQF sounds better and creates smaller files than MP3. If your computer struggles with MP3, it'll choke on VQF, which requires a faster processor. Both formats are pretty close in sound quality and size, but MP3 is more widely accepted. Check out www.vqf.com for more info.

Finally, some sets of files end in rar or r00. These files are pieces of the shn format. Although relatively obscure, this format is gaining momentum, so head to www.softsound.com for the full scoop. (That's where you can get a copy of Shorten, which renders these files playable.)

Chapter 2

Turning Your Computer into an MP3 Machine

C an your computer keep up with MP3? After all, computers were designed for playing with numbers, not playing back Jimi Hendrix leads.

Compressing guitar riffs into MP3 files takes lots of processing power. Converting those MP3 files back into tunes also takes lots of on-the-fly oomph.

Processor power alone isn't enough. After the MP3 rush consumes you, your MP3 collection will begin clogging your hard drive. Huge hard drives will begin catching your eye at the computer store. Or maybe you'll need Iomega's solution of swappable cartridges: Iomega's Jaz system stuffs around 500 MP3s onto a single cartridge — and you can play back and record songs to and from the cartridge.

Thinking about creating audio CDs with your favorite songs? Then you'll want a CD drive that can write to compact discs as well as read from them.

This chapter's both a computer doctor and mechanic. It helps you examine your computer to see where it needs a little more muscle. Then it provides instructions for bringing it up to snuff, whether it's adding a new CPU, a hard drive, an Iomega Jaz drive, or a better sound card.

Actually, this chapter's an accountant, too. Some of these upgrades can be downright expensive, so keep this formula in mind: If your planned upgrades cost more than 60 percent of a new computer's price tag, pull out the credit card and buy a new computer. (It's what you really want, anyway.)

Computing Muscle Required for MP3

To create or play MP3s well, you need a Pentium or a very fast 486 running Windows 95, Windows 98, or Windows NT 4. Add at least 16MB RAM, a high-quality sound card, and a pair of amplified speakers.

The less powerful your PC, the longer it will take to create MP3s. Some under-powered PCs will strain during playback, adding distracting skips and pops to the music. The least powerful computers can't create MP3s; they can only play them back.

- ✔ Although IBM-compatible computers currently rule the MP3 market, they're not the only MP3-compatible computers. Apple fans can create and play MP3s on a PowerMac running System 7 or above. The Teletubbie-inspired iMacs can also make and play MP3s with their PowerPC engine.

- ✔ Some Windows CE palmtops can play back MP3 tunes, but they can't create them. Not all of these little gizmos play in stereo, either; check Chapter 21 before you buy.

- ✔ Music-loving programmers have been busy; you can find MP3 players for DOS, Windows 95, Windows 98, Macintosh, Amiga, OS/2, BeOS, Solaris, Linux, FreeBSD, SunOS, IRIX, HP-UX, AIX, and other UNIX platforms. Check out www.xaudio.com or www.mp3.com for an MP3 player that supports your specific processor.

- ✔ Programmers constantly create new programs for creating and playing MP3 files. The latest ones usually appear on www.mpeg.org, listed under Audio Players.

Do I really need a Pentium III?

A Pentium III is basically a Pentium II with some extra graphics capability. MP3 players needn't worry much about graphics, so there's little reason to worry about upgrading to a Pentium III strictly to play MP3s. A Pentium II works fine, as does a fast Pentium or Pentium Pro.

Choosing the Right CPU Upgrade for Your Computer

Upgrading a computer's Central Processing Unit or *CPU* seems easy enough. You remove the case, pull out the old chip, push in the new one, and screw the case back on. The problem is dealing with the disappointment when you first turn on the computer — doubling your computer's processing speed rarely makes it run twice as fast.

Your computer's speed depends on many things, including its amount of memory and hard drive speed (and the amount of free space left on it). Even a slow graphics card can hold back your computer's performance.

Don't be surprised if that new CPU only speeds up your computer by 25 percent. And if that new CPU doesn't increase the speed by at least 100MHz, the results probably won't be noticeable enough to warrant the upgrade.

Several companies make upgrades for your CPU; Table 2-1 shows what they offer for the price.

Table 2-1	CPU Upgrades		
This Company . . .	*and This Product . . .*	*Upgrades This to This*	*Approximate Cost*
Intel (www.intel.com)	Pentium II OverDrive processor	Upgrades 150–166MHz Pentium Pro Processor to 300–333MHz Pentium II	$599
Evergreen (www.evertech.com)	Evergreen Spectra	Upgrades 75 MHz and faster Pentiums to 400 MHz with an AMD K6-2 chip	$199
Evergreen	Evergreen MxPro	Upgrades 75MHz and higher-speed Pentium PCs to 233MHz with MMX instructions	$129
Evergreen	Evergreen 586	Upgrades 486SX, DX, SX2, and DX2 PCs to 133MHz 586	$75
Kingston (www.kingston.com)	TurboChip 366	Upgrades 166MHz chips to 366MHz AMD-K6-2	$200

(continued)

Table 2-1 *(continued)*

This Company . . .	and This Product . . .	Upgrades This to This	Approximate Cost
Kingston	TurboChip 233	Upgrades Pentium 75MHz and up to 233MHz with MMX	$130
Trinity Works (www.trinityworks.com)	PowerStacker 5x86	Upgrades 486 DX2, DX, SX2, or SX systems to four times their clock speed, up to Pentium 75MHz speed	$150
Trinity Works	PowerStacker with MMX 180 or 200MHz	Upgrades most Pentium 75/90/100/120/ 133 systems to Pentium MMX 180 or 200MHz	$350

✔ The newer the chip, the more expensive it is to upgrade. That's why it costs less to upgrade a 486 to a Pentium than it does to upgrade a slow Pentium II to a faster Pentium II.

✔ Before buying an upgrade chip for your computer, check the chip's Web site for a list of incompatible systems. The upgrade chips don't work with all computers; some come with programs to determine eligibility.

✔ If your computer is more than four years old — or if the chipmaker recommends it — make sure that your computer is running the most current BIOS available before adding the new CPU. The Web site of your computer's manufacturer usually carries a program to update a computer's BIOS.

When upgrading your computer's CPU, keep in mind the following:

✔ **Tools:** One hand, a screwdriver, and the replacement CPU's manual.

✔ **Cost:** Anywhere from $75 to $600, depending on the power.

✔ **Stuff to watch out for:** Static electricity can zap a CPU. Tap your computer's case to ground yourself before touching the CPU. If you live in a particularly dry, static-prone area, wear rubber gloves — the kind that doctors and dentists wear these days.

Follow these steps to upgrade your computer's CPU to a faster model.

1. Check the manual or the upgrade manufacturer's Web site to make sure your upgrade chip is compatible with your computer.

Installing an incompatible CPU into your computer can destroy it. Check the manufacturer's guarantees and compatibility list carefully before ordering and installing the chip.

While you're looking around in the manual and on the Web site, check to see whether you need a BIOS upgrade, as well.

2. **Unplug your computer, and remove the cover.**

   If you live in an area with static, buy a "grounding wrist strap" to fasten between your wrist and the computer's case.

   No static problem? Then just touch the case to ground yourself before starting.

3. **Find your computer's Central Processing Unit (CPU) on the motherboard.**

   Your computer's processor is usually the largest black square thing on the motherboard — the large plastic sheet everything plugs into.

4. **Remove the original processor.**

   Some chips come with a little lever. Pull the lever, and the old processor pops out, ready for replacement. Other chips need to be pried out with a little metal tool. (The cheap tools usually come inside the new CPU's box.)

   A socket with a little lever is called a Zero Insertion Force (ZIF) socket. A lever-less socket is a Low Insertion Force (LIF) socket.

5. **Examine the holes in the socket and the pins in the CPU.**

   Make sure that you're putting the right CPU into the socket. The pins and holes should line up exactly. Check the replacement CPU's instructions; chips requiring a socket with a lever won't work if there's no lever.

6. **Line up the chip's pins over the socket's holes, then gently push the processor into the socket.**

   Don't bend any pins. Please. And don't push too hard; sometimes a motherboard can crack, making you head back to the computer store and frown while buying a new one.

7. **If your new processor came with a cooling fan, install it per the installation instructions.**

   The more powerful your processor, the more it heats up. (Just ask the guy at the airport with a laptop on his lap.) Some upgrade chips need a tiny fan to keep them cool. In fact, some chips come with a fan mounted right on their backs.

8. **Close the socket handle, if necessary, screw the cover back on your computer, plug it in, and see whether it runs more quickly.**

   Hopefully, you'll notice a difference in computer speed, especially when converting all your Oily Squash CDs to MP3s.

Installing a Card

Whether you're installing a basic-level sound card or a SCSI card controller for an Iomega disk drive, the steps remain the same. And they're surprisingly easy, too. This section shows how to install a new card, whatever species it may be.

Many multimedia computers come with four speakers, ready to play back Sensurround sound. Although four speakers may sound cool for a while, Sensurround was really designed for DVD players that play back movies recorded with Sensurround. The technology doesn't really make MP3 songs sound any better.

To install a new card, keep in mind the following:

- ✔ **Tools:** One hand and a screwdriver.

- ✔ **Cost:** Anywhere from $50 to $300 and more.

- ✔ **Stuff to watch out for:** Cards are particularly susceptible to static electricity. Tap your computer's case to ground yourself before touching the card. If you live in a particularly dry, static-prone area, wear rubber gloves — the kind that make cool snapping sounds when you yank them on your fingertips.

Be careful not to bend the cards while installing them. Doing so can damage their circuitry.

Cards are pretty easy to install. They're self-contained little units. For example, they suck electricity right out of that little slot that they plug into. You don't need to plug special power cables into them. (A wire from some CD players connects to some sound cards, however, to route the sound directly to the card.)

Cards come in several different lengths and standards. Make sure to buy the right type of card for your computer. Usually the choice runs between PCI and ISA cards. (PCI slots are always shorter than ISA slots and usually white; ISA slots are always longer than PCI slots and usually black. Check your computer's manual to be sure.)

Cards are delicate. Handle them only by their edges. The oil from your fingers can damage their circuitry.

Also, those innocent silver dots on one side of the card often conceal sharp metal pokers that can leave scratches across the back of your hand.

Some cards are longer and fatter than others. You may need to rearrange some of your existing cards to accommodate new cards of different lengths and thicknesses.

To install a card, follow these steps:

1. **Turn off your computer, unplug it, and remove the cover.**

2. **Find the slot that is the right size for your card.**

   See the row of slots along the inside of your computer? Some are already filled with cards. And see the row of slots along the back of your computer, where wires plug into the backs of the cards? Your new card will plug into a slot adjacent to the other cards. A sound card's holes and ports will then be accessible from outside of the PC.

   Examine the slots closely, then examine the slots along the bottom of your card. Slots vary in size; you need one that will fit your card *exactly*.

   Don't confuse your computer's expansion slots — the ones where the cards plug in — with its much-smaller memory slots, where the RAM chips slide in.

   If you have a lot of room, keep your cards spaced as far apart as possible. Doing so keeps them a little cooler.

3. **Remove the slot's cover.**

   Unused slots have a little cover to keep dust from flying in through the back of your computer. With a small screwdriver, remove the screw that holds the cover in place. Don't lose the screw! You need it to secure the card in place.

   Dropped the screw in there "somewhere"? Turn the computer on its side and shake it gently until the screw falls out. You can't leave it inside there, or it may short-circuit something important.

   Removed the dropped screw? Keep it handy, as well as the little cover bracket. You'll want to replace the cover if you ever remove the card.

4. **Push the card into its slot.**

   To spare yourself some possible aggravation, first check your card's manual to see whether you need to flip any of the card's switches or move any of its jumpers. Then you won't have to take the card back out if it's not working right.

   Holding the card by its edges, position it over the slot, as shown in Figure 2-1. The shiny silver edge with the holes in it should face toward the *back* of your computer.

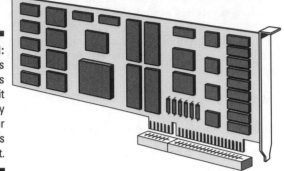

Figure 2-1: The card's two tabs should fit perfectly into your computer's slot.

Slots come in several sizes. Modern computers come with PCI slots and an occasional ISA slot. PCI slots are shorter; ISA slots are longer. Your card can only fit into one of the slots, so compare the tabs on the card's bottom with the holes in the slots.

Push the card slowly into the slot. You may need to rock it back and forth gently. When it pops in, you can feel it come to rest. Don't force it!

Don't leave any cards resting against any other cards. Doing so can cause electrical problems, and neither the card nor the computer will work.

5. Secure the card in the slot with the screw.

Yep, all those expensive cards are held in place by a single screw. Make sure that you *use* a screw, however; don't just leave the card sitting there. Cards need to be grounded to the computer's case. Without a secure connection, they may not work.

6. Plug the computer back in, turn it on, and see whether the Windows Plug and Play feature recognizes and installs the card.

Windows usually recognizes newly installed cards and sets them up to work correctly.

7. If it works, carefully put the cover back on. You're done!

If the card still doesn't work, you probably have to run the card's installation software. Still doesn't work? Then try the following:

- Check the manual to make sure that the card's switches and jumpers are set right.

- You may have to run the card's software and then reboot your computer before it will work. That's because the software puts a driver in one of your computer's special areas. Your computer reads that file only when it's first turned on or when it's rebooted.

- Make sure that the card is seated securely in its slot and screwed in reasonably tight.

- ✔ Make sure that the card's in the right slot, and that each of its copper-colored tabs fits firmly into a slot.

- ✔ It can take some fiddling to get a card working right. The key is not to get frustrated.

- ✔ Nine times out of ten, the problem lies with the software. The card is sitting in the slot correctly, but the software is conflicting with some other software or not talking with the card.

- ✔ If the card still doesn't work, root around in its box for the manual. Most manuals list a technical support phone number that you can call for help.

Installing a Larger Hard Drive

It happened ever so slowly. But suddenly, your huge, 8GB hard drive has only 500MB of free space. And you still need to convert your new Broccoli Fungus CD.

It's no secret why your hard drive suddenly shrunk. MP3 files are huge. Sure, they're compressed files, but that doesn't mean they'll fit on a floppy. The Beatles' "I Am the Walrus" eats up 4MB.

If you're turning your computer into a music player, it's time for a second hard drive. Huge, fast hard drives now cost less than ever. Best yet, most large drives come with much-appreciated installation software to start the drive spinning.

The problem comes when figuring out which type of drive to buy. Manufacturers created drives according to more than a dozen different standards over the years. Today, two standards prevail; SCSI and EIDE. Being less expensive, EIDE currently rules the market; unless you already have a SCSI drive, buy EIDE.

(By the way, EIDE stands for Enhanced Integrated Device (or Drive) Electronics. Yawn.)

Also keep in mind the following tips:

- ✔ When buying a second drive, do yourself a favor and pick up a copy of PowerQuest's PartitionMagic software at the same time. The software makes it easy to install your new hard drive as your C: drive, change your existing hard drive to your D: drive, and then copy all the information from D: to C:.

- ✔ It takes more hard drive space to create an MP3 than to merely listen to it. Converting an entire CD at once can require 500MB of space. Get the largest hard drive you can afford. Then buy one a little bit bigger.

> ✔ Before installing a second hard drive, do these chores: Back up your hard drive, and write down your CMOS settings from your computer's Setup area. (It's mentioned when your computer first boots up.) Use the Control Panel's Add/Remove Programs icon to make a Windows Startup disk. Dig around for your original Windows CD. (You may need the CD's secret password code for installation, too; it's often on a sticker on the CD case, as well as with your manual.

Installing or replacing an EIDE hard drive

Tools you need: One hand, a screwdriver, and a system disk.

Cost: Roughly $200 to $400; super-high-capacity ones can cost $600 or more.

Stuff to watch out for: If you're replacing your current hard drive, make sure that you have a system disk on hand. You need some of the programs on that disk.

Don't like fiddling around inside of computers? Most computer shops will install your new drive for around $50 in labor costs.

When installing a new drive, make it your C: drive, or *master* in computer parlance. (The master drive is the one that the computer looks at first and boots from.) The new drive will probably be faster, making Windows run faster, as well. Your old drive then becomes your secondary drive, or *slave*. You need to move a little jumper on the second drive, shown in Figure 2-2, to make that drive work as the slave.

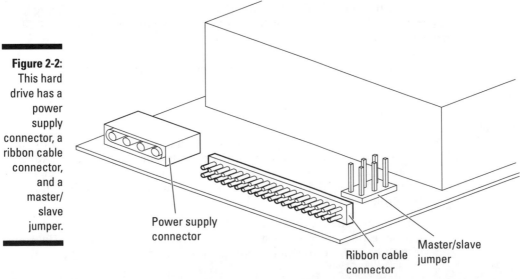

Figure 2-2: This hard drive has a power supply connector, a ribbon cable connector, and a master/slave jumper.

Power supply connector

Ribbon cable connector

Master/slave jumper

Okay, what's the complicated stuff?

If your system's more than a few years old, it may need a little preinstallation work. Most computers older than 1994 couldn't handle a hard drive much larger than 500MB. Later, the limits moved up to 2GB, then 8GB. Now, with hard drives even larger, computers face a new set of problems.

Pre-1994 computers may need both an updated BIOS and a new controller card. Newer computers may need only an updated BIOS. Sensing problems, some manufacturers bundle installation software with their hard drives, written especially to "fool" the computers into ignoring any bothersome size limits.

So, what do you do? Find out any limits your computer model places on hard drive size. Its manuals or the manufacturer's Web site may have answers. While on the Web site, download a flash BIOS update, if needed. This piece of software updates your computer's BIOS, allowing it to read and write to larger drives.

Finally, to get the most out of your fancy new EIDE UltraDMA drive, make sure your computer has a built-in UltraDMA interface. If it doesn't, buy an UltraDMA controller card (around $60) to squeeze the most performance from your new drive.

Some hard drives automatically set themselves up for one hard drive if they're set up as the master. You may have to check the drive's manual on this one.

You may need rails to mount your hard drive inside your computer. Some drives come with mounting rails; others don't. If you're replacing an old drive, you can often unscrew its old rails and swipe them. Otherwise, you may need to head back to the store to buy some. (They're usually pretty cheap.)

The following steps show you how to install a second hard drive, or replace your existing drive.

1. **Create a System floppy.**

    Insert a blank floppy disk in your A: drive, and open the Control Panel. Choose the Add/Remove Programs icon, click the Startup tab and choose Create disk.

    Without a System floppy, you may not be able to replace your old hard drive.

2. **Make sure that your current hard drive is error-free, then back up its data. Turn off and unplug your computer and remove the case.**

    Start by running the Windows ScanDisk program to ensure your hard drive is error-free. Open My Computer, right-click the drive you want to replace, and choose Properties. Click the Tools tab, and choose the Check Now button. Doing so finds and repairs errors.

Next, back up your hard drive before removing it. You don't want to lose any of your data.

Before removing your computer's case, turn it off and unplug it.

Remove the computer's case by removing the screws holding it on.

3. **Remove cables from the old drive.**

   Adding a second EIDE drive: If you're adding a second drive, *don't* remove the cables from the old drive. Instead, check out the flat ribbon cable connected to the first drive. Do you see a second, unused plug on it? If not, head back to the store for a new ribbon cable. It needs to have *two* connectors. (Most already do, luckily.) You second-drive installers can now jump ahead to Step 6.

   Hard drives have several cables plugged into them, including the following:

   Ribbon cable: The ribbon cable leads from the hard drive to its controller card or the motherboard. The cable pulls straight off the drive pretty easily.

   Power cable: The smaller cable is made of four wires that head for the power supply. Power cables come in two sizes, as shown in Figure 2-3. Like the ribbon cable, the power cable pulls straight off the drive's socket; it usually takes a *lot* more pulling, though. Don't pull on the wires themselves; pull on the cable's plastic connector. Sometimes a gentle back-and-forth jiggle can loosen it.

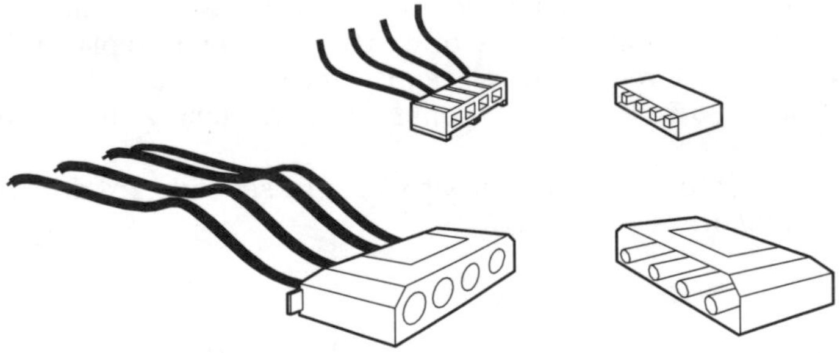

Figure 2-3:
Your hard drive uses one of these two sizes for the power cable.

4. **Remove the mounting screws holding the drive in place.**

   Some drives are held in place by two screws in front. Other drives are held in place by screws in their sides. The screws on one side may be hidden from view by a particularly long card, or even another drive mounted on its side. That means you have to pull out the card or remove the obstructing drive just to get at the screws!

5. **Slide the old drive out the computer's front.**

   After you remove the old drive's cables and screws, you can slide the old drive out of the computer. Give it a gentle tug.

Some drives slide out toward the computer's center; be sure not to gouge your motherboard while pulling out the drive.

Replacing a controller card: Will your new drive need a new controller card? Then pull out your old controller card. Look for the card where all the ribbon cables end up. Found it? Pull all the ribbon cables off, including the ones heading for your floppy drives. See that tiny screw holding the controller card in place? Remove the screw and pull the card straight up out of its slot.

6. Slide the new drive in where the old one came out.

Adding a second drive? Slide it into a vacant bay, which usually is next to the first drive. Check your computer's manual; you may be able to mount the drive on its side in a special spot inside your computer.

If you're replacing drives, your new drive should slide in place right where the old one came out. Doesn't fit? If the new drive is smaller than the old one, you need to add rails or mounting brackets to make it fit.

When handling drives, be careful not to damage their exposed circuitry by bumping it into other parts of your computer. Also, be sure to touch your computer's metal case to get rid of any static electricity before picking up your drive.

7. Add the new controller card if necessary.

Are you replacing an older drive with an UltraDMA EIDE drive? Then you may need a new controller card to go with it.

Handling the card by its edges, push it down into the slot where the old controller card sat. Then fasten it down with the screw. (You can find card installation instructions earlier in this chapter.) Check the controller's manual; you need to push ribbon cables onto the controller's connectors for your floppy disks and hard disk.

8. Attach two cables to the hard drive.

Try sliding the drive out a little bit to connect the two cables more easily. Figure 2-2 shows where each cable connects to the drive.

Ribbon cable: The plug on the ribbon cable should push onto little pins on the end of the drive. The other end of the cable goes either to the controller card or to a socket on the motherboard. (The edge of the cable with the red stripe connects to pin number one.)

If you're installing a second hard drive, the ribbon cable should have a spare connector on it. (If not, head back to the store.) It doesn't matter which connector goes onto which drive; the computer looks at the drives' master/slave jumpers to figure out which one is drive C:.

Adding a second drive: If this is your second drive, look for its master/slave jumper. Make this second drive the master drive. You can see the jumpers in Figure 2-2. The drive's manual tells you where to put the jumper. Make your old drive the slave drive.

EIDE drives usually come configured as master drives. If you're installing just a single EIDE drive in your computer, you usually don't need to mess with any of the jumpers.

Power supply: The power supply cable fits into the drive's socket only one way. Even so, check the ends to make sure that you're not forcing it in the wrong way. Check out Figure 2-2 to make sure that you've found the right power cable socket.

Power supply cables come with both large and small connectors. The connectors are supposed to fit only one way, but the small ones often fit either way. The trick? Look for the number 1 somewhere near the drive's little socket. The power supply connector's red wire fastens onto the number 1 prong.

9. **Replace the screws.**

   Cables attached? Master/slave jumper set? Then fasten the drive in place with those little screws. Make sure that they are short screws to prevent damage to the inside of the hard drive.

10. **Replace the cover, plug in the computer, and turn it on.**

    Chances are, your hard drive won't work right off the bat. Hard drives must be prepared before they start to work, unfortunately. Take a deep breath before heading for the next step. Exhale. Now move on; it's time to break in that new hard drive.

Breaking in a new hard drive

Here are the last few hoops you need to jump through before your computer starts speaking to its new hard drive. If the hard drive comes with installation software, rejoice: You may not need to mess with this stuff. Otherwise, here's the scoop:

1. **Set the CMOS.**

   When your computer starts up, it usually says to press a certain key or sequence of keys to enter its Setup program. Enter the Setup program, find the hard drives area, and set both hard drives to "Auto." If your BIOS is new enough, your computer automatically detects the two drives and sets them up correctly.

   Your computer's Setup program is where your computer keeps track of the equipment connected to it. It needs to know what kind of hard drive you installed before you can use it.

   When your computer starts up, four things can happen:

   • Some drives come with installation programs. Run the program, and everything is taken care of. In fact, some programs even copy your old drive's contents onto your second drive.

- Some drives check the CMOS to see what hard drive your computer expects to find. When you choose Auto, it automatically sets itself up to run properly. Blissfully simple! Move on to Step 2.

- Other drives let you pick *any* hard drive that's listed in your computer's CMOS table. Choose any drive that's the same capacity (in megabytes) as your new drive, and all will be fine. A bit bothersome, but still workable

- The pickiest old drives make you look for information buried in their manuals. Specifically, you need to look for the drive's recommended *cylinders, heads,* and *sectors.* Then you need to plug those numbers into your CMOS's *user-defined* area. Yeah, it's a little complicated. But if you're lucky, one of the first three options work.

2. **Partition the drive.**

Partitioning a drive completely wipes out any information stored on it.

When you finish setting the CMOS, you need to *partition* your new drive. Many drives come with a program for partitioning your new hard drive. Partitioning the drive divides it into chunks, assigning a letter to each chunk. You can divide your master drive into C: and D:, for example, assigning E: to your slave drive.

PowerQuest's PartitionMagic software, seen in Figure 2-4, lets you change your partitions later on — even if you've already installed Windows and other programs — so don't worry if you want to rearrange your partitions later.

Figure 2-4:
Power Quest's Partition-Magic software makes it easy to partition hard drives — even when they already contain information.

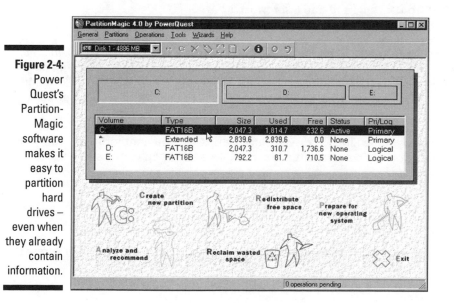

3. **Format the drive.**

The Disc wizard or drive installation programs bundled with most new EIDE drives automatically handle this as part of the installation process.

Formatting a disk completely wipes out any information stored on it.

4. **Copy your information to the new drive.**

If you replaced your drive, reinstall Windows and use the backup program to copy your old drive's information to the new drive.

If your new drive is now C: and your old drive is D:, use PowerQuest's PartitionMagic to copy everything over. (The Windows plain old "Copy" command can't handle this kind of thing.)

Installing a New Compact Disc Drive

Most CD drives created after 1998 let you make MP3s from your CDs. But to create your own CDs with your favorite MP3s, you need a CD drive that reads *and* writes to a CD.

Whether you want to install a regular CD drive or a CD-Recordable drive that writes to CDs, follow the steps later in this section.

When you install an internal CD or CD-R drive, keep the following in mind:

- ✔ **Tools:** One hand and a screwdriver.
- ✔ **Cost:** Anywhere from $50 to $300.
- ✔ **Stuff to watch out for:** Compact disc drives come in two types, *internal* and *external.* The external ones are little boxes that take up room on your desk. The internal ones slide into the front of your computer like a floppy disk. Both internal and external drives are usually either EIDE or SCSI.

Both kinds come with a card that plugs into one of your computer's slots, although some EIDE CD drives plug straight into the motherboard. You had better pop the cover and make sure that you have an empty slot before doing anything else.

To install an internal CD or CD-R drive:

1. **Turn off your computer, unplug it, and remove its case.**
2. **Plug the CD drive's card into one of your available slots and screw it down.**

Card installation gets its due earlier in this chapter.

3. **Slide the CD drive into the front of your computer.**

   You need a vacant drive bay, which is an opening where your disk drives normally live. The drive should slide in the front.

4. **Connect the cables.**

   First, connect the cable between the CD drive and the card you installed in Step 2. It should fit only one way.

   Next, rummage around the tentacles of wires leading from your power supply until you find a spare power connector and plug it into your CD drive. CD drives usually use the small-sized connector shown back in Figure 2-2.

   Finally, connect the thin audio cable from the drive to the input jack on your system's sound card.

5. **Screw the drive in place.**

   Although some drives screw in from the sides, most fasten with two screws along the front.

6. **Replace your computer's cover, plug the computer in, and turn it on.**

   When Windows boots up, it may recognize the new CD drive and automatically install it for you. If not, move to Step 7.

7. **Run the CD drive software.**

   The software should take over the rest of the installation chores and show you how to make your own CDs. (Chapter 11 covers that, as well.)

Some CD drives use SCSI ports and cards. If you don't have a SCSI card in your computer, stick with an EIDE CD drive.

If you already have a SCSI card in your computer, things can get either better or worse. Here's why:

- ✔ **The Good News:** SCSI ports can chain a handful of other SCSI devices, which means that you can connect your new CD drive into the chain. For example, if your hard drive connects to a SCSI card, you don't need the CD drive's card. Just add the CD drive into the hard drive's SCSI cable, saving time and, more importantly, a slot.

- ✔ **The Bad News:** Different brands of SCSI ports aren't always compatible with each other. Sometimes they work; sometimes they don't. Before investing in SCSI devices, call the manufacturers to be sure that the devices can all get along.

Choosing and Using an Iomega Disk

Iomega's dada-sounding Zip, Jaz, and the laptop-ready Clik drives are thick plastic disks that hold from 100MB to 2GB of information. Because they're removable, they've become the closet shoeboxes of MP3 storage.

Zip drives cost less, but they hold only 100MB. The speedy new Jaz drives shown in Figure 2-5 hold 2GB, making them the CD-burner's dream. A 2GB drive holds roughly 500 MP3s, or about 50 CDs, give or take a handful.

Figure 2-5:
The latest Jaz drives hold 2GB of storage, or about 500 MP3 songs apiece.

And they're speedy. You can play songs directly from the Jaz drive. You can even record songs to them. ("Record the baby through a microphone," brags Iomega's Web site.)

They're also expensive. But because so many people use them, they've become an industry standard.

A Jaz drive comes with very detailed installation instructions, so these steps just give you an idea of what to expect:

1. **Check your SCSI connection.**

   A Jaz drive requires a SCSI connection. You can link it to an existing SCSI card in your computer, or, lacking that, install a SCSI card for the drive. (Buy Iomega's brand of SCSI drive; it's specifically designed for the quickest file transfers.)

2. **Turn off the computer, unplug the power cord, and remove the computer's cover.**

3. **Slide the Jaz drive into an empty drive bay.**

   You may need to screw some mounting brackets onto the drive, one on each side, or the drive won't slide in correctly. (Don't screw the drive into the bay yet.)

4. **Connect a power supply cable.**

5. **Connect the SCSI cable.**

   If you already have an existing SCSI card, connect the closest connector from the wide, flat SCSI cable onto the Jaz drive. (It fits only one way.) Or, if you had to install your own SCSI card, connect the cable from the card to the Jaz drive.

   The SCSI cable has two connectors, one for your Jaz drive and the other for future devices. Attach the packaged plug to the empty port, or the drive probably won't work.

6. **Screw the Jaz drive into the drive bay.**

7. **Check your connections, and replace the computer cover.**

8. **Plug in your computer, turn it on, and insert the Jaz disk.**

9. **Insert the installation CD into your drive and run the installation program.**

   Your Jaz drive shows up as a new drive letter, waiting for you to copy information to it. Jaz drives aren't cheap, but they're fast and convenient. Let's hope somebody lets you mount a car MP3 player in the dash that takes Jaz drives. Choose from 50 CDs to match the traffic.

Part II

Downloading and Playing MP3 Files from the Internet

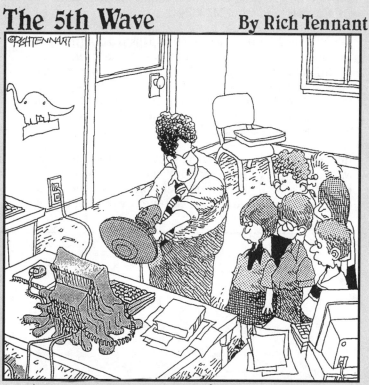

"Next time, let me know when you're going to download a 'Red Hot Chili Peppers' MP3 file."

In this part . . .

This book's first chapter contained a crash course of MP3 information — the type of stuff for people who don't have time to read entire books. The second chapter showed how to soup up your computer so it's ready to create, play, and store MP3 files.

Now it's time for the meatier stuff. This part of the book explains how to locate free MP3 files on the Internet, download them, and play them on your computer. Plus, it takes a look at the portable MP3 players that let you listen to your favorite songs while kick-boxing, parachuting, sitting on a mountain top, or simply standing more than ten feet away from your computer.

Best yet, this part of the book shows how to share your MP3 collection with the world: You can join the cutting-edge crowd who have set up their own MP3 radio station on their computer to broadcast tunes over the Internet.

Chapter 3

Finding the Best Free MP3 Files

● ●

In This Chapter

▶ Finding new MP3s from new bands

▶ Using search engines

▶ Using newsgroups

▶ Using FTP sites

▶ Finding "spoken word" MP3 files

▶ Determining which sites *don't* use MP3

● ●

he Internet is stuffed with hundreds of thousands of MP3s. Unfortunately, it's stuffed with millions of other files. How can you separate the wheat from the chaff?

Or, forgetting the breakfast cereal metaphors, where are all these darn MP3 files hiding? This chapter explains how to unleash the Internet's built-in tools to ferret them out. The next chapters show you how to download them after you locate them.

Finding Web Sites with Free MP3s from New Bands

Never tried Pleasantville Mountain Shampoo? If you had a free sample in a little plastic pack — and you were out of regular shampoo — you just might give it a try.

How about those "trial" magazine offers, where you get a free issue or two? If you hate it, you write "cancel" on the invoice, and mail it back. But if you like it, you pay the bill and keep the subscription.

Thousands of bands offer free samples of their recordings by uploading MP3 songs to the Internet. Download the MP3 song with your Web browser and give it a listen. If you hate the song, dump it or give it to a friend. If you like it, however, the band will sell you a CD full of new songs — at a price much less than you find in a music store.

That's how some of the most successful MP3 sites work. The musicians upload their songs to Web sites in the hopes that you'll like them enough to buy their CD. If you don't like them, well, nobody's lost any money.

The biggest and best MP3 site, MP3.com, offers thousands of free MP3s for downloading. Bands from all over the world upload their songs, as you can see in Figure 3-1. Choose an artist or type of music, and MP3.com shows you their offerings, ready for you to sample.

Figure 3-1:
MP3.com
offers free
MP3 songs
from bands
all over the
world.

The success of MP3.com led to many copycat sites. Many Web sites offer similar services, as shown in Table 3-1.

Table 3-1	Sites with Free and Legal MP3 Music	
Site	*Location*	*Description*
MP3.com	www.MP3.com	Try this site first. The biggest legal MP3 site, it averages more than 200,000 daily visits. It carries every type of music worldwide. Visitors have downloaded millions of songs to visitors, and the site grows daily. Contains lots of up-to-date MP3 news, hardware, software, and links to other areas.
RioPort	www.rioport.com	Created especially for Diamond's Rio portable MP3 player, this site features authorized MP3s of all genres. Dump them into your Rio, slap on the headphones, and start bopping.
Creative Labs Nomad	www.nomadworld.com	Another promo site for a portable player. Although moving along slowly, the site features downloadable MP3 music.
MusicMatch	www.musicmatch.com	MusicMatch software automatically creates MP3s from CDs in one quick step. Its Web site also features downloadable MP3s.
MP3 Box	mp3.box.sk	A fine MP3 resource from the Slovak Republic, MP3Box offers news, searches, links, and lots of general information.

Keep in mind the following when perusing MP3 sites:

- ✔ Sites in Table 3-1 carry legal MP3s. The artists have authorized the song's distribution for promotional purposes. By downloading the song and playing it — or even giving it to friends — you're not violating any copyrights. (Don't try to sell it, though.)

- ✔ Other sites aren't as discriminating. Some carry bootleg albums — illegally copied recordings intended for purchase in music stores. Still other sites carry a mix of legal and illegal files. Sometimes telling whether a song's legal or not is difficult, especially since the Grateful Dead, Billy Idol, Tom Petty, and several other artists have authorized some MP3 releases.

If you spot at least one illegal song on a Web site, chances are that site carries a lot of other illegally copied songs, too.

- ✔ Most Web sites let you download songs right from their pages; some offer links to other sites with free MP3s. Click the link — usually the underlined word — and your Web browser will take you to that site.

- ✔ When you find a good Web site that meets your needs, "bookmark" it with your browser so that you can easily find it again: Press Ctrl+D, and the site's name will appear under Bookmarks in Netscape Navigator or Favorites in Internet Express.

- ✔ To find the best new songs, search the MP3 sites and start listening. Most sites feature different new artists every week or so. You can also find recordings listed by their download rates; check out the Top 10 and Bottom 10 charts. Sample a few of each.

- ✔ Many Web sites carry links to *search engines* — programs that search the entire Internet, looking for MP3 songs. (Or other files, for that matter.) I discuss search engines in the next section.

Finding MP3s with Web Search Engines

Ever had trouble finding a misplaced book in your house? The problem increases in a library. Unless you know exactly where to look, you would never stumble upon the book you're after. That's why libraries have card catalogs and computer search systems.

The Internet's search systems are called *search engines,* and dozens of them can offer help when you search for MP3 files. Each search engine works in a slightly different way, so you often need to try two or three before finding your favorite file.

Are unsigned bands all boring?

At first thought, you may think unsigned bands are, well, boring. If they were any good, wouldn't they already be on the charts and signing deals for movie soundtracks? Nope. The music industry follows trends, hoping to make money by signing up bands that sound like the ones already on the charts. That's why the latest crop of CDs tends to sound the same.

With MP3s, you don't have to rely on a bigwig music industry exec's taste. Now, *you're* the one deciding what you like and don't like. You wear the talent agent's hat, and you can choose anything you want — even stuff that's too daring or innovative for a record company to risk releasing.

Sites like MP3.com let you thumb through the bins you'd never think of perusing at a music store. Try heading for the International section to see what kind of music people are creating in Uruguay or New Zealand. It's more fun than you may think.

The key concept here is that MP3 puts music back in the hands of you and the bands. By squeezing out the middleman, MP3 songs come without creativity filters and inflated price tags.

My favorite all-purpose search engine is `www.dogpile.com`. It searches through about 20 different search engines automatically and brings up your results from each one. If you're looking for MP3s from the Grateful Dead, for example, type **"Grateful Dead" and MP3** into the Fetch box. It should look exactly like Figure 3-2:

Figure 3-2:
Put quotes around the words `"Grateful Dead"` and add the words and MP3, just like this.

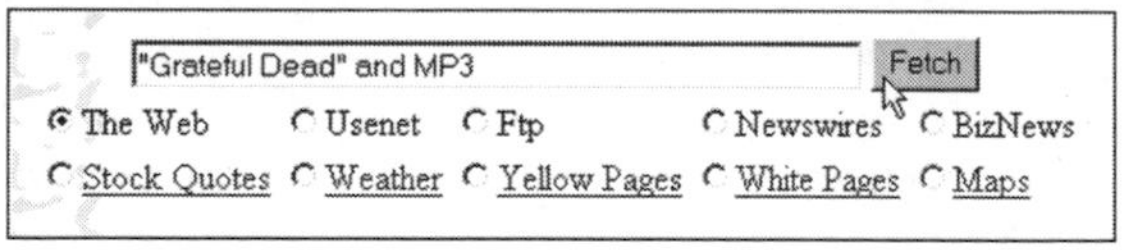

The words `Grateful Dead` should be in quotes so the computer knows to search only for those words when they appear together. The words `and MP3` tell the search engine to eliminate any Grateful Dead sites that *don't* mention the word *MP3*.

Make sure to select Dogpile's Web button, and then click the Fetch button. Dogpile compiles the results from several search engines and lists all the Web sites matching your particular search terms. The results will look something like Figure 3-3.

Scroll down the description list until you find one that claims to have Grateful Dead files. Click the site's name — it's underlined, and the search engine pulls that site onto your screen.

Check out these other search engines to locate free MP3 files for downloading. Remember, it's illegal to download copyrighted material. Stick with the songs you know are safe.

✔ As opposed to most bands, the Grateful Dead don't mind if you upload or download the band's MP3 songs. You can collect them, trade them, or even make your own CDs from them. You just can't sell them or try to make money from them. (That includes selling advertisements on a Web page that distributes them.)

✔ Dogpile remains a good bet for finding MP3s on Web pages. It can find both official and unofficial Web sites dealing with bands; some sites carry promotional MP3s.

Figure 3-3:
The Dogpile.com search engine digs through many other search engines automatically.

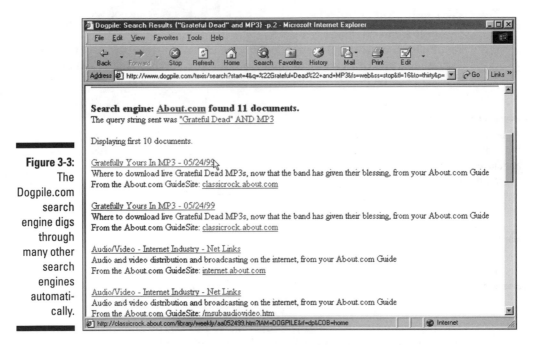

> ✔ Lycos, at `mp3.lycos.com`, caused a stir with its indiscriminate search-
> ing through the Internet for MP3 files — both legal and illegal. However,
> it's rarely accurate because most of its searches come from unverified
> FTP sites, explained a little later in this chapter.
>
> ✔ Head to `www.digMp3.com`, and click the MP3 Search button to access
> nearly ten different MP3 search engines.

Using Newsgroups in Outlook Express

One of the most esoteric — and the most reliable — ways to find MP3 files is
through newsgroups. Newsgroups work sort of like messages on a bathroom
wall. One person writes something, other people write a response, and a multi-
threaded conversation soon appears.

Those conversations appear in a special part of the Internet called *newsgroups*. And instead of merely posting words, many newsgroups exist for
people to post files and share them with the world.

Although dedicated newsgroup viewing programs like Agent
(`www.forteinc.com`) make it easy to find and download files, here's how to
make Microsoft's Outlook Express locate MP3 files (Chapter 4 shows you how
to download the files after you find them):

1. **Open Outlook Express.**

2. **Choose** <u>G</u>**o from the main menu and then choose** <u>N</u>**ew from the menu.**

3. **Right-click the word** *News* **on the bottom-right of your screen.**

   If something goes wrong up to this point, head for Chapter 4. You need
   to set up your browser so it includes News.

4. **Click the Reset List button.**

   This collects the most current list of Newsgroup topics.

5. **Type** `MP3` **into the box labeled Display newsgroups which contain, and
   press Enter.**

   A list of all the newsgroups containing MP3 appears in the box below.

6. **Select the newsgroups you would like to subscribe to, click the
   Subscribe button, and click the OK button.**

To subscribe to them all, hold down Ctrl while clicking their names. You've
now subscribed to all the Newsgroups containing MP3 files or discussions
about MP3 files.

✓ Some newsgroup postings contain messages. Just click the posting, and Outlook Express displays the words.

✓ Other newsgroup postings contain *binary* files — a file that's diced up and spread out across the several postings. That's how MP3 files are posted, and Chapter 4 shows you how to download them.

✓ Newsgroups carry lots of MP3 information posted by music lovers. Feel free to spend some time on the MP3 information groups to read the latest about MP3 players, utilities, and other MP3-related news.

✓ In addition to searching for MP3s, search for the word *dead* or other band names.

✓ The newsgroups contain some of the best and the worst of the Web. They're used by the scientists, technicians, and hobbyists as a place to gather and swap information. They're also used by pornographers and bootleggers. Stick to the files you know are legal, and avoid the ones posted illegally.

Finding MP3 Files on FTP Sites

Your computer communicates with the Internet in two very different ways. You're probably the most familiar with Web sites. Web sites use addresses like `http://www.mp3.com`.

The letters *http* stand for *hypertext transfer protocol,* which is a special way for people to put a "push-button wrapper" around the information on their Web site. Visitors click the buttons to navigate the Web site, download files, or move on to other sites.

The second method of Internet communication is called *FTP,* and it's strictly for transferring files. People simply dump files onto a site, with no easy-to-use front end. These sites have addresses that start with the letters *ftp,* usually followed by an obscure string of numbers and words like this: `ftp://123.123.123.123:21`.

Some FTP sites require passwords for entrance; others offer anonymous FTP, meaning the public can enter without having an account on the system. After they enter, they can usually download anything they see.

The person running the FTP site can shut it down at any time; some sites go up and down according to their owner's sleep schedules.

✓ FTP sites are often called servers.

✓ To find and download files from FTP sites, you need special software. Windows doesn't come with anything up to the task.

✔ You can often find FTP sites with your Internet browser. In fact, sometimes a Web site only offers downloads using FTP — the browser can't download the file. Chapter 4 explains the symptoms.

✔ Chapter 4 also explains what software to use for searching and downloading files from FTP sites.

✔ Some dedicated search programs scan the Internet for MP3 files on FTP sites. MP3Fiend (www.mp3fiend.com) for example, employs several search engines to search for a desired MP3 file. It lists the FTP address for each site containing your request, then it tries to log on to each FTP site, making sure they're up, running, and willing to let you log on and download the file. Found a valid address? (Head to Chapter 4 for information on downloading specific files from an FTP address.)

Finding "Spoken Word" MP3s

Remember, although MP3 files contain sound, they don't all contain music. Some of the most useful MP3 files contain spoken words: a person reading *The New York Times,* for example, or a stand-up comedian's routines.

You can also find entire books being read, all stored in a string of MP3 files.

Finding them is fairly easy; you'll find the best MP3s at these sites:

✔ Audible.com carries only narrated MP3 files; you can find newspapers, magazines, study guides, college lectures, and other goodies. They promise to increase the selection in the future.

✔ MP3.com also carries narrated MP3 files; you can link to Audible.com from the MP3 site.

What Are All Those Other Sound Formats?

Although MP3 is the most widely used format for storing music online, it's not the only one. The recording industry — worried that people are downloading MP3s instead of buying records — is coming up with new formats that can't be copied as easily.

Audible.com, for example, shown in Figure 3-4, stores the bulk of its "spoken word" files in a format incompatible with MP3. They sell their own portable player, the Audible MobilePlayer, for playing their files on the go. (That player doesn't support MP3, either. They've promised to convert the bulk of their files to MP3 format, but the site hasn't set a deadline.)

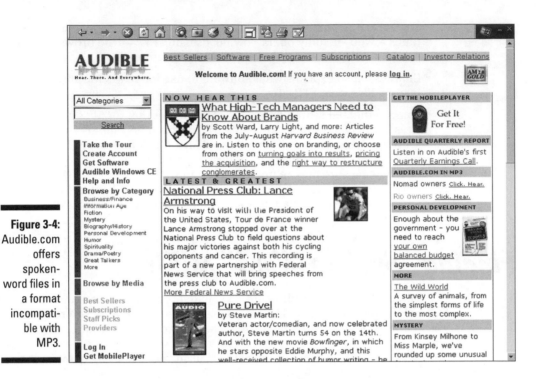

Figure 3-4:
Audible.com offers spoken-word files in a format incompatible with MP3.

LiquidAudio (www.liquidaudio.com), a distributor of commercial music, also uses its own format. When you purchase a song or CD from LiquidAudio's Web site, shown in Figure 3-5, you can then download your "Liquid Tracks" from the Web site and store them on your hard drive. Although you can play them repeatedly from your hard drive using the special Liquid Tracks software, you can copy the songs to a CD only once.

A2b music at www.a2bmusic.com uses the a2b format to sell music. After you purchase and download a song onto your computer from their site (shown in Figure 3-6), it won't play on any other computers; it must be played through its own proprietary player on your computer. Also, some free, sample songs expire after a set time. Groovy parts: Downloaded songs come with cover art, lyrics, and links to the band's Web site.

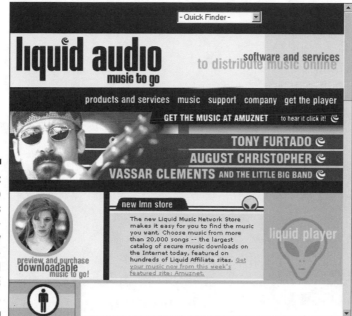

Figure 3-5:
LiquidAudio requires its own software to play music purchased through its site.

Figure 3-6:
Music purchased from A2b music can only be played on the computer that downloaded it.

Chapter 4

Downloading MP3 Files from the Internet

Chapter 3 shows you how to locate the thousands of MP3 files stuffed into the crevices of the Internet. This chapter shows you how to copy those files from the Internet to your hard drive.

Sometimes the process is simple: Just right-click the MP3 file's name, and tell your Web browser where to store the file. Other times, you may run into the abysmally elaborate procedures used by fans of FTP sites and newsgroups.

No matter which method you choose, this chapter shows you how to grab from the Internet's huge bank of MP3 files.

Don't forget to schedule a little time for your downloads, though. Even though MP3 files are one-tenth their original size, they're still pretty huge. Start the downloads, hit the sack, and listen in the morning.

Downloading MP3 Files with a Web Browser

Internet Explorer, Netscape Navigator, and just about any other Web browser can download MP3 files to your hard drive quickly and easily. Because Internet Explorer comes free with Windows 98, I cover that here.

When you spot a cool MP3 file, follow these steps to copy it onto your computer. In fact, follow these steps whenever you download *anything* onto your hard drive, including MP3 players and other utilities.

You can't get a virus from an MP3 file. (Or at least no dastardly person has figured out how to write one yet.) However, MP3 *utilities,* like any other files, can contain a virus. Check any downloaded programs with a virus checker before running them on your computer.

1. **Load Internet Explorer or Netscape Navigator and head to the desired Web page.**

   Type the Web site's address into your browser's address box, and press the Enter key.

   It's both illegal and impolite to download bootleg MP3 files. Web sites offering MP3s that have been authorized by their creators, however, are fair game.

2. **Locate the MP3 file.**

   Web sites display their downloadable MP3 files in a variety of ways. Some sites take a stark approach, displaying files by their names, date, and size, as shown in Figure 4-1.

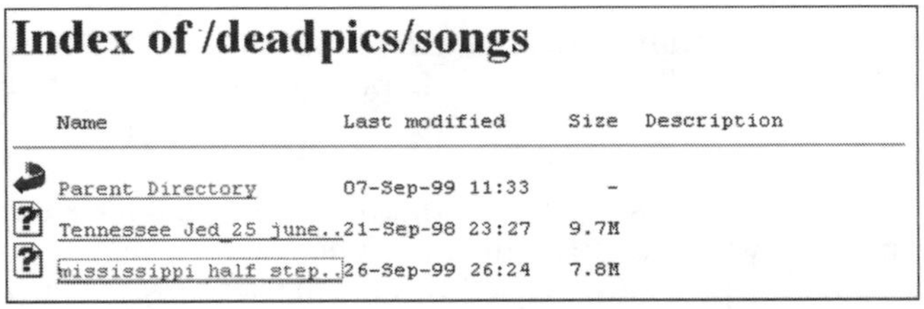

Figure 4-1:
Some Web sites arrange their MP3 files in an unpretentious list.

Index of /deadpics/songs

	Name	Last modified	Size	Description
	Parent Directory	07-Sep-99 11:33	-	
	Tennessee Jed 25 june..	21-Sep-98 23:27	9.7M	
	mississippi half step..	26-Sep-99 26:24	7.8M	

Other times, the file's name sits in the Web site itself, like in Figure 4-2.

3. **Right-click the MP3 file's name, known as its *link* in Web language.**

   When you right-click the MP3 file's name (it's usually underlined, or a different color), your browser tosses out a window similar to the one in Figure 4-3, asking you for further instructions.

4. **Choose Save Target As from the pop-up menu.**

   Choosing the Save Target As option lets you save the file to your hard drive. (Using Netscape? Then choose the Save Link As option.) The Open options, by contrast, tell your computer to begin playing the file.

Files sound best when played from your hard drive; they can lose sound quality if played straight from the Web site.

Figure 4-2: Some Web sites list their MP3 files directly on the page.

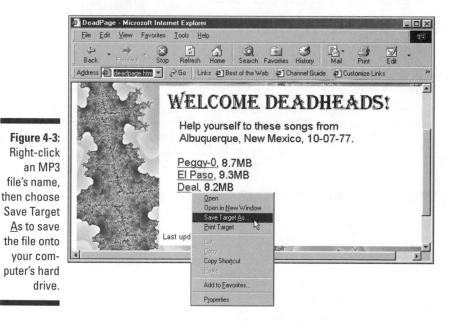

Figure 4-3: Right-click an MP3 file's name, then choose Save Target As to save the file onto your computer's hard drive.

5. **When your browser asks how to save the incoming file, as shown in Figure 4-4, create an MP3 folder (or use an MP3 folder made previously), open that folder, and click ~Save.**

To create a new folder, click the little exploding folder icon in the upper-right corner of the Save As box. A new folder appears, just waiting to be named. Name it something to describe its contents — MP3, for example — and click ~Save. The song will download from the Web site into the folder you selected.

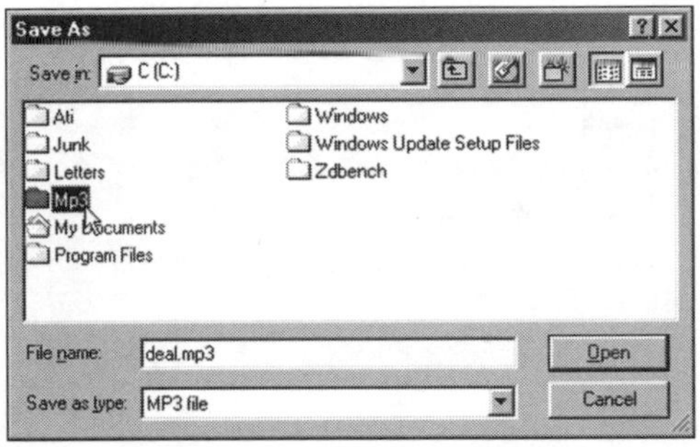

Figure 4-4:
Either
create a
new folder
to store your
MP3s, or
store your
incoming
file into an
existing
MP3 folder.

The file begins to copy onto your computer. Always helpful, your browser gauges the file's progress in a window like Figure 4-5, showing connection speed and the remaining download time.

The Web site often determines connection speed, not your modem. If the site has lots of traffic, downloads take longer, and your modem may only receive information at one-quarter of its potential.

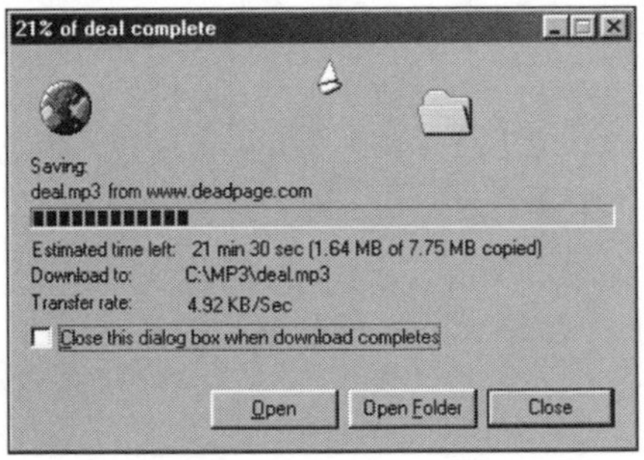

Figure 4-5:
Internet
Explorer
estimates
the amount
of down-
loading time
left, as well
as your
connection's
speed.

6. **Click OK after the program finishes downloading.**

   When you finish downloading the file, open the folder where you saved it. From there, you're ready to play it using Winamp or another MP3 player described in Chapter 5.

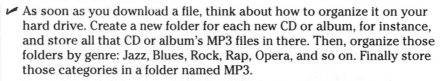

   ✔ As soon as you download a file, think about how to organize it on your hard drive. Create a new folder for each new CD or album, for instance, and store all that CD or album's MP3 files in there. Then, organize those folders by genre: Jazz, Blues, Rock, Rap, Opera, and so on. Finally store those categories in a folder named MP3.

   ✔ If a page seems to be crawling onto your screen, click your browser's Stop button and try loading the page again. Sometimes that gives your connection a kick and speeds up the connection.

   ✔ You store MP3 files on CDs in two different ways. You either store the files on a CD and play them on your computer. Or you convert the MP3 files to a different format and store them on a CD that works in your home stereo. Chapter 11 holds the briefing papers on both methods.

Troubleshooting with Your Internet Browser

Face it, Internet browsers often freak out. When you follow the downloading steps and your file doesn't appear on your hard drive, it's time to start tweaking. This section lists some of the problems you'll eventually encounter and offers a solution or two.

Instead of an MP3 file, I get an html file

This one's easy to spot. You right-click on an MP3 file, and choose the browser's Save As command. Your song appears in the box shown in Figure 4-3, but it ends with the letters htm or html instead of MP3. Your song looks like Crying_Carrots.htm, for example. Stop. Your browser jumped the gun, and the site wasn't ready to hand over the file.

Instead, the site wants you to left-click that file's name, which opens a new page of information, usually material about the song or band. The desired MP3 file is usually available for downloading on that second page. Give it another try.

My file says, "Server returned extended information"

Sometimes your MP3 file download ends in a puff of ugly smoke. Instead of downloading the file, the browser comes up with bizarre reprimands like these:

- ✔ Server returned extended information.
- ✔ The password was not allowed.
- ✔ The login request was denied.

These clues mean the Web page doesn't like to allow downloads through a mere Web browser. (The Lycos MP3 search engine is notorious for this.) Instead, the Web page is set up as an FTP site — a unique file transfer system described later in this chapter. You need a special program to download them, and it's described later in this chapter.

My file says, "A connection with the server could not be established"

This one means your file is linked to a Web page that has closed its doors. The site may be shut down temporarily while its Webmaster is picking up pizza, or perhaps the site's Internet Service Provider shut it down for offering bootleg files.

There's no way of knowing whether the site will return to life or not. Keep trying every once in a while, then give up. There are plenty of other sites out there.

Downloading MP3 Files from MP3.com

MP3.com in San Diego probably offers the largest selection of authorized MP3s from bands around the world. The site makes it easy not only to download songs, but to give them a quick listen before bothering to download the entire file.

Best yet, almost all the songs are free. If you like the band, you're free to order its CD and listen to the entire batch of songs.

When you visit MP3.com's Web page (www.mp3.com) and spot an interesting-looking MP3, the page looks like Figure 4-6.

Figure 4-6:
Depending
where you
click,
MP3.com
lets you
listen to a
song, save it
to your
computer,
or read the
lyrics.

The page offers five options, depending where you click:

- ✔ **Play:** This option immediately plays the song through your computer's speakers using your MP3 player. The file won't be saved, just played.

- ✔ **Save:** This option, shown in Figure 4-5, brings up a box that lets you choose the incoming file's location on your hard disk. After you choose a spot, MP3.com begins sending the file to its destination. The site offers one of the fastest connections.

- ✔ **Instant Play:** This option immediately plays the song, but with the RealAudio system — a format that doesn't sound as good as the other Play option. It requires its own RealAudio player, available free from www.realaudio.com.

- ✔ **Radio:** Click the band's Radio button, located next to the Radio icon beneath the band name, to hear *all* the band's songs sent to you using Instant Play. This option lets you listen to the band's chops while reading about its background.

- ✔ **Song Lyrics:** This button, it's no surprise, lets you read what that vocalist's crooning.

On your first visit to MP3, you have to fill out a short form before any of the buttons will work. The site remembers the information so you don't have to bother with it more than once.

Don't have an MP3 player? Chapter 5 evaluates the best ones on the market and explains the players included free on this book's CD.

Microsoft's Windows Media Player plays MP3 files, but not the version shipped with Windows 98. You need a version greater than 6.02, which was released April 12, 1999. (It's available at Microsoft's Web site, `www.microsoft.com` — head for the downloads section.)

Windows Media Player merely *plays* files — it doesn't save them to your hard drive. If you click on an MP3 file and Windows Media Player pops up right away to play it (as it often does in Windows 98's default setup), you're not saving the file as it plays. Windows Media Player is merely playing it. If you want to hear the MP3 song more than once, click the Cancel button and choose the Save option, instead.

Okay, Windows Media Player *does* save the file. But it renames the file with random letters and numbers and stores it in a Windows temporary directory. If you've listened to a song in Windows Media Player and you now want to save it, look for a folder starting with the letters Temp in your Windows folder. Find the newest file of a similar size to your MP3 file. Rename it to song.mp3 and see if Windows Media Player plays the song again. If so, you've found it; rename it to the correct title, and breathe a sigh of relief.

If Winamp begins playing a song when you click MP3.com's Play button, you're not saving the song, either. (Earlier versions of Winamp did this, but not the current one.)

If your browser isn't playing MP3 songs when you click the Play button, perhaps you need to choose an MP3 player. Chapter 5 helps you determine which MP3 Player Windows will automatically call into action when necessary.

Internet Newsgroups

Chapter 3 shows you how to log on to the Internet's newsgroups section; it shows how to find the MP3 newsgroups from the 30,000 other categories. But a look at the files in the MP3 newsgroups reveals something rather unsettling. The MP3 files are usually broken into small pieces — a single recording often comes spread out into 15 to 20 pieces.

Why? First, most Internet Service Providers frown when their users try to post large files onto the Internet's newsgroups. And some servers balk at any posts larger than one-half of a megabyte (500K). Because MP3 files are rather large, breaking them up and posting the pieces is an easy solution to size restrictions.

Newsgroup users download each piece of the binary file and link them back together to form the original file. Some specialized newsgroup reader programs do this automatically; so do some e-mail readers.

This section shows how to grab each piece of a newsgroup's binary file and glue them back together with Outlook Express, a program bundled with Windows 98.

MP3 files aren't the only files posted as a string of binary files on the newsgroups. Movies, music videos, and other large files suffer the same treatment.

No matter what the content, you download and recombine any type of binary file in Outlook Express by following these steps:

1. **Find the file you want to download.**

   Binary files appear as lists of files on the newsgroup; they all bear the same first name, but end in a different series of numbers, as shown in Figure 4-7.

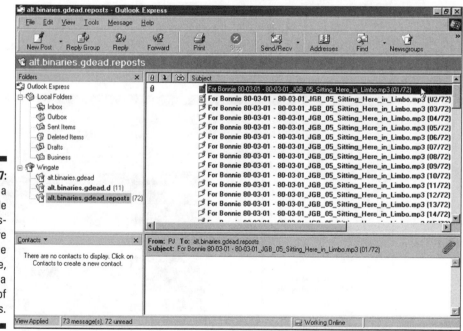

Figure 4-7: Pieces of a binary file on a newsgroup share the same first name, but end in a series of numbers.

2. Look for information about the file.

Each part of a file has a number, followed by the total number of pieces. Figure 4-7 shows the song "Sitting Here in Limbo." It's in the Grateful Dead reposts newsgroup. That means somebody had posted it already, but a fan missed the first posting, and requested that it be reposted. (Hence the newsgroup's name "reposts.")

The file names of the post seen in Figure 4-7 tells us more. "For Bonnie" means somebody named "Bonnie" requested this particular reposting. The numbers "80-03-01" mean it contains a Grateful Dead song recorded on March 1, 1980. The numbers (01/72) means the file is spread across 72 pieces. If you don't download them all and recombine them, you'll only have part of the recording.

Some postings start with the number zero rather than one. If the preceding song had a post starting with (0/72) or (00/72), that file would contain text about the post, usually describing the song, artist, and information about the recording. Although the information is helpful, it's not necessary; you don't need to combine that posting with the others in order to hear the song.

3. Select all the postings comprising the file.

In this case, click the file ending in (01/72), then, while holding down Shift, click the last file in the sequence. Outlook Express highlights all the files in the sequence (see Figure 4-8).

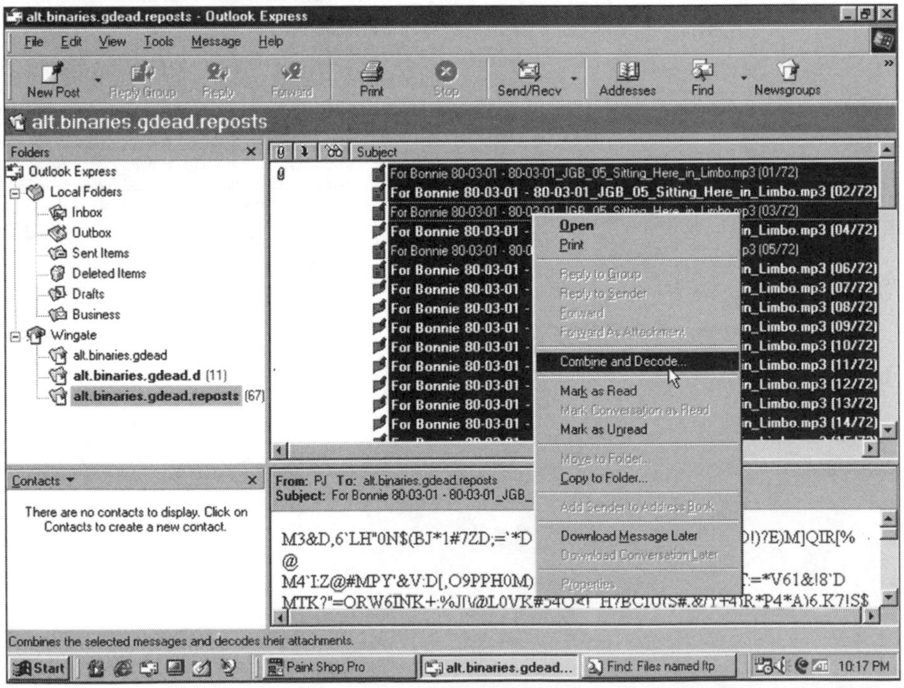

Figure 4-8: Highlight all the parts of the MP3 file listed in the newsgroup.

4. Right-click the highlighted files and choose Combine and Decode.

A window appears, asking you to drag the messages into numerical order, as shown in Figure 4-9.

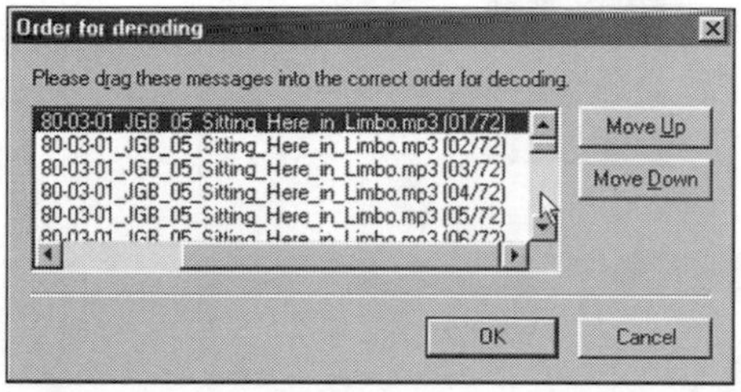

Figure 4-9:
Drag the
messages
into their
correct
numerical
order so
that the
song plays
back in the
correct
sequence.

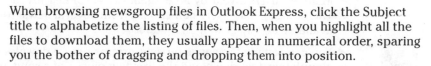

5. Arrange the selected files into numerical order.

When the Order for decoding window pops up, drag and drop the listed files until they're in the proper numerical sequence, from number one until the end.

When browsing newsgroup files in Outlook Express, click the Subject title to alphabetize the listing of files. Then, when you highlight all the files to download them, they usually appear in numerical order, sparing you the bother of dragging and dropping them into position.

Some people mess up a file name's numbers when posting. For example, their first post would be 1/72 instead of 01/72, and the second would be 2/72 instead of 02/72. Big deal? Actually, it is. When the computer sorts files numerically, it starts with 1/72, then jumps to 11/72, 12/72, and so on. If the first nine posts don't have a zero in front of their number, they are out of order, and you have to drag and drop them into their correct numerical order before combining them.

6. Press OK.

Outlook Express downloads, sorts, and squishes together all the file pieces. The file is then listed as an "attachment" to a message.

7. Right-click the file's name, choose Save As, and save your file.

The file shown in Figure 4-10 isn't officially downloaded until you save it. So either choose Save As from the File menu, or right-click the file's name and choose Save As. Choose a location for the file, and save it there.

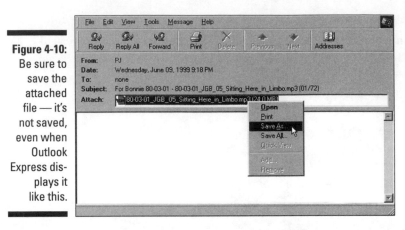

Figure 4-10:
Be sure to
save the
attached
file — it's
not saved,
even when
Outlook
Express dis-
plays it
like this.

✔ Please don't forget Step 7. The file looks as if Outlook Express downloaded and saved the file, but the file's not saved to your hard drive. If
you close that piece of e-mail without saving it, it's gone. (You can download it again, so you've lost nothing but time.)

✔ Although Outlook Express can handle newsgroup chores, it's no skilled
technician. Several third-party programs specialize in newsgroups,
whether organizing messages or downloading and reassembling binary
files with a single click.

✔ Many PC users swear by Free Agent (www.forteinc.com/agent/
index.htm). Mac users can choose from several newsgroup programs
available at www.macorchard.com/.

✔ You can sample the songs on newsgroups before downloading them
completely. Just download the first few pieces of a song, put them in
numerical order, and save the result. Winamp will play only the short
portion of the song you've downloaded.

Downloading MP3 Files from America Online

America Online users aren't shut out of the fun. If you use America Online,
you can download files from Web sites with your Internet browser using the
same steps described in the "Downloading Files with a Web Browser" section
earlier in this chapter.

To retrieve binary files from newsgroups, use America Online's Filegrabber
utility to download the files and put them back together. Here's a brief
rundown:

1. **Log on to America Online, type in the keyword** Newsgroup **and press Enter.**

   The Internet Newsgroups window appears.

2. **Click the Search All Newsgroups button.**

3. **Search for words describing your interests.**

   Type in dead for Grateful Dead, for example, and press Enter. When the Search box reveals all newsgroups mentioning the word *dead,* double-click the desired newsgroup. In this case, double-click alt.binaries.gdead to find the binary files containing MP3 songs.

4. **When the box appears, click Subscribe to newsgroup** alt.binaries.gdead.

   AOL subscribes you to the alt.binaries.gdead newsgroup — or whatever newsgroup you've searched for in Step 3.

5. **Click the Preferences button and select the box marked Show only complete binary files which AOL can automatically download and decode.**

   Clicking that button makes AOL take a look at the newsgroup, decide what files it recognizes, and display those files.

6. **Click the Save button to save your preferences.**

7. **Double-click any one of the listed pieces of a particular song.**

   Binary files are stored in pieces, as described in this chapter's "Downloading from Internet Newsgroups section." When you double-click any piece of the song, a box appears. If the box contains a button saying Download File, you're in luck. If it doesn't say that, America Online won't automatically download the file. Move on to another one.

8. **Click the Download File button.**

9. **Save the incoming file in a folder on your hard drive.**

   Choose a folder on your hard drive and click Save to begin the download.

10. **Play the file with an MP3 player.**

If all goes well, following these steps brings MP3 files to your hard drive. However, America Online isn't the most reliable or easiest-to-use source for MP3 files. Here are some problems you may run into:

✔ If you don't see the words **Download File** in Step 7, you can't download the file automatically. Also, don't choose the Download Message button, or the file won't download correctly.

✔ America Online's software sometimes won't recognize all parts of a particularly large posting. If you simply *must* have that file, you can manually download each individual piece of the file yourself. Then use a third-party program to combine and decode them yourself.

✔ When first installed, America Online automatically blocks binary downloads as part of its Parental Control feature. (Some binary files contain naughty pictures.) Whoever holds the master account for AOL needs to head for the Parental Control area and uncheck the Block Binary Downloads box.

✔ Still confused? Head for the `aol.newsgroups.help` newsgroup and look for a posting marked FAQ. That stands for Frequently Asked Questions, and the file answers questions about retrieving files from America Online's selection of newsgroups.

Downloading MP3 Files from an FTP Site

Chapter 3 explained how FTP allows people to copy files across the Internet without using an Internet browser. Instead, a grunt-worker FTP program grabs the files and copies them to your computer.

Windows 98 comes with a simplistic FTP program, shown in Figure 4-11, but you'll want a third-party FTP program to handle the chores. CuteFTP or WS_FTP fit the bill nicely.

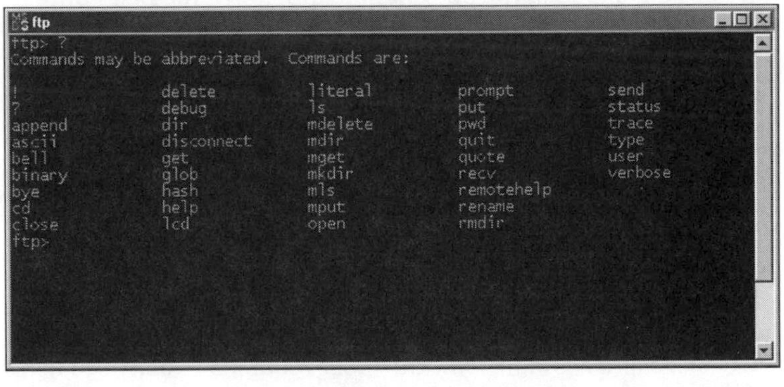

Figure 4-11: The Windows 98 built-in FTP program isn't very user-friendly.

Before telling a program to download an FTP file, dissect the FTP address's vitals, as described below.

An FTP site that's listed like this — **ftp://123.123.123.123 l:dead p:head** — reveals this information:

✔ The FTP site's address is 123.123.123.123.

✔ The login word for the site is the word **dead**. (See the letter "l" for *logon* before the word dead?) The login is similar to the user name.

✔ The password is the word **head**. (See the letter "p" for *password* before the word head?")

Sometimes that same site will be listed as ftp://dead:head@123.123.123.123. All the information is the same, but the login and password are listed up front, with the login listed first.

Here's how to download a file from an FTP site using CuteFTP:

1. **Install and load CuteFTP.**

   Download CuteFTP from www.cuteftp.com, and run the installation program. You can use the program for free for 30 days; then, some of its features stop working, and you must purchase the program.

2. **Open the program, click FTP from the top menu, and choose Quick Connect from the drop-down menu.**

   The Quick Connect window appears, as shown in Figure 4-12.

   Pressing Ctrl+C also brings up the Quick Connect window.

3. **Fill in the Quick Connect window with the FTP site information and click the OK button.**

   Suppose that you're looking for Grateful Dead tunes on this site: ftp://dead:head@24.2.55.166.

   Figure 4-12 shows the CuteFTP window filled out with that information. When you press Enter, CuteFTP automatically logs on to the FTP site using the login name and password you entered in the last step.

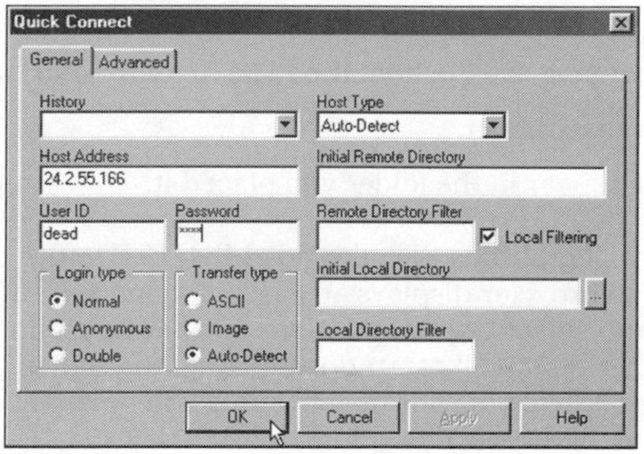

Figure 4-12: Fill in the FTP site address, the login, and the password.

4. **Place your incoming folder on CuteFTP's left side, and the song's folder on the right.**

   Each side of CuteFTP works like a mini-Explorer window. Move up or down the folders until you've placed your hard drive's MP3 folder on CuteFTP's left side, and the FTP site's Grateful Dead song folder on the right.

5. **Drag and drop the MP3 songs into your hard drive's folder.**

   Point at the song you want and, while holding down the right mouse button, point at left-hand window featuring the directory on your hard drive. Figure 4-13 shows the action. Let go of the mouse button to "drop" the file.

Figure 4-13:
Drag and drop your desired file from the FTP site's window to the folder in your own window.

```
[24.2.55.166] - CuteFTP 2.8
FTP  Session  Bookmarks  Commands  Queue  View  Directory  Macro  Window  Help

STATUS:>    Received 1856 bytes Ok.
STATUS:>    Time: 0:00:01, Efficiency: 1.81 KBytes/s (1856 bytes/s)
STATUS:>    Successfully received .Index.txt

c:\mp3                                    \GratefulDead
mississippi_half_step.mp3                 02-16-99_Planet_Drum
                                          04-20-98_Phil_Lesh
                                          06-14-85_Set_2
                                          07-08-78
                                          10-19-74
                                          6-17-91_Giant's_Stadium._N.J._SHN
                                          burned
                                          .Index.txt
                                          .Sysidx.txt
                                          01_deep_elum_blues.mp3
                                          02_friend_of_the_devil.mp3
```

6. **Click Yes when CuteFTP asks whether you're sure you want to download the file.**

   CuteFTP begins copying the file from the FTP site onto your hard drive.

7. **Close CuteFTP to disconnect.**

   Your song should appear in the folder you placed it.

To simplify the process of grabbing FTP files, load CuteFTP in the background. When your Web browser displays an FTP link to an MP3 file, right-click on the file and select Copy Link Address from the menu that appears. CuteFTP will automatically start downloading that file in the background. (CuteFTP automatically begins downloading whenever a URL or FTP address appears on the Clipboard.)

Troubleshooting Your FTP Downloads

Of course, nothing always works perfectly in the computer world. Here's how to deal with FTP foul-ups, the strange vocabulary of its users, and odd error messages that inevitably appear.

The site wants me to click on banners for passwords!

The owners of Web pages make money when people click on their site's advertisements, called *banners*. That's why many sites ask you to click on an advertisement and use a word in the banner's first sentence as the FTP password. It's a moneymaker.

What's a leech site?

Sites that let people download all the files they want are called "leech" sites. The people who eagerly scoop up all the MP3 files are called "leechers," naturally. As people begin to hoard their MP3s, offering them only for trade, leech sites become increasingly rare.

What's a ratio site?

To discourage leechers from copying all their files and running, some Webmasters require visitors to upload a file before downloading any. A one-to-five ratio means visitors can download five files for each one they upload. Most ratio sites contain bootleg MP3 files.

On some sites, a one-to-five ratio means you can download 5MB of songs for every 1MB of songs you upload.

My Internet Service Provider cuts off my connection before the download's finished!

While a file pours into your computer through an FTP site, your Internet Service Provider sometimes thinks you've lost interest, and tries to shut down your connection midstream.

Click CuteFTP's Keep Alive box in the Advanced Options area and CuteFTP sends a special command every 90 seconds that tickles your ISP connection into staying alive.

What's a reliability indicator?

Many search engines seek out and identify FTP sites carrying MP3 files. However, some of these sites aren't open 24 hours; others have shut down since the search engine found them. Many search engines use a database of FTP sites that's only updated once a week — a dead site then stays listed for a full week before being removed.

Some search engines like Lycos.com give sites a reliability rating based on how often they're up and running. The higher rating, the better chances of finding the MP3 file aboard.

The more often that an MP3 search engine double-checks its list of active sites, the more reliable its lists will be. That's why MP3Fiend, found at www.mp3fiend.com, is often the most accurate. First, it searches all the FTP sites for your requested MP3 file, then it immediately verifies all its findings to see whether any of them are up and running.

The site says "Too many users" when I try to connect

FTP sites can't let everybody connect at the same time; many limit their wares to 25 simultaneous users or less. If the site's busy, you must wait it out.

Instead of punching the button yourself every few minutes, CuteFTP has a "redial" feature that automatically tries to reconnect until it gets through.

Speeding Up Your MP3 Downloads

Downloads from Web sites, newsgroups, and FTP sites have one thing in common: They can take a long time to finish. A single MP3 file seems to average 5MB; some live Grateful Dead shows can be 20MB or more.

Here are some tips to speed up the download process:

✔ Upgrade to the newest version of your browser. I'd stay away from Internet Explorer 5.0 for the time being and stick with Internet Explorer 4.01. But get the latest version of Netscape Navigator, if you're still hanging on to that one.

✔ Buy a faster modem. If you're using a telephone line, get a 56K modem. If a cable modem is available in your area, spring for it; it can download an MP3 file in less than a minute. Call the phone company or some of the larger Internet Service Providers to check on DSL lines. Look into satellite links. *Speed* is the key word here.

✔ Don't download during the day; instead, browse the Web during off-peak hours, like early mornings or late evenings.

Chapter 5

Playing MP3 Files on Your Computer and Home Stereo

*B*y now, your computer is stuffed with MP3 songs. It's time to sit back, pop open a Pelligrino, and give your music a good listen. But which MP3 player works best? Choosing between home stereos at a music store is easy; you walk in a room and the salesperson flips the buttons.

But who has time to listen to each of the 100 MP3 players floating around the Internet?

This chapter describes the major contenders, focuses on the most popular player, and wraps things up with tips on wringing out the best sound: hooking your computer up to your home stereo, for example.

Finally, you'll find some tips on playing those MP3 files in your car. Whether you want to listen to *The New York Times* on the freeways or yodel with Jewel on the morning drive, this chapter shows how.

Using the Winamp MP3 Player

Dozens of MP3 players float around the Internet, but one player has broken rank as the clear leader. Winamp (www.winamp.com) stuffs an incredible amount of power into a relatively small package.

On the practical side, Winamp plays nearly every type of sound: MP3s, CDs, MIDI, WAV, and even WMA, Microsoft's MS Audio files. It doesn't cater to copy protection schemes, and it's free to download.

Winamp's built-in ten-band equalizer adjusts the sound; a minibrowser connects to Web pages. Winamp tunes in Internet broadcasts from MP3 radio stations around the world. Special software enhancements called *plug-ins* allow fiddling with the sound — eliminating a singer's voice, for example.

On the goofier side, plug-ins allow Winamp to be controlled with a remote control, like a TV. Visual plug-ins turn your computer screen into a sound-controlled lava lamp of swirling colors. Other utilities called *skins* decorate Winamp's look, making it as fashionable as you prefer.

Recently purchased by the investment-savvy America Online, Winamp continues to grow in speed and power. It has been downloaded more than 15 million times.

This section shows you how to wring the most sound quality from Winamp. (Mac users should download MacAMP (www.macamp.com), an unrelated, but similar program.)

Installing and running Winamp

Compared to most programs, Winamp is a breeze to install. You can either use the version included on this book's CD or download the latest version at www.winamp.com. (The programmers issue new versions almost monthly.)

Click the Web page's Download button, as shown in Figure 5-1. Your computer will grab a copy of Winamp's latest version and place it onto your hard drive.

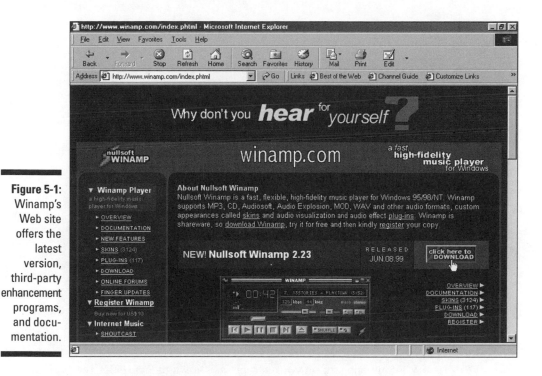

Figure 5-1:
Winamp's
Web site
offers the
latest
version,
third-party
enhancement
programs,
and docu-
mentation.

Follow these instructions to install your copy of Winamp, whether you downloaded it from the Internet or copied it from the CD in the back of this book.

1. **Double-click the program's name and click Next at the first box.**

    Winamp asks to install itself into your Program Files folder with your
    other programs. Unless this offends you, click Next; Winamp scoots
    itself onto your hard drive, then asks how it should act.

2. **Choose your settings and click Next.**

    As shown in Figure 5-2, leave all the boxes checked. You want Winamp to
    play your CDs and sounds, and you want its icons easily accessible.

    Unless you're using a network with a firewall, it's easy to choose
    whether you use a modem to connect to the Internet, a network, or you
    don't have Internet access at all. A working Internet connection lets
    Winamp identify songs from inserted CDs and ensure you're using the
    latest version.

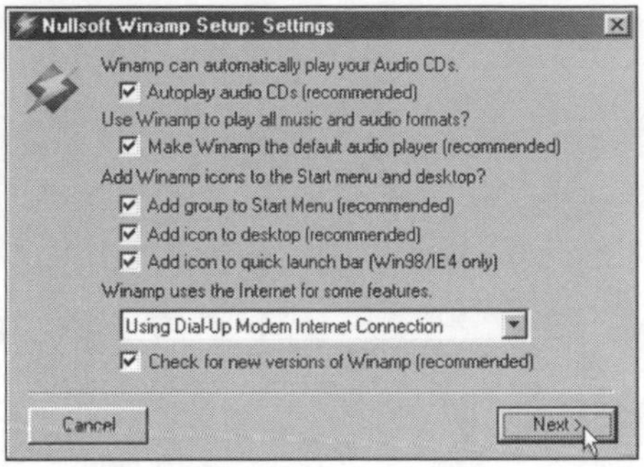

Figure 5-2:
Leave all the
boxes
checked for
peak perfor-
mance;
choose your
proper
Internet
connection,
or choose
none if you
don't have
one.

3. **Fill out the form and click Next.**

   Winamp likes to know how far its program travels, how many times
   people update, and other statistical tidbits.

4. **Click the Run Winamp button.**

   Winamp appears on your screen, as shown in Figure 5-3, ready to play
   your CDs, MP3s, and just about any other file or thing relating to sound.

Figure 5-3:
The highly
configurable
Winamp
comes with
a built-in
Internet
browser,
equalizer,
play list,
shuffle, and
other
features.

> ✔ Winamp now comes free. It used to be shareware, meaning if you like it
> enough to keep it, you're morally obliged to send its creators $10 for
> their efforts. (I sent in my $10 before it became freeware.)

✔ Winamp resembles a wall where other people hang their signs. Winamp is the framework, and users write software to add features — plug-ins and skins — to Winamp.

✔ Not too proud to embrace this group support, Winamp's Web page offers a wealth of add-on programs, plug-ins, and skins. Like most sites for products, you can also find documentation, the most current version, and online forums. (One programmer even uploaded a picture of his crashed Audi.)

✔ Like a wine club, the Winamp community often praises the virtues of past versions. Some versions run better on certain computers, or sport different features. To sample past vintages, head for Winamp Heaven (welcome. to/winampheaven). You'll find more than 50 versions for download.

✔ Winamp comes in four parts for pushing and pulling it into different configurations. The next four sections cover those parts.

Adjusting Winamp's main controls

Winamp consists of four separable windows, but it keeps most of them under wraps. In fact, Winamp works fine when shrunken to the pencil-thin waif in Figure 5-4. The main window, shown in Figure 5-5, serves as the control panel for the others; it works like the front panel of a CD player.

Figure 5-4:
Winamp's
minimalist
window.

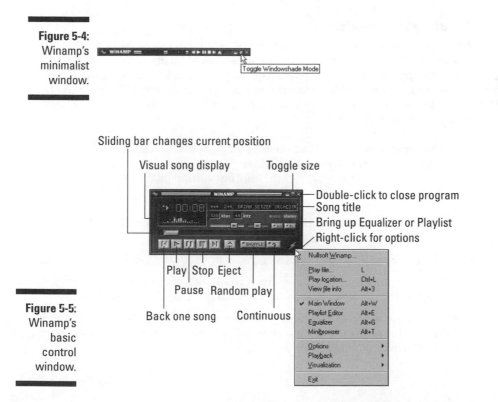

Figure 5-5:
Winamp's
basic
control
window.

Anybody with a CD player already knows the controls for moving from song to song or skipping parts of songs. Some of the others aren't as apparent. Here are a few to remember. Check out the dissected parts in Figure 5-5 for reference.

- ✔ To toggle Winamp between large or small, click the little gray button next to the cross in the upper-right corner. (The second gray button sweeps Winamp down to your taskbar.)

- ✔ Slide the longest bar back and forth to move your song's position. The second longest bar, right above it, changes volume. (It also turns from cool green to fiery orange as the volume increases.) The green bar adjusts the sound's positioning between the two speakers. It's lime green when the balance is right.

- ✔ In Figure 5-5, Winamp is currently playing back music in stereo, because the Stereo button is lit up; some older songs or live recordings light up the adjacent Mono button.

- ✔ The song in Figure 5-5 was recorded at 128Kbps and 44kHz. That's the standard sampling rate for MP3s, making them sound nearly as good as a CD.

- ✔ Click the tiny EQ and PL buttons to bring up the Equalizer and Playlist windows. I cover them next.

Adjusting the equalizer

Winamp's equalizer adjusts the volume of various frequencies in a song, making it sound better according to your physical location, your mood, or the song's particular sound. Tweak the controls yourself, moving the bars up or down to increase or decrease the volume in certain ways. Slide up the bars on the left end to increase the bass, for example; move down the right-hand bars to decrease the treble.

Click the Presets button to load custom-made sound settings, as shown in Figure 5-6. Choose the Jazz setting, close your eyes, and the band sounds as if it were playing in a smoky Jazz club. Another setting puts that same band in a church, or stadium.

- ✔ If the Equalizer isn't working, turn it on by clicking the EQ button in the upper-left corner. (It lights up when turned on.)

- ✔ The ten-band equalizer controls frequency ranges from 60Hz to 16KHz.

- ✔ Don't be impatient when switching from different preset frequency settings. It takes a few seconds for the changes to be heard in the song.

- ✔ A Preamp bar on the left side increases or decreases the sound's volume before it reaches the equalizer, which not only affects the overall sound, but the overall volume.

✔ When playing through your computer's speakers, the music may not sound much different, no matter how much you tweak the equalizer. When you hook up your computer to your stereo, as shown later in this chapter, you'll hear more subtleties in the sound.

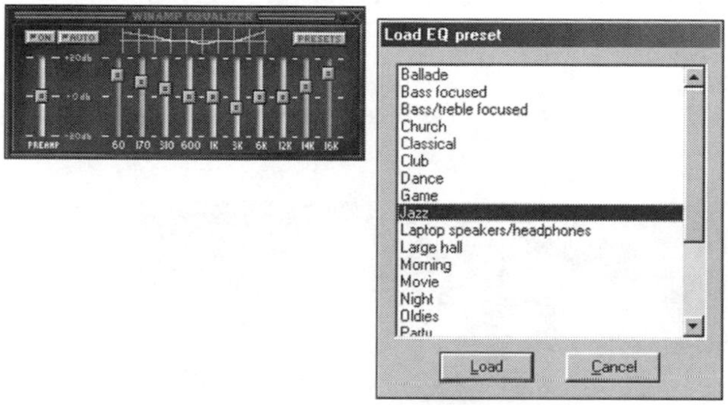

Figure 5-6:
Sliding the equalizer's bars up or down enhances a song's sound by changing the volume of different sound frequencies.

Creating playlists

Want to hear the blues all night? Or a mixture of your Miles Davis and Night Ranger? Winamp lets you create customized MP3 playlists for playback either randomly or in alphabetical order.

Creating a playlist is easy enough; drag and drop the files you want to play into the Playlist window, as shown in Figure 5-7. As the songs drop into the window, their names and lengths appear.

Not into dragging and dropping? Each of the buttons along Winamp's bottom help manage your playlist. Click the +File button, for example, to reveal a standard Windows file browser box. Choose your files, and click Open.

✔ Hold down the +File button to reveal a list of directories. Click the directory containing your MP3 files, and wham! Winamp loads every MP3 from that directory onto its playlist.

✔ To save a playlist, hold your mouse button down on the Load List button in the playlist's bottom-right corner. A menu pops up. Without releasing the mouse button, slide the mouse pointer up to the pop-up menu's Save List option. Release the mouse button, and a window pops up for you to type in the file's name.

✔ To load a playlist, repeat the process above, but slide the mouse pointer up to the Load List option, and then choose your playlist.

✔ A Winamp playlist is merely a text file. Each line consists of a file's name and path. Winamp uses the playlist as a map when pulling files from different directories. Playlist files end with an M3U extension; MP3s end with an MP3 extension.

✔ Save each of your albums in a different playlist. And organize the playlists: Stash all your Hip Hop albums in a Hip Hop folder. Then they're lots easier to find than frisking a CD tower or rummaging through shelves of plastic cases.

✔ The Misc button allows for sorting the list, creating an HTML version of the list, and other goodies. Feel free to experiment.

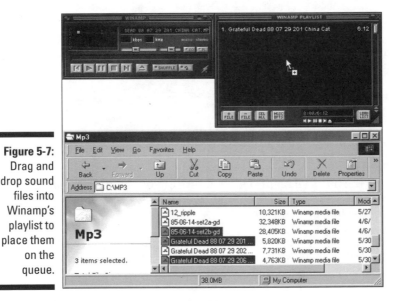

Figure 5-7:
Drag and
drop sound
files into
Winamp's
playlist to
place them
on the
queue.

Using the minibrowser

The minibrowser is a tiny Internet browser — a little window for grunt-level Web chores. A single click heads to Winamp's Web site. Another brings up Amazon's online superstore for MP3-inspired CD purchases. RollingStone.com rests another click away, complete with its handy encyclopedia for looking up unfamiliar tunes and names.

At the very bottom of the minibrowser, click the little arrow pointing up and choose Shoutcast Top 50. A quick list appears, showing the hour's most popular Internet radio stations. Click on something interesting, and you'll join the others listening through Winamp to hear an MP3 Internet radio station.

Customizing Winamp with add-ons

By now, you realize why Winamp currently plays most of the world's MP3s. Winamp is not working as-is, though, because its dedicated users have created thousands of add-ons. This section shows you how to find and install Winamp skins, plug-ins, and MP3 utilities.

Adding skins

Skins are just that — wraparounds for Winamp's face, giving it a new look. Figures 5-8 through 5-11 show a few of the roughly 3,000 available skins.

Figure 5-8:
A jukebox skin.

Figure 5-9:
The SketchAmp skin.

Figure 5-10:
A wood-grain skin.

Figure 5-11:
A Zebra skin.

When configured for Internet access, Winamp's minibrowser automatically lets you check out the latest in skins. Found some eye-pleasers? Follow these steps to wrap them around your copy of Winamp.

1. **Right-click the lightning bolt in Winamp's bottom-right corner.**

2. **On the menu that appears, click Options and choose Skin Browser.**

3. **When the Skin Browser window appears, click the (Download skins) button.**

   Winamp's Web site opens to the page containing the free skins.

4. **Pick and choose from those available, and download the zipped file directly into Winamp's Skins folder. (You don't even have to unzip the file.)**

   ✔ To load a skin, right-click the bottom-right corner of Winamp. Choose Skin Browser from the Options menu, and a window pops up to reveal all your installed skins. Click a skin's name, and Winamp quickly slips it on for your approval. Double-click, and Winamp wears the skin until you take it off, and it defaults to its basic look.

   ✔ Skins come in a wide variety of themes, including Anime, Cars, Celebrities, Drinks, Games, Music, People, Sports, TV, and just plain Ugly.

   ✔ When adding things to Winamp, start with skins. They're easy to add and remove and can't cause any real irreparable damage.

TECHNICAL STUFF

How do I create a skin?

With more than 3,000 Winamp skins to choose from, something is obvious: Skin building is a popular hobby. You can create them with the Windows built-in Paint program, but you'll prefer a graphics program like Paint Shop Pro or Photoshop.

First, head to www.winamp.com and download Winamp's Base 2.*x* Skin. Use that as a template for building your own skin. Read the "Skin-building Tutorial" for some pointers on the process.

The template contains cursor files, bitmap files and a few text files. If you don't change any of them, Winamp uses its normal features. Start editing the graphics, and Winamp begins to change its look. Beware, however; skin building requires detailed work.

To join other skin builders in group e-mail discussions, send e-mail to join-skins-dev@listserv.winamp.com. (Don't put anything in the message's subject or body; Winamp's mailing list computer just grabs your name and puts it on the list.) Soon, you'll be able to exchange messages with other skin-construction aficionados.

Using plug-ins

Skins merely change how Winamp looks. Plug-ins change what Winamp does. Check out Table 5-1 for a description of Winamp's battalion of plug-ins.

Table 5-1	Which Plug-in Does What?
This Type	*Does This*
Input	Mostly players for other sound formats: RealAudio, FM radio (with special hardware), tone generators, VQF players, and downright obscure synthesizers.
Output	Fade your songs into each other during playback. Or, remove any gaps so live recordings sound like the same show, because the applause never stops.
Visualization	"Eye candy," the site calls it, and Figure 5-12 shows it: three-dimensional graphics that dance to the sound's groove. They're meant for people who don't have to pretend they're working on their computers.
DSP/Effect	These Digital Sound Processors add reverb, chorus, strip the singer's voice, or tweak the audio in other ways.
General Purpose	Just plain weird: Infrared and TV remote controllers for Winamp, joystick and network controllers, Internet radio station tools, alarm clocks, and other Winamp-influenced bursts of creativity.

✓ For years, only well-heeled "hi-fi" enthusiasts could afford to collect the latest equipment, always testing their sound with the latest gadget. Winamp lets users play with more gadgets than they have time for. And for the most part, everything's free.

✓ To load an effect, right-click the lightning-bolt symbol in the bottom-right corner, choose Select Preferences from the Options menu, and click the desired variety of plug-in.

✓ You can configure plug-ins to your taste. Highlight your plug-in and click the Configure button. The About button reveals the plug-in's version number and author.

Brian Setzer Orchestra - The House Is Rockin'

Figure 5-12:
Winamp's
visual plug-
ins add
pulsating
graphics to
the musical
groove.

Finding Winamp's Easter Eggs

Just as painters sign their paintings, programmers often place their own digital signature onto their work. Dubbed an "Easter Egg," it's a hidden area inside the program that pops up to reveal details about the programmer.

Today, programmers hide much more than their initials, as you discover when unearthing the Easter Eggs hidden in Winamp. The problem is finding the darn things. You must enter a predetermined sequence of keystrokes in a precise order before an egg reveals itself.

Justin Frankel, head programmer of Winamp, hid two Easter Eggs in Winamp, and here's how to locate them.

Computer history buffs point back to the late 70s for the origins of Easter Eggs. Back then savvy players of Atari's 2600 game console discovered a secret room with the programmer's initials hidden in the Adventure game cartridge.

Winamp's Logo Easter Egg

After being installed and loaded, Winamp plays its "trademark" logo sound. (The one about the llama.) By entering these keystrokes, the logo appears across the top of Winamp, on its title bar.

1. **Open Winamp.**

2. **In this order, press the letters N, U, and L.**

3. **Press the Esc key.**

4. **Press the letter L.**

5. **Press the Esc key again.**

6. **Press the letters S, O, F, and T.**

Winamp's trademark Logo appears on the title bar, as shown in Figure 5-13.

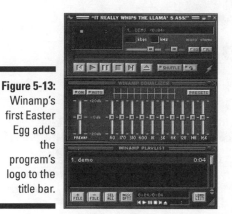

Figure 5-13:
Winamp's first Easter Egg adds the program's logo to the title bar.

Winamp Programmer's Photo and Age Easter Egg

Not satisfied with the new title bar? Here's a more elaborate Easter Egg that not only reveals the face of Justin Frankel, but his age – up to the minute.

1. **Open Winamp.**

2. **Right click on Winamp's title bar.**

   That's the area along the very top where it says WINAMP. A menu will pop up.

3. **Choose Nullsoft Winamp from the pop-up menu.**

   The About Winamp window appears.

4. **Click the Winamp tab.**

   A bizarre swirling face of a man wearing headphones appears, as shown in Figure 5-14. (No, that's not the Easter Egg. That always appears.) The next step unveils the Easter Egg.

Figure 5-14:
Click the
Winamp tab
to see a
swirling man
wearing
headphones.

5. While simultaneously holding down the Ctrl, Alt, and Shift keys, double-click the copyright notice line near the window's bottom.

The Easter Egg appears: Winamp Programmer Justin Frankel's face replaces the bizarre man, as seen in Figure 5-15. But wait, there's more, as seen in Step 6. (This only works in the shareware versions, though.)

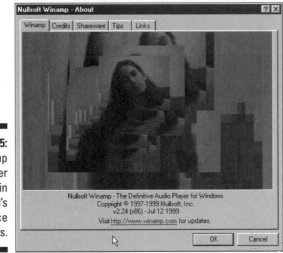

Figure 5-15:
Winamp
Programmer
Justin
Frankel's
face
appears.

6. Click the Shareware tab and doubleclick on Usage Statistics.

As shown in Figure 5-16, Justin Frankel's age appears, tabulated by the number of days.

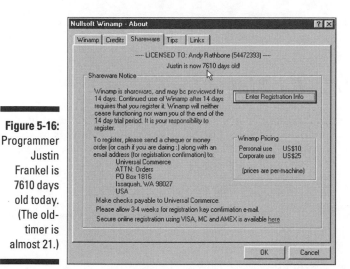

Figure 5-16:
Programmer
Justin
Frankel is
7610 days
old today.
(The old-
timer is
almost 21.)

All-in-One MP3 Players and Encoders

Winamp wins hands down at playing MP3s, but several other players can do a little more. They can *create* MP3 files as well as play them back. In fact, all-in-one software is fancy enough to warrant its own coverage in Chapter 10. Here's a quick preview:

✔ MusicMatch Jukebox (www.musicmatch.com) plays, organizes, and creates MP3s — for free. (Best yet, it's on the CD in the back of this book.) To upgrade MusicMatch to the highest quality (128Kbps), you pay $29.99.

✔ AudioSoft's Virtuosa Gold plays, downloads, organizes, and creates MP3 and other files on more than 55 compatible CD Read/Write drives. It offers a 15-day free evaluation and $29.00 for the unlimited version.

✔ RealPlayer's jukebox can create MP3s from your CDs as well as play MP3s. Like the others, it charges $29.95 to increase quality to MP3's 128Kbps standards.

The Other MP3 Players

Winamp isn't the only MP3 player out there. More than 100 programs can play MP3 files. If you're not enamored with Winamp, for some strange reason, head to www.mp3.com and head to the Software page; you'll find plenty of players to sample for just about every variety of operating system.

Here's a brief look at two of the more popular MP3 players you may run across. They don't create MP3s, just play them back.

Windows Media Player

When Microsoft entered the MP3 player race, the corporate giant simply added MP3-playback capabilities into the sound arsenal of Windows Media Player. The result, shown in Figure 5-17, still doesn't record, but it plays MP3s and a wide variety of other audio and video formats.

Figure 5-17: Microsoft's latest version of Media Player handles MP3s.

Microsoft also whipped up a new music compression format to compete with MP3. Dubbed "Windows Audio format" by Microsoft's creative titans, the new version is half the size of MP3 files, reducing download time.

It's incompatible with MP3, however, and you can't freely copy it, because it contains a rights-management system for copyright holders. The real scoop? Most people say MP3 still sounds better than Microsoft's format.

The version of Media Player bundled with Windows 95 or Windows 98 can't play MP3s. You need to download the new copy, Media Player version 6.02 or greater, released April 13, 1999. (The free program is available at Microsoft's Web site, www.microsoft.com — head for the downloads section.)

✔ Media Player is a convenient freebie, but it isn't nearly as configurable as Winamp.

✔ To find your version of Media Player, choose Programs from the Start button, click Accessories and choose Entertainment.

✔ Microsoft may be a late starter in the MP3 race, but it started late with Internet browsers, too. After a few years, it hammered the competition into the ground.

Sonique

Sonique (www.sonique.com) simply breathes cool. Figure 5-18 shows one configuration of the interface; other faceplates blink and swirl like Las Vegas neon. Sonique is coming on strong behind Winamp; the program attracts skins, features an equalizer, and uses playlists.

Figure 5-18: This free program changes shapes, supports skins and plug-ins, handles Internet Radio, and plays MP3s, as well as many other formats.

Sonique plays them all, including MP3 files, Microsoft Windows Media files, music CDs, and other formats. Check it out for kicks, and see whether you aren't hooked.

Changing Your Default MP3 Player

MP3 players have big egos. As soon as you install one, it assumes you want it to automatically play all your sound files, including MP3s, CDs, and any other piece of sound on your hard drive.

And that's the problem. What if you don't like this newcomer, and want to switch back to your old player? If you're lucky, it's as easy as clicking a button.

For example, to reassign MP3-playing rights to Winamp:

1. **Right-click the little lightning bolt to bring up the Options menu, and then choose Preferences.**

2. **Choose File Types and click the Select all button.**

   Winamp highlights all the file types it supports.

3. **Click Close, and Winamp grabs back its abilities. (To keep it from happening again, put a check in the box marked Register types on Winamp start.)**

If you're not using Winamp, or something goes wrong, here's the manual way to tell your computer what program to use for playing MP3s.

It's a rather complicated two-step process that starts by disabling the MP3 player that's currently grabbing your MP3s. The second step lets you choose another MP3 player to spring into action when you double-click an MP3 file.

Disabling your current MP3 player

First, you need to disable your current default MP3 player by following these instructions. (If you've never installed an MP3 player, jump ahead to Step 2.)

1. **Open Explorer.**

   This is Explorer the *file* browser, not Internet Explorer the *Web* browser. Right-click the Start button, and choose Explore from the menu.

2. **Choose Folder Options from the View menu.**

   Folder Options lies at the bottom of the menu.

3. **Select the File Types tab.**

4. **Find your current MP3 player in the list.**

   Look for the words **MP3 file** (used by Windows Media Player) or **Winamp media file** (used by Winamp). Your existing player may say something different. You know you've found the right one when you see the words MP3 listed after the word Extension in the window's File type details area, as shown in Figure 5-19.

5. **Click the MP3 player's area words and click the Remove button.**

   The words **Winamp media file** have been clicked in Figure 5-19, for example, and are ready to be removed with the Remove button.

   Don't stop now. At this point, Windows doesn't know what program opens your MP3 files. When you try to open one, Windows will be confused.

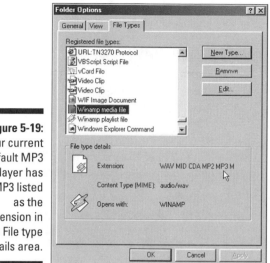

Figure 5-19:
Your current
default MP3
player has
MP3 listed
as the
extension in
the File type
details area.

Assigning an MP3 player to your MP3 files

Sometimes the wrong MP3 player pops into action when you double-click an MP3 file or play it from MP3 sites on a Web site like www.MP3.com.

Windows gives you two ways to assign a different MP3 player for your MP3 files. Try the simple method first; if that doesn't work, dig a little deeper with the second solution.

The simple way to change default MP3 players

Follow these six steps to change the MP3 player that plays your MP3 files.

1. **Click once on any MP3 file.**

2. **Hold down the Shift key and right click on MP3 file.**

3. **When the menu pops up, choose Open with.**

4. **When the list of programs pops up, choose WinAmp, Sonique, or any other MP3 player.**

   Click on the program's name to choose it.

5. **Check the box that says Always use this program to open this type of file.**

6. **Click the OK button to save your changes.**

Now, whenever you click on an MP3 file, your newly selected MP3 player pops into action to play it.

The more difficult way to change default MP3 players

If the first method didn't let you change the MP3 player that automatically plays your MP3 files, try these steps. They're more complicated, but sometimes that's what it takes.

1. **Open Explorer.**

   This is Explorer the *file* browser, not Internet Explorer the *web* browser. Right-click the Start button, and choose Explore from the menu.

2. **Click View and choose Folder Options.**

   Folder Options lies at the bottom of the menu.

3. **Select the File Types tab.**

4. **Click the New Type button.**

   The Add New File Type appears.

5. **Type the words MP3 file into the Description of type box.**

6. **Type the words .mp3 into the Associated extension box.**

   Don't forget to put the period before mp3.

7. **Type the words audio/mpeg into the Content Type (MIME) box.**

8. **Click the New button beneath the empty Actions box.**

   A window labeled New Action appears.

9. **Type open into the Action box.**

10. **Type "C:\Program Files\Winamp\WINAMP.EXE" "%1" into the Application used to perform action box.**

The above example installs Winamp as your default MP3 player. To install a different player, substitute that program's name and location for the words "C:\Program Files\Winamp\WINAMP.EXE" in Step 10. Be sure to add the "%1", complete with quotation marks, or it won't work.

If you experiment with several different MP3 players, each player tries to set itself up as the default player. Following these two procedures lets you pick the player that should automatically jump up and begin playing MP3 files.

When you first listen to an MP3 file being played back from MP3.com, a box appears. Select the option that says Open this file from its current location. Then uncheck the option that says Always ask before opening this type of file.

Connecting Your Computer to Your Home Stereo

The speakers connected to many computers sound like squawking menus at drive-up fast-food joints. To improve the sound, ditch the tinny speakers and connect your computer to your home stereo.

Run the right-sized wires between the right places, as described later, to turn your computer into a 300-disc CD player.

Tools you need: A Y-cable (a one-eighth-inch stereo plug with two RCA phono plugs, usually red and green; see Figure 5-20) and an extension cable long enough to connect your computer and stereo.

Cost: About $5 to $10, if the sound card didn't already come with the correct cable.

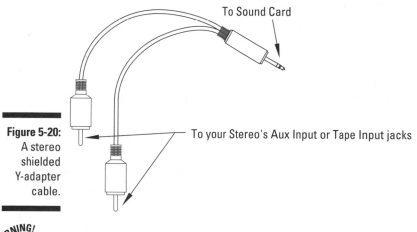

To Sound Card

Figure 5-20:
A stereo
shielded
Y-adapter
cable.

To your Stereo's Aux Input or Tape Input jacks

Keep the volume turned down on the stereo and the sound card while connecting the cables — you don't want to pop anything.

1. **Turn down the volume on your stereo and sound card.**

   Turn down the stereo's volume knob, usually pretty easy to find.

   If you can't find your sound card's volume knob — which is either somewhere on the back of the card or through its software program — simply turn off your computer (after saving your work, of course).

2. Find the correct cable.

You need a shielded Y-adapter cable, shown in Figure 5-20. This cable has a stereo ⅛-inch plug on one end and two RCA phono plugs on the other end. You can find the cable at Radio Shack. (The six-foot cord is part number 42-2481; the three-footer is number 42-2475.) Other electronics stores and some computer stores carry the cord, as well.

The package of a stereo Y-adapter cable calls it a male stereo ⅛-inch plug to two male RCA plugs.

The best sound card manufacturers throw the cord in for free; others make you head to Radio Shack. If your computer and stereo aren't very close together, pick up a 12-foot stereo cable (part number 42-2356). A 20-foot stereo cable (part number 42-2462) provides even more room. If your computer and stereo are more than 20 feet away, ask the Radio Shack salesperson how to buy the right cable and plugs to make your own extension cable.

3. Plug the ⅛-inch stereo plug into your sound card's speaker jack.

Hopefully your sound card has all its little jacks labeled so that you know which little hole does what. If it doesn't, you have to open the card's manual. Then run the extension cord between your computer and your stereo system.

If you have a carpet, push the cord into the crack between the carpet and the edge of the wall. Use the right tool for the job: a spoon handle works well. No carpet? Buy a rug. But don't leave the cord lying across the floor. If somebody trips over it, they'll pull out the plug and the music will stop.

4. Plug the cable's two RCA phono plugs into the stereo's Aux Input or Tape Input jacks.

Check the back of your stereo for some unused input jacks; you should see several pairs of stubby little metal heads. Use the Aux Input or the Tape Input jacks — whichever isn't being used.

One jack of the pair is probably red or labeled "Right" — push the cord's red plug into that jack. The other jack is probably black, white, or green — this jack is for your other plug, no matter what color it is.

Don't plug your sound card's output into your home stereo's Phono Input jack. Your stereo doesn't expect such a strong signal from that jack. (If you throw caution to the wind and plug the cord in there anyway, keep the card's volume *very* low.)

5. Turn on the stereo and switch it to Tape Input or Aux Input.

Turn the stereo's input select switch to the jack you've used, either Tape Input or Aux Input.

6. Play an MP3 file on the sound card and adjust the volume.

Gradually turn up the volume on your stereo and sound card. If everything is hooked up right, the sound should start filling the room.

If the sound doesn't start filling the room, make sure that the stereo is turned to Aux Input or Tape Input — or whatever input jack you plugged the sound card into. If the stereo isn't turned to the correct input switch, your sound card won't come through. (Oh, is the stereo plugged in and turned on?)

Your home stereo isn't always a friend. It reveals the shortcomings of a cheapie sound card, for instance, as well as an MP3 encoder that's not quite pulling its weight.

Listening to MP3 Files in Your Car

You can play MP3 files from your home stereo, from your computer, and from a portable player using headphones.

But MP3 hasn't quite broken through the final barrier — the automobile. Plenty of people are working on the situation, and automobile-based MP3 players may soon flood the market.

Until then, here are a few workarounds to consider.

Just like car stereos, dedicated MP3 players for cars can be ripped off. To avoid that, substitute your portable MP3 player. You can easily grab your portable MP3 player when you leave the car, keeping it safe. Also, some of the latest portable MP3 players use IBM's 340MB microdrive (Chapter 6), which holds six hours of MP3s.

✔ **Use a cassette player adapter:** If your car has a cassette player, check out Radio Shack's CD-to-Cassette Player Adapter (part number 12-1999). It looks like a cassette tape with a stereo cable hanging from one end. Plug the cable into your portable MP3 player's headphone jack, insert the cassette, and start listening to your MP3s through your car stereo. It sounds amazingly good.

✔ **Uses a wireless CD adapter:** Plug the cable from this small Radio Shack FM transmitter (part number 12-2051) into your portable MP3 player. Then tune your car's FM radio to the right frequency and hear your MP3s.

✔ **Buy a car stereo with a CD Input jack:** Some car stereos lack a CD player. Instead, they have a CD Input jack. Plug a ⅛-inch stereo cable (Radio Shack part number 42-2420) between this jack and your portable MP3 player to hear MP3s through your car's stereo system.

✔ **Record MP3s onto cassettes:** After you hook up your computer's sound card to your home stereo, record the songs onto cassettes. If your car has a tape deck, you're ready to roll.

✔ **Burning MP3 songs onto a CD in audio format:** Does your car have a CD player? Then convert your MP3 songs back into standard "CD audio" format and copy them to a CD. (I cover how in Chapter 11.)

✔ **Connect a portable MP3 player to amplified speakers:** Take some amplified speakers — like the ones that come with your PC — and plug a portable MP3 player into them. Carry it all to your car and start listening. To change songs, just swap new cards in and out of the portable player.

✔ **Experiment with a prototype MP3 player:** Just because you can't pick up a prepackaged MP3 player for your car at the dealer doesn't mean that they don't exist. Many people currently build automobile MP3 players. For the latest list of links, check out www.mp3.com and click Hardware. The site keeps track of the latest car MP3 players, as well as their requirements, release date, and, if available, price.

Chapter 6

Choosing and Using Portable MP3 Players

· ·

· ·

*O*vercoming skeptics, lawsuits, and abysmal distribution, Diamond Multimedia swept up the cash with its Rio portable MP3 player.

Today, Diamond faces some stiff competition, not only from other portable MP3 players, but palmtop Windows CE computers.

Which MP3 player will win? Some are only sold overseas, but aiming at the United States market; other players already appear in consumer electronics stores.

This chapter is a handicap sheet to help you separate the winners from the losers.

No matter which player you purchase, splurge on a new set of headphones. Check out a stereo shop for some lightweight sports headphones. The cheap plastic ones shipped with the players almost always stink.

Rio, RioSE, and Rio 500

Manufacturer: Diamond Multimedia.

Cost: Rio PMP300 ($149), Rio PMP300SE ($249.95), Rio 500 ($269).

Web: www.diamondmm.com.

Onboard Storage: Rio: 32MB; RioSE: 64MB; Rio 500: 64MB.

Upgradability: You can upgrade all Rios with SmartMedia cards of up to 32MB.

Connection: A "pass-through" parallel port lets you connect the Rio's connector while keeping your printer attached.

The first portable MP3 player sold in the United States, the Rio, shown in Figure 6-1, has held its lead by dropping the price and introducing new models faster than the competition.

The Rio's successor, the RioSE (shown in Figure 6-2), doubled the Rio's storage and ditched the plain black case for a hip translucent model that exposes capacitors, integrated circuits, and other electrical playgyms.

Figure 6-1:
Diamond Multimedia's Rio PMP300.

Figure 6-2:
Diamond
Multimedia's
RioSE.

Diamond's third model, the Rio 500, not only works with a Macintosh, but also supports Audible.com's narrated text format. Its file-management system works well, keeping pace with RealPlayer's Jukebox and MusicMatch.

A fourth-generation Rio player capable of using IBM's 340MB microdrive (see the end of this chapter) is due to arrive before the end of 1999.

Musicians should check out Chapter 16 for tips on how the Rio and other portable MP3 players help you practice.

Nomad

Manufacturer: Creative Labs.

Cost: 32MB version ($169.99); 64MB version ($249.99).

Web: www.nomadworld.com.

Onboard storage: Nomads come with 32MB or 64MB onboard.

Upgradability: You can upgrade both with SmartMedia cards of up to 32MB.

Connection: A desktop docking station transports information through the parallel port. (Unfortunately, you must free up the parallel port by disconnecting your printer before connecting the Nomad.)

Having more available time in the design studio, Creative Labs tossed a few more features into its MP3 player, Nomad, shown in Figure 6-3. The engineers stuffed an excellent FM tuner with programmable stations and a voice recorder into the tiny gadget's cool magnesium case.

The case not only looks cool, but it's tough, compared to the plastic used for its competitors. Magnesium's not only one of the lightest metals around, it's also flammable, strangely enough. It won't catch fire in your pocket, though. You need to slice off metal slivers and hold them under a lighter — something few people will do to their $200 toy.

Figure 6-3:
Creative
Lab's
Nomad.

On the practical side, the Nomad also functions as a huge floppy disk for moving any type of files between computers. (If you'd ever want to do such a thing.)

Unlike the Rio or most other MP3 players, the Nomad fits into a docking station. The docking station plugs into your computer's parallel port, and an adapter plugs into an electrical outlet for power. Drop the Nomad into the docking station to recharge the batteries as well as to load MP3 files.

Bummer department: The Nomad requires two rechargeable AAA batteries, which recharge through the docking cradle. It works with two alkaline AAA batteries, if you run out of power on the road, but AAA batteries are much more difficult to locate than the popular AA batteries. (The Rio and raveMP both use a single alkaline AA battery.)

Multimedia Windows CE Palmtops

Manufacturer: Casio (and Hewlett Packard, Compaq, and others).

Cost: $499 for E-100, $599 for E-105.

Web site: www.casio.com.

Onboard Storage: 16MB onboard the E-100; 32MB onboard the E-105.

Upgradability: Uses CompactFlash cards, which hold 128MB or more.

Connection: Docking cradle connected to serial port.

Casio's Cassiopeia 100-series palmtop (shown in Figure 6-4) best illustrates the merging of MP3 players with Windows CE palmtops. As MP3 players move toward the computer world with their ability to record dictations, track phone numbers, store notes, and transport files, Cassiopeia's 100-series have turned into MP3 players. They now play stereo MP3 files through their headphone jack.

Other Windows CE palmtops play MP3s in mono, unfortunately. Windows CE owners can find the latest MP3 player software at www.utopiasoft.com.

The Cassiopeia not only plays MP3s, but it also can convert MP3s into Microsoft's Windows Audio format, halving the file's size and stuffing more tunes onto the memory cards.

Check out Chapter 21 for more tips on playing MP3s through a Cassiopeia.

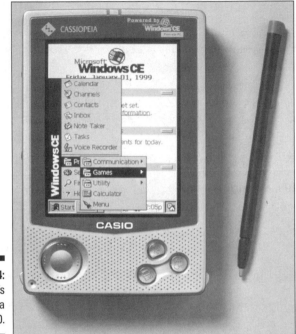

Figure 6-4:
Casio's
Cassiopeia
E-100.

Mpman

Manufacturer: Eiger Labs/Saehan Information Systems, Inc.

Cost: $179 suggested retail price.

Web: www.mpman.com.

Onboard Storage: MP-F10: 32MB; MP-F20: 64MB; MP-F30: 64MB; MP-H10 sports a tiny hard drive.

Upgradability: The cards use SmartMedia memory cards except MP-CL10, which uses Iomega's 40MB removable Clik drives.

Connection: Parallel port.

Figure 6-5 shows the Mpman MP-F10, the Asian-and-European equivalent of the United State's Rio. Eiger labs provided the world with its first portable MP3 player in February, 1988, and has since pulled several other models out of the bag, including the MP-F20, shown in Figure 6-6.

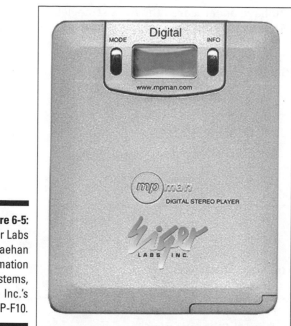

Figure 6-5:
Eiger Labs
and Saehan
Information
Systems,
Inc.'s
MP-F10.

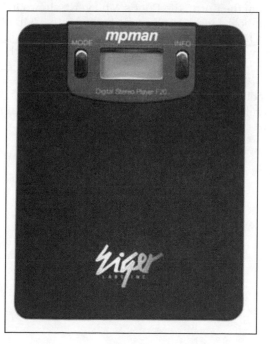

Figure 6-6:
Eiger Labs
and Saehan
Information
Systems,
Inc.'s
MP-F20.

In fact, the Mpman might have underscored the Rio's stranglehold had it been able to reach the United States at the same time as it hit the Asian and European markets.

The Mpman aims for the low-end market, with a low price and minimum features.

Mplayer3

Manufacturer: Pontis.

Cost: $195.

Web: www.mplayer3.com.

Onboard Storage: No onboard storage.

Upgradability: Slots for two multimedia cards.

Connection: Serial interface for PC connection.

Taking a step away from the norm, the Pontis Mplayer3, shown in Figure 6-7, doesn't bother with onboard memory. Why be locked into 32MB of onboard storage, the designers figured, when memory cards hold increasingly larger sizes as the technology develops? In fact, the industry predicts the new Multimedia cards, described later in this chapter, will soon hold 128MB.

"In view of the extremely fast developments on the storage medium market," the company's press release says, "there would have been a great danger that the Player would have soon become outdated."

Flash cards holding 32MB are common, with larger sizes to follow. The Mplayer3 will be ready for them.

Figure 6-7:
Pontis
Mplayer3.

raveMP

Manufacturer: Sensory Labs.

Cost: $199.

Web: http://www.ravemp.com/ravehome.html.

Onboard Storage: 64MB built-in.

Compatibility: 16MB or 32MB flash memory cards.

Connection: Parallel port docking station.

The raveMP does the same as the others and more — hopefully causing a price-and-features war that's good for everybody. The raveMP (shown in Figure 6-8) plays MP3 files, like the others, but does much more. When playing songs, its three-line, 16-character LCD screen displays the current song title, artist name, and song length.

A built-in microphone records up to four hours of voice messages; head to the electric memo area to store thousands of telephone numbers for quick access. It even stores memos and text files for reference on the road. My unit came with quick Korean phrases to use on the go. (It's made in Korea.)

My unit maxed out as I stored the first 16K of "Jane Eyre." I read three paragraphs — 16 characters at a time — before giving up with the tiny screen size. Stick with telephone numbers and other short items.

Its software also lets you transport large binary files back and forth to other computers, provided they also have the raveMP software. If this came with a FM tuner to listen to after you've grown tired of your hour of music, it could have been a real winner. As it stands, it's an awkward organizer.

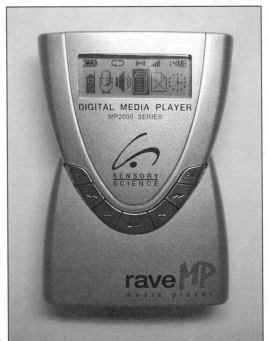

Figure 6-8:
Sensory
Labs'
raveMP.

JazPiper

Manufacturer: RFC Singapore.

Cost: $189.

Web: www.jazpiper.nl.

Onboard Storage: 32MB built-in memory; upgradable to 64MB with SmartMedia cards.

Connection: Parallel port.

When playing music, JazPiper's graphic LCD display features the artist name and song title (see Figure 6-9). But it also records voice memos and stores up to 250 phone numbers. It uses AAA batteries. Ho hum.

Figure 6-9:
RFC
Singapore's
JazPiper.

It's currently selling in the Netherlands, and should arrive in the United States shortly.

I-JAM

Manufacturer: IJAM Multimedia Corporation.

Cost: $99-199.

Web: www.ijamworld.com.

Onboard Storage: No onboard memory; uses Multimedia cards.

Connection: Parallel or USB.

Hey, the I-JAM, shown in Figure 6-10, comes in nine groovy colors (I like Purple Haze), and it includes an FM radio. With backlighting for nighttime listening and a low price, it's worth a listen.

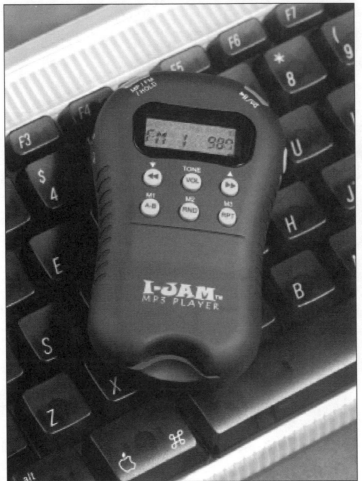

Figure 6-10:
Multimedia
Corporation's
I-JAM.

Lyra

Manufacturer: RCA.

Cost: $200.

Web: www.lyrazone.com.

Storage: No onboard memory; includes 32MB CompactFlash memory.

Connection: Parallel port unit dumps onto CompactFlash card.

The Lyra (shown in Figure 6-11) is built for the future. First, it skips the onboard memory in favor of CompactFlash memory, which is rapidly expanding in capacity. The Lyra can also download software plug-ins to play different audio formats as they evolve.

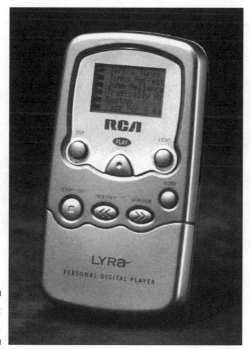

Figure 6-11:
RCA Lyra.

Nex

Manufacturer: Frontier Labs.

Cost: unknown.

Web: www.frontierlabs.com.

Storage: 64MB onboard memory.

Connection: Parallel port.

The Nex, shown in Figure 6-12, is waiting for takeoff. This itty-bitty player uses SmartMedia cards, features a backlit LCD screen, and offers separate bass and treble controls. Toss in separate bass and treble controls, fast forward/rewind, and AAA batteries for power, you have a player that's not much different from the zillions of others out there.

Figure 6-12:
Frontier Labs Nex.

Storage Devices

PCs can fall back on their standard floppy disk, but no standard storage card exists for PDAs; different brands use one of three: CompactFlash, SmartMedia, and MultiMedia cards. They're all relatively easy to find, because digital camera owners have grabbed them for several years.

The well-developed camera market has spawned loads of cool accessories and quick file-transfer methods, discussed later in this section.

CompactFlash

Cut a standard PC-Card in half, and you have the size of a CompactFlash card. Used by many portable MP3 players, cameras, and other gadgetry, CompactFlash cards store information without requiring a battery (see Figure 6-13).

CompactFlash cards come in two sizes: Type I and the slightly thicker Type II. Although a Type I works fine in a Type II slot, a Type II doesn't fit into a Type I slot. Not even if you push real hard.

Currently, a Type I CompactFlash card (used by most portable MP3 players) stores up to 128MB, whereas a Type II CompactFlash card (used by some second-generation players) holds up to 160MB.

> ✔ CompactFlash cards can survive a ten-foot drop. (Your MP3 player might not, but you can still salvage the CompactFlash card.) Under average use, the card will last more than 100 years without losing data.

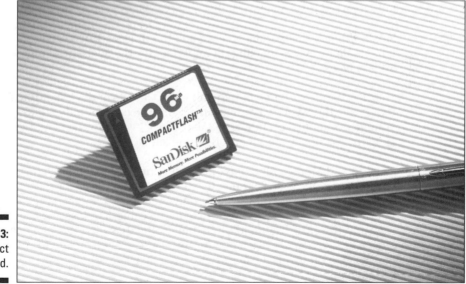

Figure 6-13:
Compact
Flash card.

- ✔ Although CompactFlash cards are a bit larger than SmartMedia or MultiMedia cards, they're less expensive, especially at the higher capacities.

- ✔ IBM's 340MB microdrive (discussed later in this section) fits into a Type II slot.

- ✔ Head for the CompactFlash Association at www.compactflash.org for all the information you could ever want to know about CompactFlash cards. You can find even more information from the card's creator, SanDisk, at www.sandisk.com.

- ✔ SanDisk began cranking out CompactFlash cards in late 1995, giving them a headstart compared to other types of tiny storage devices.

- ✔ To transfer information quickly between a CompactFlash and your computer, check out some of the PC-Card adapters. Slide the CompactFlash card into the end of the PC-Card, slide the PC-Card into a PC-card slot like the ones on a laptop, and you have immediate access to the CompactFlash data. Check out www.simpletech.com/flash/intro.htm for more information.

SmartMedia

Toshiba came up with the Solid State Floppy Disc Card (SSFDC), that's thankfully referred to as a SmartMedia card (see Figure 6-14).

Smaller than a CompactFlash card and the thickness of a credit card, they fit into smaller devices, making them perfect for the ever-shrinking portable MP3 players.

SmartMedia cards come in two voltages: 3.3 volts and 5 volts. Hardly anything uses the 5-volt card anymore. (Turn the card with its shiny side up; the voltage is stamped on that side. Also, the 3.3-volt card has a notch on its right side; the 5-volt card has a notch on the left side.)

The Rio and Mpman MP3 players use *proprietary* SmartMedia formats for copyright protection. That means you can't swap the cards with your digital camera or other MP3 players. Not only that, after you format the cards for your MP3 player, you can't use them in the camera unless the camera can reformat the card. Diamond offers beta software called RioDiag.exe at its Web site (www.diamondmm.com/products/drivers/rio.html) to reformat the card back to standard format, but it's not guaranteed.

Figure 6-14:
SmartMedia
card.

Some PC-Card adapters claim to transfer information quickly between a SmartMedia card and your computer. While these work with cameras, they don't work with most MP3 players. Make sure the adapter works with your MP3 player before opening your wallet. Check out www.simpletech.com/ flash/intro.htm for more information.

MultiMedia

The designers of the CompactFlash recently came up with the MultiMedia card — a postage-stamp-sized card created to compete with the SmartMedia card (see Figure 6-15). It's the tiniest storage device available.

It's new, and a few overseas MP3 players use it, but it's hard to tell if it will catch on. In the meantime, plenty of MultiMedia card enthusiasts hang out at www.mmca.org.

Figure 6-15:
MultiMedia
card.

IBM's microdrive

IBM invented the hard disk drive and sold the first one in 1956. Now it has turned its magnifying glass upside down to shrink a hard drive. *Really* shrink it. IBM's new 340MB microdrive, shown in Figure 6-16, fits into a Type II CompactFlash card that can easily fit between your toes.

As the size goes down, however, the price goes up. A microdrive kit including a 340MB drive, a PC Card adapter for a standard PC Card slot, and a field case retails for $499.

The microdrive's whirling platter is the size of a large coin, and the whole thing weighs less than a AA battery. Yet it stores six hours of near CD-quality audio. Here are some more interesting facts:

- ✔ Diamond Multimedia plans to release a Rio supporting the new drive, letting consumers store more tunes than ever before.

- ✔ Now, the bad news. Whirling hard drives consume much more electricity than memory cards. Don't count on powering the thing with a single AA battery, like some of today's MP3 players.

- ✔ For more information about IBM microdrive products, race to www.ibm.com/storage/microdrive.

Figure 6-16:
IBM's
340MB
microdrive.

Chapter 7

Listening To or Setting Up an MP3 Radio Station

• •

In This Chapter

▶ What's a SHOUTcast radio station?

▶ What equipment do I need?

▶ Listening to SHOUTcast

▶ Webcasting through SHOUTcast

• •

*I*f you've perused some of the earlier chapters, you're well aware of how MP3 technology turns PCs into jukeboxes packed with music. It lets you stuff tunes into tiny gizmos with a belt-clip for on-the-road bopping.

But there's even more: MP3 lets anybody with a copy of Winamp — the connoisseur's MP3 player — tune in to the hundreds of MP3 radio stations available on the Internet.

After reading this chapter, you'll know how to tune in those stations and you'll be able to link Winamp to a Web site called SHOUTcast, which gives you the chops to create your own radio station, capable of attracting listeners worldwide.

What's a SHOUTcast Radio Station?

Nullsoft, the corporate arm of the folks who created Winamp, created SHOUTcast to let Winamp users share their musical tastes with the world.

Tuning in to an Internet radio station is pretty easy. First, make sure you've installed a copy of Winamp. (Use the copy in the back of this book, or grab an updated copy at www.winamp.com.) Next, log on to SHOUTcast at www.shoutcast.com. As shown in Figure 7-1, SHOUTcast currently has 1,441 listeners tuned in to 524 Internet radio stations. Click a station, and start listening. The next section describes the process in more detail.

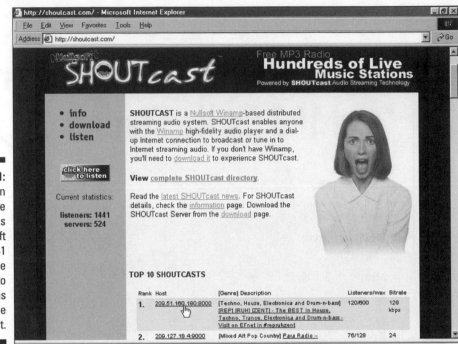

Figure 7-1:
As shown by the statistics on the left side, 1,441 listeners are listening to 524 stations through the Internet.

✔ Radio stations aren't *broadcast* through the Internet. The term "broadcast" refers to airwave transmissions. No, SHOUTcast's stations are being *Webcast*.

✔ A SHOUTcast radio station is essentially an Internet "feed" from somebody's copy of Winamp. Basically, you're listening to that person's Winamp playlist.

✔ After adding additional software, you can configure your copy of Winamp to Webcast its playlist over SHOUTcast. Depending on the speed of your connection, you're limited to anywhere from one listener to several hundred.

✔ It's more complicated to Webcast your own station than it is to listen to an existing station. You can still do it, though, as you find out in an upcoming section.

✔ The faster your modem, the better the stations will sound when listening. The same goes for Webcasting: Faster modems let more people listen.

✔ Yes, this stuff is legal and it's free — unless you're making money off of it, in which case Nullsoft humbly requests you to contact sales@shoutcast.com for information on how to pay the obligatory $299 commercial fee.

✔ You can listen to SHOUTcast through a proxy server, if you're stuck behind one of those complicated network things. You can also listen from behind a firewall, if some kind network administrator opens a hole for you.

What Equipment Do I Need for SHOUTcast?

Forget about the transmission towers, stacks of paperwork, and legal fees. To listen or broadcast on SHOUTcast, you need the following equipment:

✔ A computer that's powerful enough to play MP3s through Winamp (covered in Chapter 5).

✔ A copy of Winamp Version 2.05 or above. (You can use the version on the CD bundled with this book or download the latest version from www.winamp.com.)

✔ You also need a modem. You can listen with a 28K modem, although the sound improves considerably as your modem speed increases.

✔ To set up your own station, download the required software on SHOUTcast's Web site at www.shoutcast.com.

✔ If you're trying to Webcast through SHOUTcast with a dial-up connection, you can reach only one listener. Your modem simply isn't fast enough. Bummer. To reach more listeners, you need ISDN, DSL, a cable modem, or something even faster.

Listening to SHOUTcast

It's easy to listen to SHOUTcast Webcasts. Make *sure* that you've installed a copy of Winamp. Nullsoft created Winamp and SHOUTcast to work together. Sonique added SHOUTcast support, too, but it doesn't work with RealPlayer or Windows Media Player. And Macintosh users are left out completely, unfortunately.

After you install your copy of Winamp, follow these instructions to tune into a station:

1. **Make sure that Winamp has registered the .PLS file extension.**

   After installation, Winamp is configured to play MP3s and most other file types. But make sure that Windows knows to send the SHOUTcast Webcast to Winamp. Open Winamp, and press Ctrl+L. Then make sure that PLS is selected in the list along with MP3 and other optional file types.

2. **Head to SHOUTcast at** www.shoutcast.com, **as shown in Figure 7-1.**

   You needn't move past the first page to begin listening.

3. **Choose a station matched for your modem speed.**

   Figure 7-2 shows a blow-up of Figure 7-1, showing how to figure out information about each station.

   Before picking a station, look at its *bit rate* — the number in the last column. Be careful to choose a station that your modem can handle. A modem with a dial-up connection should choose a 24 Kbps station, for example. If you start receiving skips or gaps in the sound, choose a station that's Webcasting at a lower bit rate.

Figure 7-2:
Point and click on the string of numbers (or the word Listen), and Winamp begins playing that station.

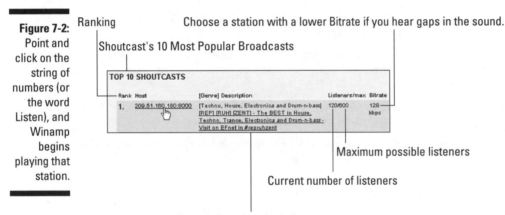

Ranking

Choose a station with a lower Bitrate if you hear gaps in the sound.

Shoutcast's 10 Most Popular Broadcasts

Maximum possible listeners

Current number of listeners

Description of station's format.
(Click on underlined words to visit Web page.)

4. **Click the mouse on a station's address.**

   Notice how the mouse pointer becomes a little hand as it points at the string of numbers under the word *Host* in Figure 7-2. Those numbers designate the *address* for that particular station. Click the address, and Winamp begins playing the station. (Sometimes, the word *Listen* appears above the string of numbers; if so, click that instead.)

5. **Configure your browser, if needed.**

   This last step takes place only the first time you tune in to a station.

   Internet Explorer: When you first click on a SHOUTcast station, Internet Explorer sends a message, shown in Figure 7-3, asking whether it should Open this file from its current location or Save this file to disk. Select the first option — opening the file — and uncheck the box marked Always ask before opening this type of file.

Figure 7-3:
When
Internet
Explorer
first
receives a
SHOUTcast
Webcast,
choose the
Open box
and
uncheck the
box marked
Always ask
before
opening this
type of file.

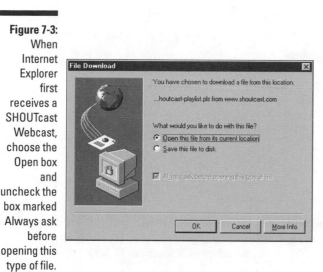

Netscape Navigator: When you first click a SHOUTcast station, Netscape brings up the box in Figure 7-4 with four buttons: More Info, Pick App, Save File, and Cancel. Click Pick App. When the box shown in Figure 7-5 appears, type the location and name of Winamp. (If you chose the Winamp defaults during installation, you should type `C:\program files\winamp\winamp.exe`.)

Your computer loads Winamp and begins playing the station.

If that station turns out to be a drag, click a different one. After a few moments, Winamp will begin playing the new station's sounds. (And because you've configured your browser, the station will play automatically. No need to repeat Step 5.)

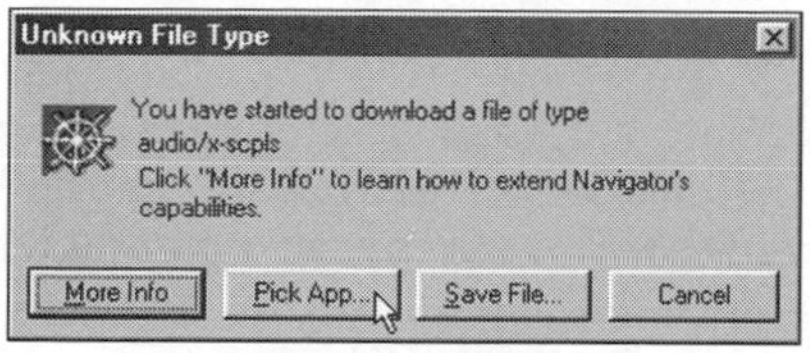

Figure 7-4:
When
Netscape
first
receives a
SHOUTcast
Webcast,
click the
Pick App
button.

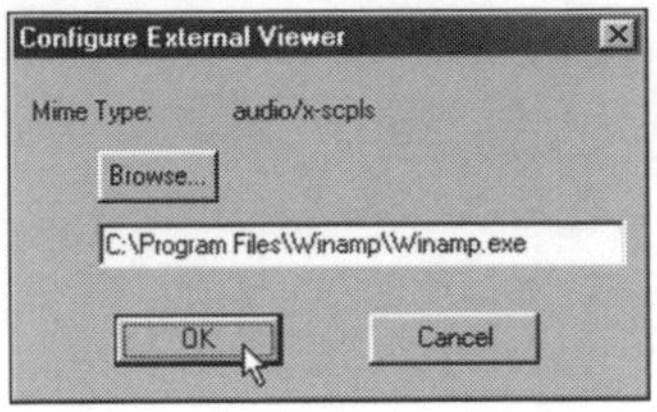

Figure 7-5:
After
choosing
the <u>P</u>ick App
button, pick
Winamp by
typing its
location and
name into
this box.

Configure External Viewer   [x]

Mime Type: audio/x-scpls

Browse...

C:\Program Files\Winamp\Winamp.exe

OK   Cancel

✔ Write down the address numbers of your favorite station. Then, to hear the station quickly, open Winamp and press Ctrl+L to bring up the Open Location box. Type in the address and press Enter.

✔ The next time you load Winamp, the program remembers which station it previously played. Click the Winamp play button — the same button that starts playing MP3 files — and, depending on your type of Internet connection, Winamp will begin playing the station.

✔ Check out a cool utility called MP3Spy at www.mp3.com. It lists all the available stations, rates them by signal strength, and lets you chat with the DJ and other listeners. (If anybody's actually tuned in to that station.)

✔ While you're checking out utilities, an up-and-comer called FreeAmp claims to work with SHOUTcast, too. Apparently a Macintosh version is in the works. Check it out in your spare time at www.freeamp.org.

✔ When listening with a low-speed, dial-up modem connection, any sort of Web surfing or page flipping often causes skips in the sound. The solution? Get a cable modem, or don't Web surf while listening.

✔ Using a proxy server on a network? You can still listen, if you tell Winamp about it. Load Winamp, press Ctrl+P, and click Setup. Under Internet Settings, click the button marked Using LAN Internet connection. Then type your Proxy into the box labeled HTTP proxy: 'Server:Port'. I use Wingate to let all my networked computers share a single cable modem, so I type wingate:80.

✔ Modems rarely receive information at their labeled speed. A 56K modem can't receive a 56 Kbps SHOUTcast Webcast. That's because 56K modems usually receive around 32K to 40K per second, depending on the quality of the Internet connection. Similarly, 28K modems can handle 24 Kpbs and lower SHOUTcasts. Luckily, SHOUTcast carries stations Webcasting at a variety of rates to support many modems.

Finding New SHOUTcast Stations

When you first log on to SHOUTcast, the page displays the Top Ten stations rated by the number of listeners. Plenty more stations await your ears, though. To find them, click the words *View complete SHOUTcast directory*. (Or click the picture of the shouting woman.) When the screen in Figure 7-6 appears, click the List Servers menu to choose between different types of stations.

To see every station currently running, choose All, as shown in Figure 7-6.

When the All page appears, it displays a wide variety of stations using different modem rates and music types. The station at the top of Figure 7-7, for example, would only be accessible to super fast modems — 128K or faster.

In the Listeners/max column, SHOUTcast says that station supports 600 listeners, with 110 current listeners. The station directly below it — Para Radio — sends its Webcast stream at 24 Kpbs, so it's designed for listeners with 28K modems. (Seventy-six people are currently tuned in, with plenty of room for more.)

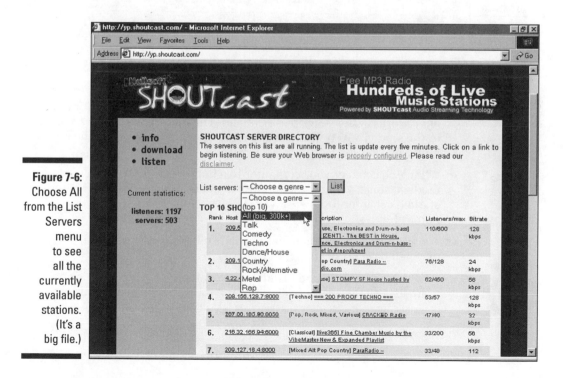

Figure 7-6:
Choose All
from the List
Servers
menu
to see
all the
currently
available
stations.
(It's a
big file.)

![Screenshot of SHOUTcast Server Directory in Microsoft Internet Explorer]

http://yp.shoutcast.com/cgi-bin/newlistserv.cgi - Microsoft Internet Explorer - [Working Offline]

File   Edit   View   Favorites   Tools   Help

Address http://yp.shoutcast.com/cgi-bin/newlistserv.cgi   Go

Nullsoft
SHOUTcast
streaming audio system

- info
- download
- listen

SHOUTCAST SERVER DIRECTORY

Searched for: **ALL** (found 499 servers)

List servers: – Choose a genre –   List

server IP	[genre] description now playing	listeners/max @ bitrate	average listen time uptime
Listen 209.51.160.180:8000	[Techno, House, Electronica and Drum-n-bass] [REP] [RUH] [ZENT] - The BEST in House, Techno, Trance, Electronica and Drum-n-M[Techno, House, Electronica and Drum-n-bass]	110/500 @ 128 kbps	14m 38s 1d 17h 19m
Listen 209.127.18.4:9000	[Mixed Alt Pop Country] Para Radio -- http://pararadio.com	76/128 @ 24 kbps	6m 37s 3h 50m
Listen 4.22.4.3:8000	[Techno,House] STOMPY SF House hosted by nabi.net	58/450 @ 56 kbps	13m 55s 1d 01h 10m
Listen 208.156.128.7:8000	[Techno] === 200 PROOF TECHNO ===	53/57 @ 128 kbps	15m 39s 9h 39m
Listen 207.66.185.90:8050	[Pop, Rock, Mixed, Various] CRACKED Radio Notorious BIG - Mo Money Mo Problems	40/40 @ 32 kbps	N/A 2d 04h 01m
Listen 216.32.166.94:6000	[Classical] [live365] Fine Chamber Music by the VibeMaster-New & Expanded Playlist	33/200 @ 56 kbps	40m 39s 5h 52m

Figure 7-7:
The station called Cracked Radio has reached its limit of 40 listeners, meaning nobody else can tune in.

When a station reaches its listener limit, its listing of listeners turns red, letting you know it's currently unavailable.

✔ To find out more information about a particular station, look for underlined words in the Description column. The underlined words are a link to the station's Web site. The site often displays the name of the currently playing song.

✔ When you connect your computer to a home stereo and use a cable modem, some Webcasts sound just as good or better than an FM radio station. (Chapter 5 shows how to hook up your computer to your home stereo.)

✔ Always choose a station using a speed suitable for your connection rate, or you'll have problems.

Be sure to download and install MP3Spy at www.mp3.com. This cool program lists all the available stations and rates them by signal strength.

My modem keeps disconnecting me after a half hour!

As you kick back and listen to Internet radio stations, some Internet Service Providers think you've forgotten that you've logged on. So, they automatically disconnect you. That leaves their phone line open for somebody else to call.

Also, Windows sometimes tries to protect you by disconnecting your connection, as well.

How can you stop this radio rudeness? Unfortunately, different ISPs handle the situation in different ways. Some cable modems offer 24-hour service — you can listen all the time without problems. Other services just dump you when you haven't used the service for a while.

Dial-up connections cause the most problems. Here are a few solutions to avoid the dastardly dial-up disconnect.

The simplest solution is to watch for the ISP's automatic disconnection warning, and click "Do not disconnect." Distracting, but livable. If you *do* get disconnected, click the play button on Winamp, and it will automatically try to connect and play the same station.

Although you can't always stop your ISP from disconnecting you, you can make sure Windows doesn't do the disconnecting. Try these settings for Windows 95 and Windows 98.

For Windows 95:

1. **Click the Start button and choose Control Panel from the Settings option.**

2. **Double-click the Internet icon.**

3. **Select the Connection tab.**

4. **Remove any check mark in the box next to Disconnect if idle for __ minutes.**

5. **Click Apply.**

6. **Click OK.**

For Windows 98, Second Edition:

1. **Click the Start button and choose Control Panel from the Settings option.**

2. **Double-click the Internet Options icon.**

3. **Select the Connections tab.**

4. **Select the Settings button.**

5. **Click the Advanced button.**

6. **Remove any check marks next to options saying Disconnect.**

7. **Click OK.**

For Windows 98, First Edition:

The sequence for Windows 98 is the same as for Windows 98, Second Edition, except for a few areas. Windows 98's Control Panel icon is labeled "Internet" in Step 2, for example. In Step 6, there's only one option labeled Disconnect, so make sure that one's not clicked.

To tell which edition of Windows 98 you have, right click on your desktop's My Computer icon and choose Properties. A window appears listing your particular version.

Okay, is this radio stuff legal?

Like most anything else, SHOUTcast can be used legally and illegally. The Recording Industry Association of America offers its own position on the legality of Webcasting at this Web site: `www.riaa.com/weblic/wl_faq.htm`.

Basically, the situation boils down to this: A relatively new law simplifies the way Webcasters obtain licenses from artists and record companies for their copyrights. Webcasters must meet certain conditions to use the recordings legally:

✔ They can't play too many songs by the same artist within a certain period of time.

✔ They can't preannounce the times when they're going to play certain artists.

✔ They can't keep playing the same sets of songs over and over.

✔ They can't use artists to endorse advertisements.

✔ They can't encourage listeners to copy their Webcasts.

✔ They can't Webcast bootlegs or illegal copies of sound recordings.

Sound recording copyright owners may negotiate with Webcasters to receive royalties based on marketplace value. If Webcasters and copyright owners do not agree on a rate, an arbitration proceeding determines rates.

"Marketplace value" is the key issue. So far, nobody's defined what that term really means. And until it goes to court, we probably never will.

If the Webcaster meets all these conditions, they must send a $20 filing fee to the Library of Congress.

Again, check the RIAA's Web page for more detailed information.

Setting Up a SHOUTcast Radio Station

When you've grown familiar with listening to Webcasts, and you're ready to set up your own station, these instructions will put your tunes on the Net.

If you're on a network and running on a proxy server, you can't Webcast. It just won't work.

1. **Log on to SHOUTcast's download page at** `www.shoutcast.com/download.html` **with your Internet browser.**

   The Web page shown in Figure 7-8 appears; it contains all the necessary enhancements for Webcasting needed for Winamp.

2. **Make sure that you're using Winamp 2.05 or newer.**

   Feel free to use the copy included on this book's bundled CD. Or grab a new copy by heading to the Winamp Web site (`www.winamp.com`). Take a shortcut there by clicking the word HOMEPAGE on the SHOUTcast download page you reached in Step 1.

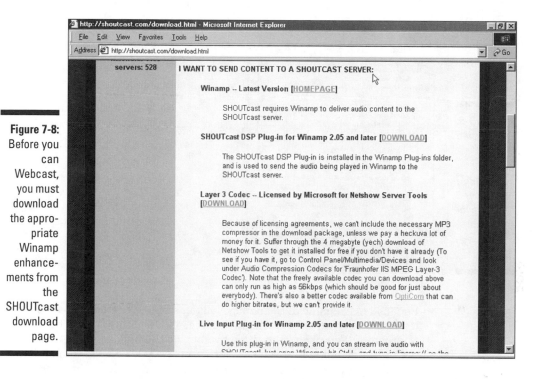

Figure 7-8:
Before you
can
Webcast,
you must
download
the appro-
priate
Winamp
enhance-
ments from
the
SHOUTcast
download
page.

Already have a copy of Winamp? Make sure it's Version 2.05 or higher by watching the program as it first loads. The version number should appear where the song's title normally appears. Or click the little box in the program's upper-left corner. Click the words Nullsoft Winamp; when the window appears, read the version number on the screen's third line. (The letter v is in front of the version number.)

3. **Download and install the SHOUTcast DSP plug-in for Winamp.**

   From SHOUTcast's download page (as shown in Figure 7-8), find the line mentioning SHOUTcast DSP Plug-in and click the word DOWNLOAD. Your browser downloads the file to whatever directory you choose. (Or download it from Winamp's Web site; it's called DSP_SC.ZIP.)

   Unzip the file with WinZip or another unzip program and copy it to your Winamp Plug-ins folder. (Winamp plug-ins get their due in Chapter 5.)

   This particular plug-in sends the music currently played by Winamp to the SHOUTcast server, where it can be Webcast.

4. **Download and install Layer 3 Codec — Licensed by Microsoft for Netshow Server Tools.**

   Now you need a special MP3 decoder. First, see whether your computer already has it: Open Multimedia from the Control Panel, click the Devices tab. Look under Audio Compression Codecs, as shown in Figure 7-9, for Fraunhofer IIS MPEG Layer-3 Codec.

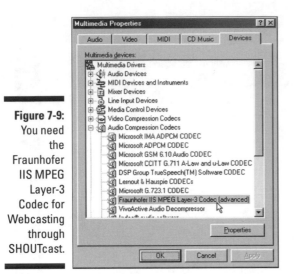

Figure 7-9:
You need
the
Fraunhofer
IIS MPEG
Layer-3
Codec for
Webcasting
through
SHOUTcast.

Because of licensing agreements, Nullsoft can't offer this free decoder on its site. The solution? Download the free, 4MB Netshow Tools from Microsoft's Web page. (Get there by clicking the link, as shown in Figure 7-8.) After downloading, click the program, NSTOOLS.EXE, to install the decoder. (Ignore the rest of the program.) The decoder allows you to Webcast as high as 56 Kbps — a reasonably decent rate.

5. Load Winamp and configure the station.

When Winamp loads, press Ctrl+P to bring up the Preferences window, as shown in Figure 7-10, and click DSP/Effect to configure the plug-in installed in Step 3.

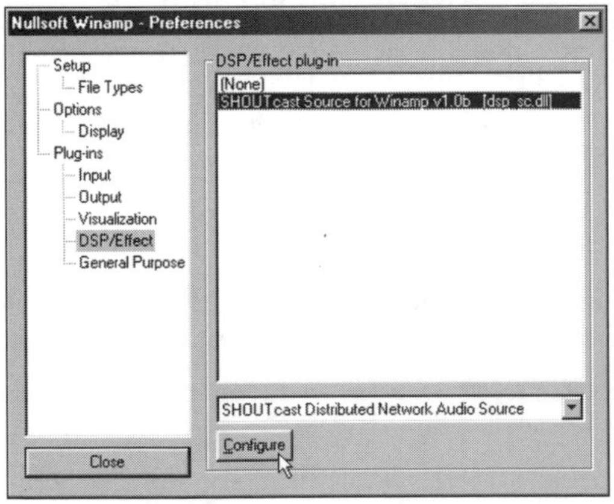

Figure 7-10:
Press Ctrl+P
to bring up
the Winamp
Preferences
window.

Click SHOUTcast Source for Winamp, as shown in Figure 7-10, and click the Configure button; when the box shown in Figure 7-11 appears, you need to do five things.

Change the password. (You don't even have to remember it; it will always appear in the box.)

- *Don't* change the Encoding format area.

- Make sure that the Public server button is checked.

- Fill out the Description of your station.

- Fill out the Genre box, which describes the type of music you'll be playing. (The information in the Description and Genre boxes show up in the SHOUTcast list for listeners to view.)

When you're done, the box will look something like Figure 7-11. Click the OK button to save your changes.

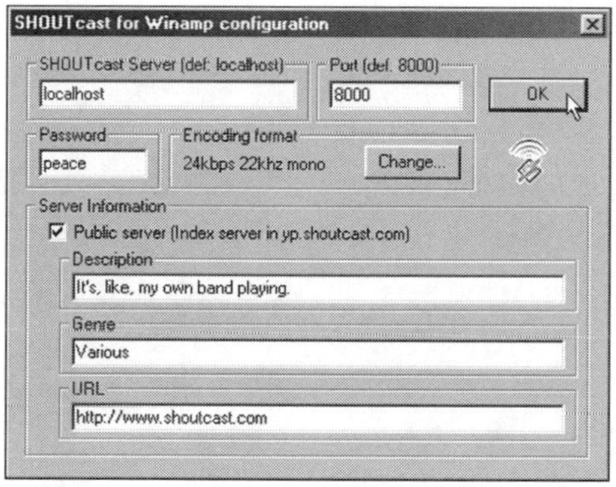

Figure 7-11:
Fill out the plug-in's configuration box like this.

6. **Download the SHOUTcast Server for your computer.**

   Chances are, you'll want the first file on the list: SHOUTcast WIN32 server; it's for Windows. (Servers for other types of operating systems, like Linux, appear here as well.)

   Unzip the file shoutcast-win32-101.zip into a folder named SHOUTcast. It should contain three files: sc_serv.exe, sc_serv.ini, and readme.txt.

   The readme.txt contains detailed instructions, if you're into that sort of thing. Sc_serv.exe is the actual program, and sc_serv.ini contains program settings. In fact, you change those settings in the very next step.

7. **Edit the sc_serv.ini file in Notepad, and save the file.**

   Most of this file consists of comments and instructions. (Any line beginning with a semicolon or "[" symbol is a comment or label, and shouldn't be changed.) Only the following lines need an ogle:

- **PortBase=8000**: Make sure that this number is the same as the number entered into the Port box in Figure 7-11. (Because you probably didn't change it in Step 5, you won't need to change it here.)

- **MaxUser=:** Choose a conservative number of maximum users for your server. Multiply your modem's speed by 0.9, and divide by your bit rate — 24, as defined by the Encoding format area in Step 5. For example, a 56K modem's dial-up connection would support two users.

- **Password=**: This must be the same password entered in Step 5.

- **Logfile=**: This is the file used for storing connection information. Leave it as-is.

Make sure that all the things you enter here correspond to what you entered in Step 5.

8. **Load the Server by double-clicking the Sc_serv.exe file in the SHOUTcast folder.**

    The server leaps to the screen, waiting for you to run Winamp.

9. **Run Winamp, and begin playing some songs.**

    Your SHOUTcast Server Monitor window shows the new station, called Turnips, being logged onto SHOUTcast, as shown in Figure 7-12.

Figure 7-12:
The SHOUTcast Server Monitor window shows that my hot new station, called Turnips, is now Webcasting; it's attracted one out of 20 possible listeners through my cable modem.

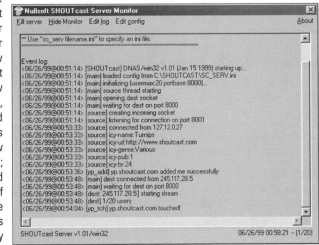

✔ For live Webcasts, download the Live Input plug-in. It lets you Webcast live audio — talk shows, band jams, whatever. After downloading the plug-in into your Winamp Plug-in folder (as described in Chapter 5), open Winamp, press Ctrl+L, and type `linerec://` to Webcast live audio. MP3Spy offers live Webcasting help at `www.mp3spy.com/server/mic.shtml`.

✔ SHOUTcast offers some promos that do play along with your playlists — things like, "Milking our bandwidth for all it's worth with SHOUTcast streaming audio!"

✔ Be sure to check out MP3Spy after you get your station on the Web. It makes it easier to attract listeners.

✔ Interested in Webcasting? Check out `www.saint.simplenet.com/shout`. From there, you can find Webcasting stations, radio stations, TV stations, and Webcams all over the world.

Part III
Creating Your Own MP3 Files

The 5th Wave   By Rich Tennant

"Oh yeah, that's it! Add a little more bass!"

In this part . . .

When I was a nerdy little kid, I collected TV theme songs. Whenever a show started, I ran up with my Radio Shack tape recorder, put the microphone up by the TV's speaker, and recorded shows like *The Beverly Hillbillies, The Jetsons*, and *Rockford Files* — if I could stay up that late.

Now, as a nerdy adult, my equipment and tastes have changed. Instead of a cheap tape recorder and microphone, I copy songs from CDs onto my computer, creating MP3 files in the process.

This part of the book shows how to turn CDs into MP3s, but it also covers creating MP3s from albums and tapes. It even shows how to take your vacation movies of a Hawaiian beach, convert the sound into MP3, and loop it — layering your room with a relaxing environmental ambience.

And if you do have a hankering for the *Go Speed Racer* theme song, this part of the book shows how to capture it.

Chapter 8

Ripping and Editing Songs from a CD, TV, Tape, or Microphone

. . . .

In This Chapter

▶ Understanding and using Ripper software

▶ Ripping sounds from a CD

▶ Recording sound from the TV

▶ Recording sound from a tape

▶ Recording sound from a microphone

▶ Editing recorded music or sound

. . . .

*R*ipping basically means copying sounds from a CD onto your hard drive. MP3 aficionados use the word "ripping" because they're tearing sound off the CD, and placing it onto your hard drive. Besides, "ripping" sounds more cool than copying.

This chapter shows you how to rip CDs into your computer, where you convert it into an MP3 file. It also shows you how to record albums, camcorder soundtracks, TV shows, videotapes, or anything else that makes some noise.

If you're looking for the simplest method of converting CDs into MP3s, head for Chapter 10; it covers software designed especially for turning CDs into MP3 files in one easy step. But if you're making MP3s from something other than CDs, or you're looking for tips to make the cleanest rips possible, stick around.

Why Use a Ripper?

Creating an MP3 requires two steps. First, you rip the sounds from the CD onto the hard drive. Then, you encode those copied sounds into MP3 files.

When you rip the sounds into your computer, the Ripper software stores the CD's music files in a WAV format. (Chapter 1 describes the differences in file formats.)

Your computer plays WAV files without problem through either Winamp or Windows Media Player. Why not stick with WAV files? Because WAV files are huge, uncompressed files of 40MB to 50MB or, in the case of a rocking Grateful Dead live version, 200MB.

Converting the WAV files into MP3 files is called *encoding.* (Encoding gets its coverage in Chapter 9.)

In the early days, MP3 creators always used two pieces of software, one for ripping and the other for encoding. Today, all-in-one software like MusicMatch, AudioCatalyst, and RealJukebox perform both chores at once: You insert the CD, and the software automatically transforms the songs directly into MP3 files.

✔ Some MP3 makers dislike all-in-one software because they lose control over the sound quality. When the software automatically turns the CD's songs into MP3s, it bypasses the WAV file step, which leaves no way to edit the WAV file to correct any flaws in the rips.

✔ Plus, not everybody rips CDs exclusively. Some people convert their aging album collection into MP3s for easier storage and to get rid of that stinky mildew smell.

✔ Ripping has nothing to do with *Raster Image Processing,* also called *RIPping,* which refers to the conversion of a PostScript file to a high-resolution bitmap used in fancy printing work. Ripping doesn't hurt the CD, either.

✔ Popular sound-editing programs like Cool Edit ($50 at www.syntrillium.com) and the even-cooler SoundForge ($499 at www.soundforge.com enhance, filter, and clean up dirty WAV files. They remove "pops" from an album, for example, or fix CD rips that don't sound "right."

How Do I Rip Songs from a CD?

Start the Ripper software, insert the CD, choose the songs, and click the software's Copy option. The software grabs the CD Audio (CDA) straight from the CD and saves the sound as a WAV file on your hard drive.

You don't even need a sound card; the CD's music (which is already stored as numbers on the CD) becomes numbers on your hard disk.

Ripping CDs, known technically as Digital Audio Extraction (DAE), doesn't work on all CD players, unfortunately — especially the older ones. MP3.com's CD drive compatibility list at `www.mp3.com/cdrom.html` lists drives able to withstand the rigors of ripping. If your drive can't, it's time to buy a new one. (Chapter 2 shows how to install it.)

The latest list of Ripper software lurks at `www.mp3.com/software/ windows/cdrippersrest.html`. Figure 8-1 shows one popular ripper, WinDAC, ripping a CD. Some Rippers are free, others are shareware, and still others are commercial.

Figure 8-1: WinDAC, a popular ripper, prepares to copy a 39.65MB song onto the hard drive, where it can be encoded into an MP3 file.

Track	Playtime	Starttime	Drivespace nee...	Copyprotection	Pre-Emphasis	Tracknumber
Track01	00:03:23.13	00:00:02.00	34.18 MB	Yes	No	1
Track02	00:07:22.59	00:03:25.13	74.49 MB	Yes	No	2
Track03	00:01:42.52	00:10:47.72	17.28 MB	Yes	No	3
Track04	00:02:48.74	00:12:30.49	28.43 MB	Yes	No	4
Track05	00:03:35.73	00:15:19.48	36.33 MB	Yes	No	5
Track06	00:03:55.51	00:18:55.46	39.65 MB			6
Track07	00:07:20.03	00:22:51.22	74.03 MB			7
Track08	00:05:06.36	00:30:11.25	51.56 MB			8
Track09	00:09:44.23	00:35:17.61	98.30 MB			9
Track10	00:05:35.61	00:45:02.09	56.49 MB			10

Play
Copy track(s)...
Copy track(s) (Classic Mode)...
Copy range...
Rename track

CD inserted | Playtime 00:03:59.62 h:m:s.f | Actual track : 02

The songs on the CD shown in Figure 8-1 range from 17.28MB to 98.30MB. Ripping the entire CD at once would require more than 500MB of hard drive space.

✔ WAV files consume lots of room. If your hard drive lacks at least 100MB of free space, rip the songs one at a time. Encode the ripped song to MP3 format, delete its WAV file, and move on to the next file.

✔ Hard drive not big enough? Chapter 2 contains tips on installing a second drive or using an Iomega Jaz drive, a standard for audio storage.

✔ Bought a blazingly fast 24x speed drive? It'll never rip audio that quickly. That rating shows how fast the drive *reads* a CD's information. Rippers need a CD to *send* data. In fact, for the best quality rips, choose single speed. If you try to rip at too fast a speed, the sound file often contains skips and pops.

✔ Immediately after ripping a CD, listen to the WAV file in Windows Media Player or Winamp. If the sound has skips, pops, unwanted noise or other distortion, tell the software to rip at a lower speed.

✔ Feel free to clean up a CD's WAV file using any of the sound-editing programs discussed later in this chapter.

Connecting Sound Cables to Your Computer

Whereas ripping refers to copying sound off a CD — and bypassing the sound card in the process — you need the sound card when creating MP3s from a turntable, TV set, VCR, camcorder, or microphone.

To grab audio from those sources, you record it through your sound card: Connect the output cables from your sound source into the Line-In jack on your sound card.

This section shows how to connect the cables and record the sound onto your hard drive.

Tools you need: A Y-cable (see Table 8-1) from the sound source to the stereo.

Cost: About $5 to $10, if the sound card doesn't come with the correct cable.

Stuff to watch out for: Sound cards rarely label their jacks well. Instead of using big letters, they use bizarre pictures or weird circles. And if the jacks on the back of your sound card aren't marked, you'll have to dig around for the manual.

Follow these steps to connect a cable from your album, tape, VCR, or TV set to your sound card's input jack for recording:

1. **Turn down the volume on your sound card and sound source.**

   You don't want to hear any speaker-shattering pops when pushing cables into jacks.

2. **Find the correct cables for your sound device and your sound card.**

   Different components use different cables; Table 8-1 shows what cable to use. Although most stereo stores carry these cables, Radio Shack is always a good last resort.

Table 8-1	Cables for Connecting a Device to a Sound Card	
This Device...	*Needs This Cable*	*Radio Shack Part Number*
Turntable, VCR, tape deck, or stereo TV	Y-cable with one pair of RCA jacks on one end and a ⅛-inch stereo plug on the other.	42-2481 for six feet; 42-2475 for three feet
Mono TV	Y-cable with a single RCA jack for the TV and a ⅛-inch plug on the other.	42-2444
Camcorder	Y-cable with two RCA jacks for the camcorder and one ⅛-inch stereo plug for the sound card.	42-2481 for six feet; 42-2475 for three feet
Microphone with ¼-inch plug	Plug the microphone's cord into a ¼- to ⅛-inch plug adapter, then plug it into the sound card's MIC jack.	274-047 for adapter
Microphone with ⅛-inch plug	Plug the microphone directly into the sound card's MIC jack.	No adapter needed

3. **Connect one end of the cable to your sound device.**

   Check the back of your VCR, camcorder, turntable, stereo, or TV for output jacks. You should see a pair of stubby little metal heads (RCA jacks) along one side. If it's not stereo, there's only one little stub. If you're lucky, they're labeled.

   Take the Y-cable adapter, like the one in Figure 8-2, and plug the cable's two RCA jacks into those output jacks, making sure that the red jack goes into the red plug. (That's for the right speaker.)

4. **Connect the cable's ⅛-inch plug into your sound card's Line In jack.**

   Make extra sure the cable doesn't mistakenly push into the other nearby jacks.

5. **Adjust the mixer levels.**

   Now, start playing your turntable, camcorder, or whatever else you're trying to record. This is where recording becomes an art: You carefully adjust the volume level through the Windows mixing board while watching the recording software's volume level to make sure the incoming sound is not too loud or soft.

Figure 8-2:
The ⅛-inch plug goes into your sound card's Line-In jack; the two RCA jacks connect to the VCR, camcorder, turntable, or other device.

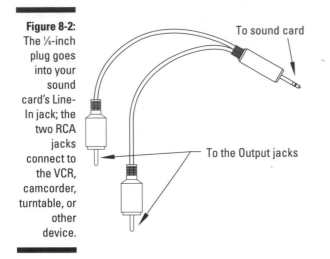

To sound card

To the Output jacks

To see the Windows built-in mixing board, double-click the speaker icon in the screen's bottom-right corner. When the mixing board appears, choose Properties from the Options menu, as shown in Figure 8-3.

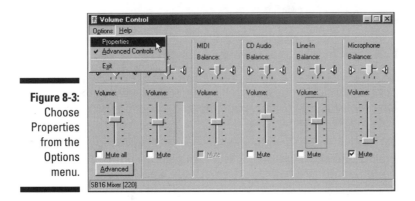

Figure 8-3:
Choose Properties from the Options menu.

Because you want to record the incoming sounds, choose Record from the Properties window. Click in any empty box to put a check mark inside it; doing so shows all the options of what you're able to record.

Click OK, and the Recording Control window appears; because you're recording from the sound card's Line-In jack, select the Line-In box, as shown in Figure 8-4.

Figure 8-4:
Choose the
Line-In box
and slide
the meter up
or down
until the
recording
level looks
right in your
recording
software's
meter.

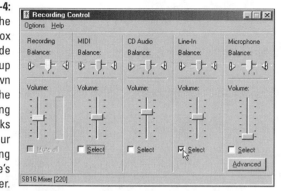

Now turn on the volume meter — sometimes called a VU meter — on your recording software — Cool Edit, in this case. Slide the mixing window's Line-In bar up or down until the sound level in its adjacent meter looks just right: The Windows meter should stay below the red levels, and the recording software's meter should come close to — but not reach or surpass — 0 on the control bar.

See how the mouse pointer slides the bar up or down in Figure 8-5? When you slide the bar to adjust the volume coming in through the Line-In jack, the volume meter along the bottom of Cool Edit moves back and forth accordingly.

6. Listen in through your sound card's speakers.

The incoming sound should begin playing through your sound card's speakers.

- If you don't hear anything, check the sound card's mixer software. Make sure that the Line In or Line button is checked, and the controller is slid up about halfway.

- Keep checking your cable connections, as well. You're always aiming for the sound card's Line-In jack. Don't use the Mic jack for anything but microphones, or it sounds awful.

- To listen to your computer through your home stereo's speakers, head for Chapter 5. It shows you how to connect cables in the opposite direction.

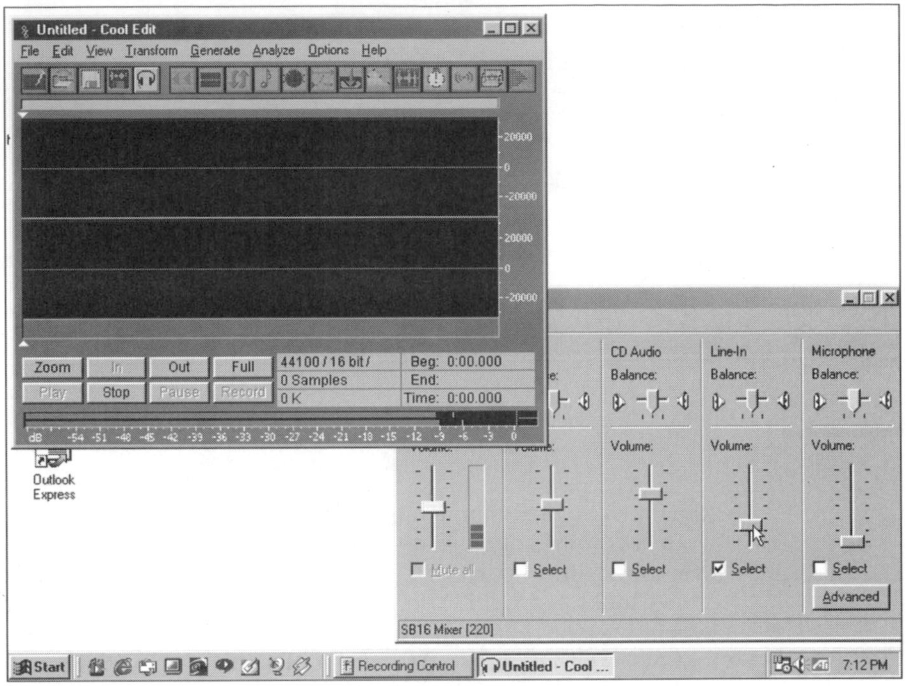

Figure 8-5:
Choose the
Line-In box
and slide
the meter up
or down
until the
recording
level looks
right in your
recording
software's
meter.

Recording Songs from Albums

Albums may be a joy for listening, but they're too big for easy storage. Plus, you always worry about when it's time to change the needle. Playing any rare singles? Don't they deteriorate each time they're played?

Converting albums to MP3 has several other advantages: Because the sounds originated from an album, the MP3 has that warm feel of vinyl — none of that sterile CD feeling. Almost any portable MP3 player can play a full album.

Some "all-in-one" MP3 packages record albums and convert them to MP3s on the fly, but that skips the WAV stage, leaving no way to remove any recording flaws before the final encoding.

These steps show how to record songs from an album and save them as WAV files — where you can touch them up before turning them into MP3.

1. **Clean the album.**

   The cleaner the album, the cleaner the sound. Try these cleaning tips:

   • Wash both sides of the album with a lint-free cloth. Most music stores sell record-cleaning brushes designed expressly for removing dust.

- To remove extra-stubborn goo from the grooves, try a mixture of 50/50 rubbing alcohol and distilled water. Lacking that, small amounts of baby shampoo can do the trick. Be sure to rinse well.

- Always wash the record with a circular motion; don't scrub "across grain" as it might scratch the grooves. When you finish cleaning, dry the album and only touch it by the edges.

- If it's an important album — a rare import, or an old 78 — check the phone directory for professional record cleaning services found in many big cities. They can often vacuum any extra-persistent grunge from the vinyl.

2. **Clean the turntable's needle.**

   Wipe it off with the little brush that comes with the turntable. Lost yours? Pick one up at the music or stereo store. They're cheap.

3. **Connect the turntable's output cables to your sound card.**

   See the "Connecting Sound Cables to Your Computer" section, earlier in this chapter.

4. **Adjust your recording level.**

   See the long black bar along the bottom of Cool Edit in Figure 8-4? That's the recording monitor. It flashes according to the incoming volume levels.

   Start playing your album and watch the monitor. If it flashes too close to the top, turn down the volume going into the sound card, or use the sound card's mixer program to turn down the incoming sound. (I cover how in this chapter's "Connecting Sound Cables to Your Computer" section.)

   If the level's too high, it will distort; if it's too low, you'll hear background noise. Take your time to find the right level before recording.

5. **Start the recording software.**

   Begin recording using Cool Edit, or another recording-and-editing package. (MusicMatch can also record albums, as described in Chapter 10, but it can't edit the resulting WAV files.)

6. **Play the album.**

   Be sure to press the Record button on your recording software *before* playing the album. Don't worry about the initial pop when the needle falls onto the record, or the empty space before the first song. You edit out those sounds later, as described in the "Editing a Recorded Sound" section.

- Hear a persistent humming sound in the background? Try plugging your computer and turntable into the same outlet. (Use an adapter, if needed.) The two devices then share a common ground.

- Remember to record at a level that's very close to the 0 on the recording level — but never too close. Otherwise, the recording won't sound loud compared to others, like MP3s created from CDs.

- Recording an old mono album? You might only hear the sound on one speaker. You can correct this with sound editing software, however, as explained later in this chapter.

- Record the entire album's first side, and save that as a WAV file. Then do the same with the flip side. It's easier to separate the tracks into separate files using Cool Edit, Sound Forge, or other sound-editing software.

- In the eyes of the law, converting albums to MP3 files isn't any different from copying CDs. You can keep the file for your own personal use, but don't give it away or sell it, or you might be violating copyrights.

Recording from Tapes, Camcorders, a Microphone, or TVs

Recording from TVs, audio tapes, or videotapes works the same as recording from an album. Why would you want to? Well, perhaps you want an MP3 file of that hot new band playing on David Letterman in the wee hours.

Or maybe you videotaped something with an exciting soundtrack. (You would be surprised at the sound quality from today's camcorders.)

Here's how to copy the sound from the TV show or tape to your hard drive, where it can be cleaned up and converted to an MP3 file.

1. **Connect the sound source's output cables to your sound card.**

   I describe how in the "Connecting Sound Cables to Your Computer" section, earlier in this chapter. Basically, you connect the Output cables of your sound source to your sound card's ⅛-inch Line-In jack. Table 8-1 shows the required cables.

   Remember that *everything* plugs into the sound card's Line-In jack except a microphone. Microphones must plug into the sound card's Mic jack.

2. **Adjust your recording levels and start recording.**

   Check out the Steps 4 and 5 in the "Recording from an Album" section; everything's the same. Make sure that you begin recording *before* your sound begins playing. You can always edit out any unwanted garbage later, but if Jeff Beck starts playing before you push the recording software's Record button, you're out of luck.

3. **Press the Stop button when through.**

   Grabbed the sound? Hit the Stop button on the recording software, and get ready to clean up the sound, as described in this chapter's "Editing a Recorded Sound" section.

Just because you can grab a TV performance off the air doesn't mean you own it. The same goes for a band playing at a local street fair. You can keep the soundtrack for your own personal use, but don't give it away or sell it, or you might be violating copyrights.

Editing Recorded Music or Sounds

After you record the music or sounds and save them as immense WAV files on the hard disk, you can convert them straight to MP3s using the Encoder programs described in Chapter 9.

But while the file's still in WAV format, there's no excuse not to touch it up a little bit. Remove those clicks and pops from the album; edit the TV sequence so it starts the moment David Letterman says, "And now, here's . . ."

Here are some tips for editing WAV files down to the best possible recording.

Making mono recordings play on both speakers

When recording from a mono source — a single microphone or a TV with only one speaker — the computer fills only one side of its stereo signal with the sound.

Ripping audio from the Internet

Saving audio or music sent in a "live stream" from the Internet is a copyright violation. That's why sound programs won't let you save incoming RealAudio programs. (I guess you could stick a microphone next to your PCs speaker, but it wouldn't sound very good.)

Versions of Winamp before Version 2.10 could save streamed MP3 files, but that function is disabled in the current versions. Older versions of Windows Media Player save streamed MP3 files in your Windows Temporary folder, if you take a peek.

You can't get true stereo from a mono recording, but you can fake it.

Tell your sound editing software to copy the recorded track onto the other, empty track. For instance, if the sound's only recorded on the right side, duplicate it to the left side, too.

The sound editing software can match up the two tracks so they're identically positioned. Save the resulting file, and your mono sound will now play over both speakers. It's still not stereo, but it's better than only one speaker.

Cutting out the bad parts

When you record something through a sound editor like Cool Edit, the software shows a pictures of the sound waves, like in Figure 8-6.

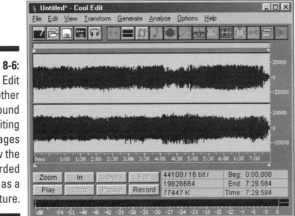

Figure 8-6: Cool Edit and other sound editing packages show the recorded sounds as a picture.

In a way, sound editing software works like word processing software. You position the cursor in different places to cut and copy sections, or move segments to different locations.

The first editing step is to find the beginning and end of your recorded sounds so you can trim off the unnecessary sounds. Use the software's Zoom or Magnify commands to magnify your view of the sound. That gives you a better picture of when sounds start and stop.

A tall wave means a loud sound; very small waves (or no waves) mean no sound.

Figure 8-7 shows a live recording in Cool Edit. Notice how the sound wave comes to an abrupt stop near where the cursor points in Figure 8-7? That's the end of the song, and you can delete anything past that point. Double-check by clicking at the ending point, and pressing the Play button. The software plays any sounds past that point, letting you make sure they're not needed.

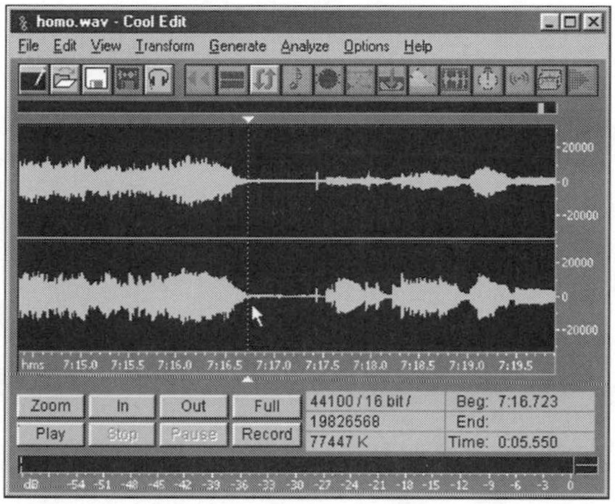

Figure 8-7:
Cool Edit shows where the sound file ends; the remaining wave can be trimmed.

Highlight all the sound waves past your chosen ending point; press the Delete key, and Cool Edit chops it out.

Here are some more editing tips:

✔ Listen to your file from the beginning to see when it actually starts. Click at the actual starting point, highlight the material in front of it, and delete it, too. Your resulting file is now trimmed to its exact size.

✔ Prefer a nice fade out on a recording? Choose where you would like the fade out to begin, highlight the sound from that spot onward, and choose the software's fade option. The software will make the sound fade away, like the ending of many songs.

✔ When dealing with a noisy recording, check your sound editing software's filter and noise reduction menus. Many of them can not only reduce the pops of a crackling album but cut out some hiss from tapes.

✔ The more money you spend on your sound editing software, the more tricks it has for manipulating your sounds. Sound Forge may be expensive, but it's full of features not found on less-expensive software. It has plenty of Undo features, so you can go back to normal if an experiment goes awry.

Chapter 9

Completing the MP3 File with an Encoder

*C*hances are, you won't need to read this chapter. If you're just converting your CDs into MP3s, move ahead to Chapter 10. It covers software designed expressly for that purpose.

But if you're converting something besides a CD — or you want to convert a WAV file into an MP3, this is the spot.

Besides, this chapter explains all that codec stuff you're bound to hear MP3 fans talk about.

What's a Codec?

Short for compression/decompression, a *codec* is the computer coding used to compress a file and then expand it when needed. MP3 stands for MPEG-1, Layer 3 because that's the name of the MP3 *standard* — the official name for the original codec used for creating MP3 files.

MP3 began in 1987 when Germany's Fraunhofer Institute and France's Thomson Consumer Electronics found a new way to compress video. They transferred the compression mechanism to audio, and the MPEG organization liked the concept so much they declared the codec a standard — MPEG-1 Layer 3, or MP3.

In fact, the timing of MP3 caught the recording industry by surprise. Until fairly recently, computers weren't powerful enough to compress CD-quality audio into such easily saved files. The creation of MP3 matched the timing of Pentium computers and fast modems, leading to a worldwide MP3 sonic boom of popularity on the Internet.

✔ MP3 certainly isn't the only type of codec. Sound and video can be compressed in many ways. However, MP3 is one of the best ways to compress sound while still retaining almost CD-quality sound.

✔ Interesting Factoid: France's Thomson Consumer Electronics, one of the creators of MP3, is putting out the Lyra portable MP3 player under the RCA brand name. Lyra's picture and description await in Chapter 6.

✔ Files aren't the only things using codecs. So does streaming audio — music that flows into your computer over the Internet. Compressing the audio before sending it saves download time, because the receiving computer can decompress the audio upon arrival.

✔ MPEG stands for Moving Pictures Experts Group, a bunch of programmer-types who think up new ways to compress things, and then think of imaginative new names to call them: MPEG-1 Layer 3, for example, as well as MPEG-2, MPEG-4, and MPEG-7. The group deals with video as well as sound.

✔ MPEG-1 comes in several layers, but MP3 uses only the Layer 3 standard. It sounds better than other standards (Layers 1 and 2) because it's more complex, requiring more processing power to handle the compression and decompression chores.

✔ You'll find more technical information than you can stomach at the MPEG Organization's Official Web site, `drogo.cselt.stet.it/mpeg/`, as well as the more easily readable `www.mpeg.org`.

Okay, how do they compress an MP3 file's sound?

Human hearing isn't perfect. Dogs can hear more accurately; that's why they start howling several minutes before the fire engine passes by.

MP3 takes advantage of the human ear's imperfections by editing out the sounds and tones humans can't hear. It does that by taking the audio file and dividing it into a bunch of separate frequency bands. The software then examines the bands and decides which portions of the bands are inaudible to the average human.

Imagine an agitated piano player sitting at a broken piano. You'd hear the player's fingers pounding at the keys, as well as occasional grunts of frustration. When you fix the piano and it begins to play, the sound masks out the once-audible grunts and finger noises.

Similarly, a particularly loud sound in a song masks out lower-volume sounds. So, when the compression software examines the layers of sound frequencies, it saves the loud layer, but discards the adjacent layers containing quieter sounds.

By eliminating sounds on the inaudible frequencies, MP3 reduces the file's size. Humans won't notice much, if any, difference, but your dog might. Don't use MP3 on music your dog enjoys.

Which Codec Is Best?

Just as gourmets never agree on the best wine — or even the best way to create wine — programmers can never agree on the best codec — the backbone of MP3.

All files encoded using MP3 technology must be able to play on all MP3 players. However, just as different types and brands of cassette tape work in everybody's player, different types of codecs can create MP3 files that play on all MP3 players.

And just as each brand of tape is made of the basic components, nearly every codec is based on the original programming work done by Fraunhofer. In fact, Fraunhofer has shut down several encoding programs for alleged copyright violations. Other programs pay a license to Fraunhofer to use their technology.

Some codecs start with the Fraunhofer codec, but alter it slightly, changing the way it compresses the sound into the MP3 standard. Some codecs require more time and processing power, but create better-sounding MP3 files. Others are quick, but not as effective.

Because Fraunhofer charges licensing fees for the use of its technology, you rarely find any free encoding software for creating high-quality MP3s. (The free versions usually only encode at lower quality rates.)

- ✔ All encoder software uses a type of MP3 codec to convert standard audio files (WAV files, as described in Chapter 9) into MP3 files, shrinking the file to the defined MP3 standards.

- ✔ Because Fraunhofer came up with the original MP3 codec, it's generally regarded as one of the best quality, and it's usually the basis for other MP3 codecs.

- ✔ Bunches of MP3 codecs are out there — Xing, BladeEnc, and others. To choose the best, simply listen to them all and choose the one that sounds best to you. Try listening through headphones, or ask around on the newsgroups described in Chapter 4.

Using an Encoder

All encoders work the same way. First, choose your WAV file (anything ripped using the steps in Chapter 8), and choose the quality level. Then press the Encode button and twiddle your thumbs for a while.

Choosing the quality level is pretty much a no-brainer. The MP3 standard calls for files to be encoded at 128 bits, 44kHz, stereo. If you want your songs to sound the best, use those settings.

✔ Not all encoders let you create MP3 files at those settings, however. In fact, many shareware versions of programs use that fact to encourage people to register and pay for program. When you send in the money, the program lets you encode at the standard 128 bits. RealAudio's RealJukebox, for instance, encodes at 96 rather than 128 bits. MusicMatch does something similar.

✔ The freely available Fraunhofer codec used by the Windows latest version of Media Player can only encode up to 56 bits per second, and 22kHz stereo. If you buy the advanced codec from Opticom (www.opticom.de) for $49.95, you can reach the normal MP3 quality levels.

Can I install one codec for *all* my programs to use?

Some codecs don't come built into separate programs. Instead, they're Windows "plug-ins" known as Audio Codec Managers (ACM). Once installed, any Windows audio recording program can use the ACM — Cool Edit, Sound Forge or even Windows Sound Recorder — to create MP3s.

You'll find a free Fraunhofer ACM codec by installing Windows Media Player 6.0 (available at the download section of www.microsoft.com) or by downloading Microsoft's Net Show development, as described in Chapter 7.

The freebie ACM Fraunhofer codec can decode 128-bit or better MP3 files — it sounds great. However, it only allows encoding up to 56K at 22,050kHz stereo, which is far from the average quality MP3 file. To up the quality to normal levels, you must buy the advanced codec from Opticom (www.opticom.de) for $49.

Chapter 10

MusicMatch Jukebox's All-in-One Software: From CD to MP3

• •

• •

Some software performs one task, then stops, waiting for the next program to take over. CD rippers, for example, copy music from your CD onto your hard drive. The encoders then go to work, converting the ripped WAV files into MP3s.

MusicMatch Jukebox, by contrast, does everything at once: When you insert the CD and push a button, a window appears, listing the song titles. Click the songs you want encoded, and the software automatically converts them into MP3s.

Best yet, MusicMatch Jukebox comes free on the CD in the back of this book. This chapter shows you how to install it and put it to work.

Installing MusicMatch Jukebox

Follow the steps below to install MusicMatch Jukebox, the software installed on this book's CD.

MusicMatch Jukebox works only on Windows 95, Windows 98, and Windows NT 4 or newer operating systems. Plus, your computer must be a Pentium 166MHz or faster. Without one, the software will probably give up during the installation process. Finally, some older CD-ROM drives can't handle "ripping." If your drive has trouble, it may need an upgrade.

The MusicMatch Jukebox installation process doesn't differ much from most software packages. Feel free to follow the directions on the screen, referring to these steps if you encounter a head-scratcher.

1. **Close any programs before you begin the setup process.**

   Do this before installing *any* program. Sometimes programs share resources, and when a new program tries to butt in, everybody's unhappy.

MusicMatch
Jukebox 4

2. **Insert the Installation CD into your CD ROM drive, and double-click the MusicMatch icon.**

   The MusicMatch icon looks like the one in the margin.

3. **Click the Next button at the Welcome screen.**

4. **Read the, uh, 15-page License Agreement and click Yes.**

   Accept the terms? Then click the Yes button. Don't like the terms? Then click No, which means no software for you.

5. **Click the Next button to choose the installation folder.**

   Almost all Windows programs like to install themselves in the Program Files folder on your C: drive. By clicking Next, the software creates a MusicMatch Jukebox 4 folder in the Program Files folder.

6. **Click the Next button and choose where to store your newly created MP3 files.**

   Choosing Next means MusicMatch will store all your MP3s in a Music folder on your C: drive, inside the program's folder. The program stores each CD's group of MP3 files into a different folder, making things easy to find later.

7. **Choose where you would like the MusicMatch icon stored on your Start button, and click Next.**

   Whew! The program copies itself to your hard drive.

8. **Choose whether MusicMatch should be your default MP3 player.**

   When you double-click an MP3 file, do you want MusicMatch to play the song? Or do you have another player, like Winamp, that you prefer? Click Yes to make MusicMatch play them; click No to let another player handle the chores. (I prefer Winamp, so I click No.)

9. **Choose whether MusicMatch should play your playlists.**

   The .m3u files are playlists — lists of MP3 files. Some people don't even have playlists. I click No, allowing Winamp to keep playing my playlists. (That works better for SHOUTcast, too, as described in Chapter 7.) If you want MusicMatch to handle your playlists, click Yes.

10. **Choose whether MusicMatch Jukebox should play your CDs.**

   This one doesn't really matter. Winamp can play CDs, as can a host of other Windows programs. I let Winamp keep playing mine, so I click No.

11. **Click the Yes button so MusicMatch restarts your computer, and then click the Finish button.**

   Whew! You've finally installed MusicMatch. Your computer needs to restart so it can find the program and make sure everything is in order.

   When your computer comes back to life, an icon for MusicMatch Jukebox rests upon your desktop, ready to be clicked into action.

Putting MusicMatch to Work

MusicMatch Jukebox does a lot more than offer one-step conversion of songs into MP3 files. If your computer's hooked up to the Internet, MusicMatch automatically dials into a database of album names and titles. After locating your particular CD's contents, MusicMatch Jukebox automatically names each MP3 appropriately.

If that's not enough, the program also fills in the MP3's Tag information, as discussed in Chapter 18. Click a few more buttons, and MusicMatch grabs the CD's cover from the Internet, and stores it with your MP3s, ready to display when playing back the songs.

The next few sections show how to make MusicMatch automate tasks that once took hours of work.

The Recorder: Making an MP3 file from a CD

MusicMatch can convert an entire CD all at once, or just grab the songs you want. Either way, follow these steps to rev up MusicMatch's MP3 creator and start creating MP3s.

1. **Start MusicMatch by double-clicking its icon on your desktop.**

   Or start MusicMatch from your Start button, depending on where you told the program to lodge itself in Step 7 of the Installation process. The program leaps into action, as shown in Figure 10-1.

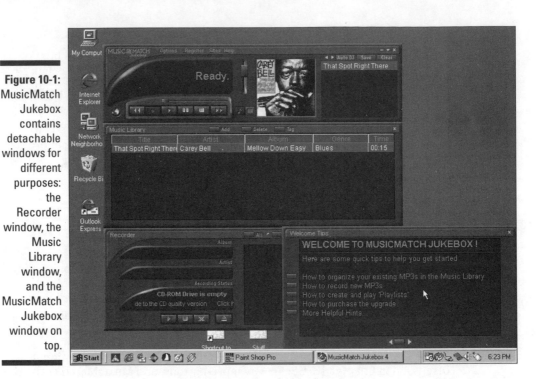

Figure 10-1:
MusicMatch
Jukebox
contains
detachable
windows for
different
purposes:
the
Recorder
window, the
Music
Library
window,
and the
MusicMatch
Jukebox
window on
top.

Just like Chapter 5's Winamp, MusicMatch consists of several detachable windows. The bottom-right corner is the Welcome Tips box. Feel free to click some of the tips to become familiar with the program.

The Welcome Tips box partially covers the Recorder box. Only necessary while creating MP3s, the Recorder box lists a CD's songs. The Music Library box, in the middle, is where the MP3s stay organized by CD for easy access.

Don't see MusicMatch's Recorder window? Choose View from the MusicMatch window's Options command, and select Show Recorder.

Finally, the MusicMatch Jukebox sits on top, ready to play any selected CDs or MP3s.

2. Close the Welcome Tips box.

Click the little arrow in its top-right corner. To keep it from reappearing, click in the box marked Show Welcome Tips at start up; that removes the checkmark, and the box no longer appears.

3. Insert the music CD into your CD-ROM drive.

When the CD is inserted into the drive, MusicMatch uses your Internet account to dial up CDDB (www.cddb.com), a database of CD titles and their songs. Figure 10-2 shows how it correctly identified Jimi Hendrix' Electric Ladyland CD, and automatically entered all the CD's song titles.

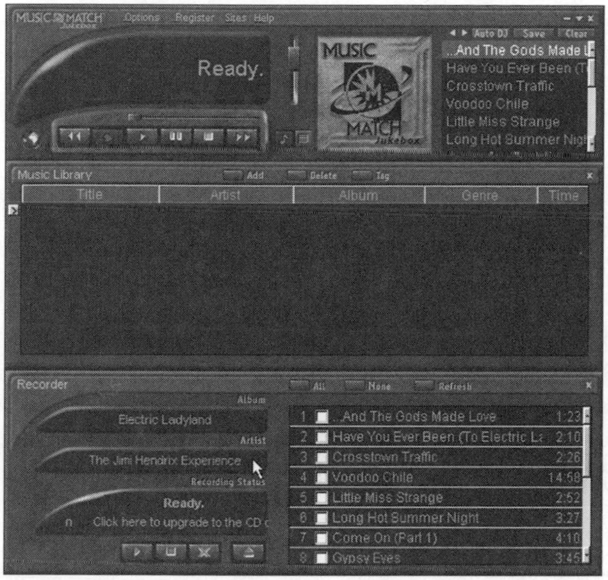

Figure 10-2:
MusicMatch
uses an
Internet
connection
to identify
the CD's title
and songs.

No Internet connection? Feel free to type in the titles yourself.

4. **Choose the songs to be converted, or click All to select them all.**

   Click in the box next to a song to mark it for conversion to MP3. Clicking the All button, right above the songs, selects all of them.

5. **Click the Record button to begin converting songs to MP3 files.**

   The first time MusicMatch creates MP3 files, it must examine your CD's configuration, as shown in Figure 10-3. Click the OK button and wait for 10 to 30 seconds for the program to finish. (You have to do this only once.) The program then converts the songs, storing the MP3 files in the folder you selected during Step 6. (Chances are, they're stored in C:\Program Files\MusicMatch\Music.)

   ✔ As the program encodes your CD's songs, it lines them up in the Music Library Window, shown earlier in Figure 10-1, and adds them to the Music Library for easy access later.

   ✔ If your new MP3 file sounds weird, you may be pushing your processor too hard. MusicMatch Jukebox rips and encodes in a single step, so it requires more processing power than plain encoders.

   ✔ Don't use your laptop with MusicMatch. The CD-ROM drives built into laptops are built for energy conservation, not smooth reading. Laptops play MP3s okay, but usually do a terrible job of creating them.

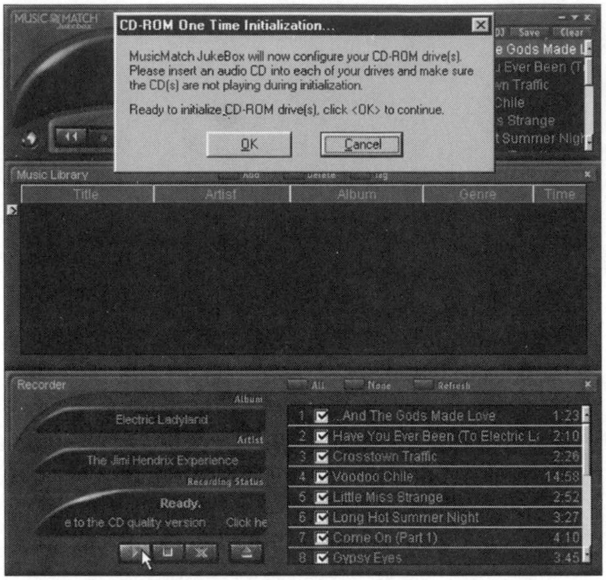

Figure 10-3:
When first
used,
MusicMatch
Jukebox
examines
your
CD-ROM
drive to
make sure
everything
is okay.

✔ MusicMatch is considered shareware, which means the program works, but it works better when you register it. Currently, the program only converts at 96Kpbs, not the 128Kpbs standard. That's called "near-CD quality" by the software, but it's not the best sound possible. A $29.99 registration fee buys a secret code; when entered into the program, it instantly unlocks the goodies, letting you encode MP3s at the standard 128Kpbs rate.

✔ Some people intentionally encode files at 96Kpbs or lower. The files will be smaller, letting you squeeze more of them into a Rio or Nomad. Actually, you probably can't tell the difference between the two formats when on a skateboard doing a one-footed, nose-boned tailgrab.

Music Library: Playing MP3 files

MusicMatch displays your MP3s in a list in the Music Library window, just like books stacked on a shelf. But the files are a lot easier to organize than CDs or albums.

First, notice the words Title, Artist, Album, Genre, and Time along the top of the Music Library window. Click any of those words to sort the MP3s in the list. Clicking Name, for instance, sorts the songs by name. Click Album, and the songs are sorted by their CD's name, bringing all the CDs together in the list.

Or if you're looking for short songs, click Time to list them all by length.

Selecting songs works just like selecting files in Windows. Hold down Ctrl and click files to select them one by one. Or click one file, hold down Shift, and click another file to highlight files in between.

After you select files, drag and drop them into the Playlist window, as shown in Figure 10-4. Click the Play button (the buttons look just like they do on a tape recorder) and the selected files begin to play.

Don't see the Music Library window? Choose <u>V</u>iew from the MusicMatch Library's <u>O</u>ptions menu, and select Show <u>M</u>usic Library.

Adding CD art and tag information

Here's a little trick. MP3 files come with a special tag containing the song's title, album, and other information. MusicMatch automatically fills out most of that as soon as you encode the CD.

But here's how to grab the CD's cover art, as well. You don't need a scanner, and you don't even have to use your CD's original art. Just follow these steps and MusicMatch automatically displays your CD's cover art whenever it plays a song from that CD.

1. **Drag any MP3 song from your newly encoded CD to the Music Library to the play list in the upper-right corner of the MusicMatch Jukebox.**

   Figure 10-4 shows the action.

Figure 10-4:
Drag the song that needs art to the play list window.

2. **Choose <u>B</u>uy CD site from <u>S</u>ites menu in the MusicMatch Jukebox's window.**

   Don't worry, you're not going to buy a CD you already own. MusicMatch has worked out a secret deal with Buy CD site that becomes clear later.

3. **When the Buy CD site appears in your Internet browser, type your CD's name in the Title box.**

   The Buy CD site has two boxes at the top; one is marked Artist, the other is the Find It box. You can type the name of your CD's creator into the Find It box and click the button to find every CD by that artist.

   A quicker way is to click in the little arrow by the Artist box; when the drop-down menu appears, choose Album Title. Just type your CD's title into the Find It box, and click the adjacent button.

   When your CD appears in the Web site, you'll also spot the treasure: a picture of the CD's cover, ready for the taking.

4. **Right-click the cover, choose <u>C</u>opy from the menu, and close your browser.**

   As shown in Figure 10-5, choose <u>C</u>opy to copy the CD's cover to the Windows Clipboard. Close your browser; you don't need it anymore.

5. **Choose <u>E</u>dit from the MusicMatch <u>O</u>ptions menu, and choose the <u>P</u>aste/Tag art from clipboard option.**

   Wham! Your CD cover appears in MusicMatch, as shown in Figure 10-6.

Figure 10-5: Right-click your CD's cover from the Web page, and choose Copy to copy the art to the Windows' Clipboard.

Options Register Sites Help
Ready.
Auto DJ Save Clear
...And The Gods Made Lc

Figure 10-6: Your CD cover appears in MusicMatch.

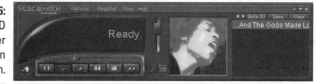

6. **In Music Library, click the song you dragged to the playlist and choose Tag.**

   Now it's time to fill out your newly created MP3s' Tag information, making sure they're all linked to the new art file. When you click Tag, a window pops up. It's filled out with the title of the song, its album, and the newly acquired art, but you can add more, as shown in Figure 10-7.

7. **Fill out the Tag form and choose Update Tag.**

   Notice how most of the boxes have a tiny checkbox next to them? (The arrow points to one in Figure 10-7.) If you're filling out a box that applies to every song on the CD — the CD's Art, or the Record Year, for example — click that tiny box.

   Then, when you click the Update Tag button, MusicMatch uses that information to automatically fill out the tags for the other songs.

   By assigning artwork to one file, and then updating that tag to include all the other songs on the CD, every song from that CD will display the artwork.

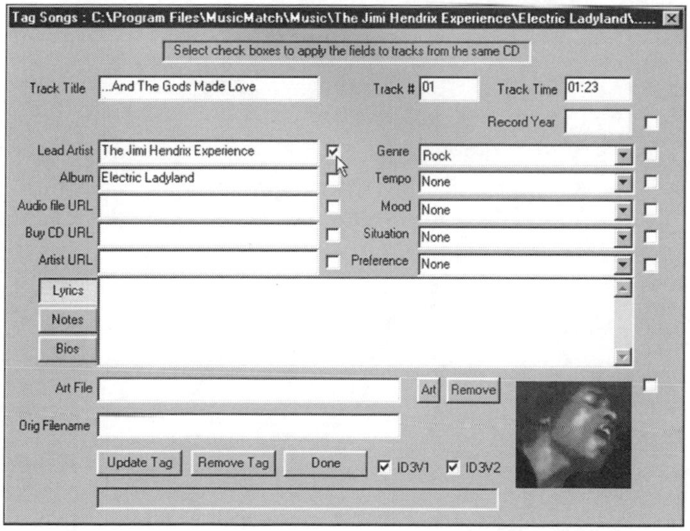
Tag Songs : C:\Program Files\MusicMatch\Music\The Jimi Hendrix Experience\Electric Ladyland\.....
Select check boxes to apply the fields to tracks from the same CD
Track Title
...And The Gods Made Love
Track #
01
Track Time
01:23
Record Year
Lead Artist
The Jimi Hendrix Experience
Album
Electric Ladyland
Audio file URL
Buy CD URL
Artist URL
Genre
Rock
Tempo
None
Mood
None
Situation
None
Preference
None
Lyrics
Notes
Bios
Art File
Art
Remove
Orig Filename
Update Tag
Remove Tag
Done
ID3V1
ID3V2

Figure 10-7: Fill out the Tag window to assign information, including the cover art, to each file from the CD.

Creating MP3s from Albums or Other Sources

MusicMatch creates MP3s from albums, camcorders, or anything else that makes a noise.

Connect a Y cable from your audio source, and plug it into your sound card's Line-In jack, as described in Chapter 8. Then perform the following steps:

1. **Choose Recorder from the Music Match Jukebox's Options menu.**

2. **Choose Source from the menu that emerges, and select Line In.**

3. **Turn on your sound source — start playing the album, turn on the camcorder, or whatever else you're recording — and quickly press the Record button on MusicMatch's Recorder.**

The program automatically transfers the incoming sound into MP3 format, skipping the WAV file in the process.

Chapter 11

Saving MP3 Songs on a CD

● ●

● ●

*C*ompact discs may look the same, but they come in a wide variety of formats. Each format is designed for a different task. You can't buy one disc that does it all. In fact, you can't even buy a compact disc drive — a *CD-ROM drive* — that does it all. There are too many different formats for a drive to understand.

Understanding CD Formats

The next few sections explain the types of CDs on the market, what you can do with them, and when they're simply not up to the task.

CD-R discs

Short for *CD-Recordable*, these have also been labeled *WORM* discs by the People Who Like Letters Department. WORM stands for Write Once, Read Multiple. That means data can be written to them once, then read many times.

For years, CD-R discs ruled the CD world. Music CDs, as well as software programs, came on CD-R discs. Although the discs themselves were relatively cheap, the machines that made them — the CD *burners* — cost oodles of dollars.

Today, many computers come with inexpensive CD-ROM drives that can write information to discs. Known as Read/Write drives, these drives copy or *burn* files onto a blank CD-R disc. They can also read discs, just like their predecessors.

These Read/Write drives can't sling data as fast as their predecessors, though. If you replace your 32X CD-ROM drive with a Read/Write drive for burning CDs, you'll notice it's slower at reading CDs. (And burning CDs takes much, much longer than reading them.)

When choosing a new CD-ROM drive — or when buying discs to feed it, keep the following points in mind.

- ✔ When a blank CD-R disc is full of information, the fun is over. The disc can't be reused, like a floppy disc. You can't erase the freebie CDs that America Online sends out and use them for storing your own data.

- ✔ Luckily, the price of CD-R discs keeps spiraling downward. You can buy a bag of bulk CD-R discs for about dollar a piece.

- ✔ MP3 users must choose between two formats when burning information onto CDs. They either store MP3 files onto the CD, or they store audio files. The two formats are completely different. One is a computer file, and can only be played back in a computer. The other is digital audio that can be read in any regular home stereo CD player.

- ✔ If you burn MP3 files onto a CD, you can fit several hundred songs onto the CD. However, that CD only plays back on your computer. To play MP3 songs on your home stereo, you need to decompress the MP3 files and convert them to audio files. That means you can only fit about a dozen or so songs onto a CD.

- ✔ The CDs designed for playback on a home stereo are known as Red Book CDs. Why? Because those players use an oddly named standard called "Red Book." The CD players sold in stereo stores are designed to play CDs that use the Red Book standard — and nothing else.

- ✔ The market is slowly seeing a few home stereo MP3 players. These look like regular CD players, and they connect to your home stereo, but they play songs in the MP3 format. That means you can burn a few hundred MP3 files onto a CD, push the CD into the home stereo MP3 player, and hear several hours of songs. The player decompresses the songs before sending the music to your amplifier. Unfortunately, they're still in the development stages, or I'd stick a rebate coupon in the back of the book.

- ✔ Keep an eye on MP3.com's hardware section for the latest developments on home stereo MP3 players.

CD-RW discs

After a few years, computer technicians tired of discs that couldn't be reused like floppy discs. So they created a new technology called CD-Rewritable (CD-RW) discs. These discs can be written to, erased, and written to again.

Some older CD-R disc drives can't handle the new format, but it's quickly gaining acceptance among manufacturers. And all CD-RW drives can read CD-R discs.

However, CD-RW discs don't have much use among MP3 users because the discs cost so darn much — three to five times as much. And just as most people don't throw away their CD collections, little reason exists to erase a collection of MP3 files.

Besides, a home stereo can't read CD-RW discs, no matter how the information is stored.

Although CD-R and CD-RW discs can both be written to, only CD-RW discs can be erased and written to again. CD-R is used for permanent storage; CD-RW is for temporary storage — yesterday's backup files, for instance, which are replaced with today's backup files.

DAM CDs

Most CD-ROM drives can play CDs containing MP3s as well as the audio CDs from the music store.

But your home stereo isn't as versatile; it can only play audio CDs. However, MP3.com, the most popular MP3 Internet site, has come up with a new method known as *DAM*, or Digital Audio Music CDs.

These compact discs take advantage of an MP3 file's small size. So, MP3.com burns a CD with the audio files, then fills the leftover space with those same songs in MP3 format.

That gives you the best of both worlds. You can put the CD in your home stereo to play the audio songs, or you can play both the MP3 and audio versions on your computer's CD-ROM drive.

In fact, you can even copy the CD's MP3 files to your computer for playback on your hard drive.

Some older CD players and CD-ROM drives can't play DAM CDs. In fact, some CD-ROM drives won't be able to spot the MP3 files in Windows Explorer file manager. You may need to upgrade your CD-ROM drive to take advantage of this format.

Before buying a new CD-ROM drive, try the DAM disc on several computers. You may just have a bad disc.

Creating MP3 CDs to Play on Your Computer

The concept sounds easy: Just copy the MP3 files to your CD as if it were a floppy disk. Unfortunately, it's not always easy in reality. Different brands of CD-ROM drives come with different types of software.

CD-burning software can write to drives in a couple different ways:

- **Packet writing:** Your software should support this type of writing in order to make a CD full of MP3 files. Just like the name sounds, packet writing software sends information to the CD in packets — it copies information file by file, then stops. You can add more later, if you want. Not all CD recorders support packet writing, and not all CD-ROM drives can read packet-written discs. The feature must be built-in to the drive.

- **Track at Once:** This method writes a single track to the disc and stops, leaving a few seconds' pause before writing the next track. Use this method for creating audio CDs from MP3 files that have been converted to WAV files.

Your best bet is to use the best software for the job: Adaptec's DirectCD (www.adaptec.com). My computer came with Adaptec's CD Wizard for writing files onto my Philips CDD 3610 R/W drive. The software lets me write files to the disc, or create audio CDs.

When buying a new CD recordable drive, check the box for the bundled software. Adaptec often packages a version of its software with the drive.

Here's how to use Adaptec's CD Wizard to copy MP3 files onto a blank CD-R disc.

1. **Insert the blank CD-R disc into the CD recordable drive.**

2. **Click Adaptec's little CD icon in the lower-right corner of your screen.**

   Adaptec's software places a little CD icon in the corner of your screen. By choosing Adaptec's icon, you immediately see the status of your CD, as shown in Figure 11-1.

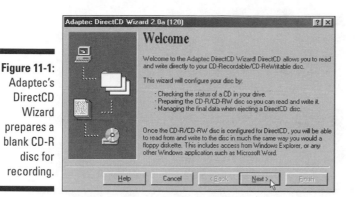

Figure 11-1:
Adaptec's
DirectCD
Wizard
prepares a
blank CD-R
disc for
recording.

3. **When the Welcome screen appears, shown in Figure 11-1, click Next.**

4. **Choose your CD-R drive from the file browser window, and click Next.**

   This one is pretty much a no-brainer. Most people have a single CD-R drive. In my case, shown in Figure 11-2, the drive is G:. Adaptec describes it correctly as holding a blank CD-R disc that's possible for conversion to DirectCD format, which is the packet writing format necessary for copying MP3 files onto the disc.

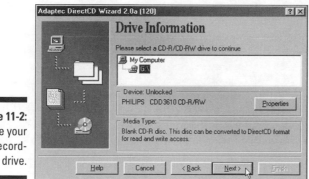

Figure 11-2:
Choose your
CD-record-
able drive.

5. **Choose the DirectCD option from the menu and click Next.**

   Here, Adaptec offers two choices, as shown in Figure 11-3. The DirectCD format allows reading and writing to the CD from Windows Explorer, whereas the Easy CD Creator writes audio files to the CD. To store MP3 files on the disc, choose the DirectCD option to allow packet writing.

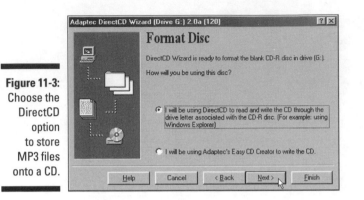

6. **Type a name for the disc into the box and click Finish.**

Just as you need to name a folder, you need to name a disc. The disc is named MP3 Disc, as shown in Figure 11-4. When you click Finish, the program formats the disc and puts it under the DirectCD's packet writing system.

7. **When the disc is ready, click OK.**

After the software spends a few minutes formatting the disc, it finishes up with an announcement that it's through. Click the OK button to continue. Now, when you look at the disc in My Computer, like in Figure 11-5, you see the amount of storage space available. But wait — the CD says it has 650MB of space on the box, but there's only 619MB free space.

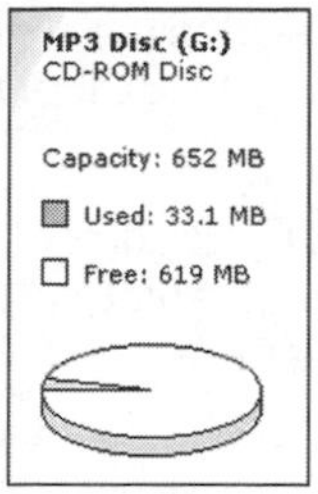

Figure 11-5:
Although a
CD-R disc
has 650MB
of space,
only 619MB
is available
for storage.

MP3 Disc (G:)
CD-ROM Disc

Capacity: 652 MB

☐ Used: 33.1 MB

☐ Free: 619 MB

That's because the file management overhead requires 33.1MB of space. Windows uses that space to keep track of a file's location on the disc, its name, and other vital statistics.

8. **Drag and drop the MP3 files from your hard drive onto the disc.**

Select your MP3 files from wherever you've stored them on your hard drive, drag them over to the disc, and let go of the mouse button, as shown in Figure 11-6. Windows immediately begins copying the files.

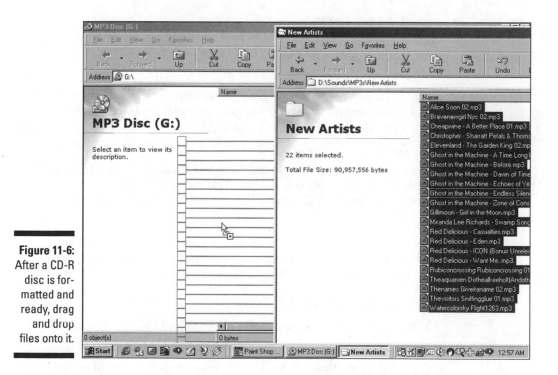

Figure 11-6:
After a CD-R
disc is for-
matted and
ready, drag
and drop
files onto it.

✔ For the best sound — especially with slow computers and hard drives — defragment the hard drive first. Right-click the hard drive's icon in My Computer, choose Properties, and select the Tools tab. Click the Defragment Now button to start the process.

✔ Adaptec's software makes working with CDs nearly foolproof. As soon as you insert a CD, it automatically checks the disc's format, letting you choose how it should be treated.

✔ The packet writing software doesn't require the entire disc to be filled at one session. You can add some new ones every day. Feel free to add as many MP3 files as you want until the disc is full.

✔ Many CD writers don't support packet writing, forcing you to write all your MP3 files to the disc at once.

✔ When you start to eject the disc, Adaptec gives you the option of "organizing" the disc so it can be read by other computers, or leaving it "as-is," so it can be written to again when you insert it. Unless you want other computers to read it, leave it as-is. You can always make Adaptec organize it when it's full.

Creating MP3 CDs That Play on Your Stereo's CD Player

If you copy a bunch of MP3 files onto a CD, it will play fine on your computer — but your home stereo's CD player will ignore it. CD players like their music uncompressed, not squeezed down like an MP3 file. The solution is to decompress the file.

Luckily, you can decompress the file using MusicMatch — the all-in-one MP3 creator bundled with this book. You can find those instructions in Chapter 10. After you transform MP3 files into WAV files, save them in a folder, ready for easy access.

Then follow these steps to turn the WAV files into audio files and copy them onto a disc. CD-Recordable drives come with different types of software; these steps use Adaptec's Easy CD Creator, available at www.adaptec.com.

1. **Convert the MP3 files to WAV files.**

   You can do this with MusicMatch, as described in Chapter 10.

2. **Insert the blank CD-R disc into the CD recordable drive.**

3. **Click Adaptec's little CD icon in the lower-right corner of your screen.**

   Adaptec's software places a little CD icon in the corner of your screen. By choosing Adaptec's icon, you immediately see the status of your CD, as shown in Figure 11-1, earlier in this chapter.

4. **When the status screen appears, click Next.**

5. **Choose your CD-R drive, and click Next.**

   This one's pretty much a no-brainer. Most people usually have a single CD-R drive. In my case, shown in Figure 11-2 earlier, the drive is G:. Adaptec describes it correctly as holding a blank CD-R disc.

6. **Choose the DirectCD option from the menu and click Next.**

   Here, Adaptec offers two choices, as shown in Figure 11-7. The DirectCD format allows reading and writing to the CD from Windows Explorer, whereas the Easy CD Creator writes audio files to the CD. To create an audio CD, choose the Easy CD Creator option.

Figure 11-7:
Choose the
Easy CD
Creator
option to
create an
audio CD
that plays
on your
home
stereo.

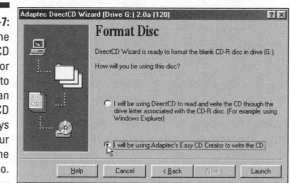

7. **Choose Audio CD from the Easy CD Creator's Welcome screen that appears.**

   At this point, the CD Wizard passes control to the Easy CD Creator Wizard, which asks whether you want to store data files or audio files on the CD. Choose the Audio CD button, as shown in Figure 11-8.

Figure 11-8:
Choose the
Easy CD
Creator's
Audio CD
button.

8. **Select the WAV files to be copied to the CD and click the A̲dd Now button.**

   Use the browser to select the file containing the WAV files you created in Step 1. MP3 files won't do — they must be WAV files. Click the A̲dd Now button, as shown in Figure 11-9.

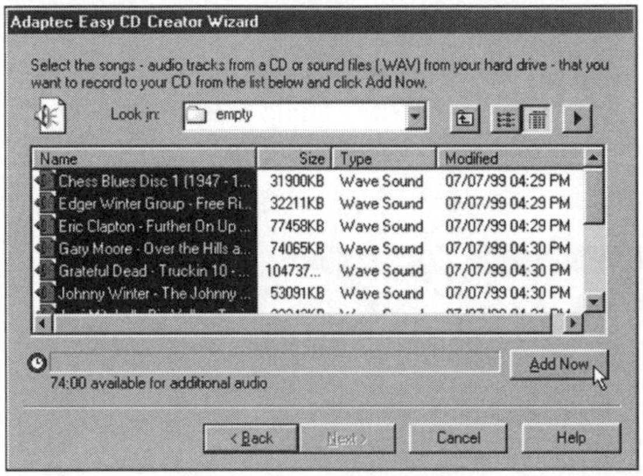

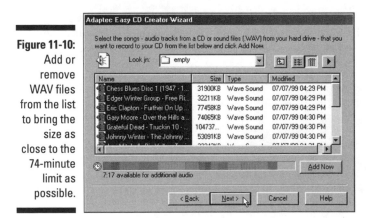

Figure 11-9:
Choose the WAV files you con-verted in Step 1 and click the A̲dd Now button.

9. **Add any additional WAV files that will fit on the disc and click N̲ext.**

   After clicking A̲dd Now in Step 8, Easy CD Creator adds the songs to its list, as shown in Figure 11-10. A stripe along the bottom of the front window shows the songs' size; beneath the stripe, the program shows the amount of time left on the CD. You can add or remove WAV songs to bring the total to 74 minutes — the disc's total capacity.

Figure 11-10:
Add or remove WAV files from the list to bring the size as close to the 74-minute limit as possible.

10. **Name the disc and its contents and click Next.**

   After you select the songs, type in a title for the disc, as well as the artist. If you're creating a mixture, type Miscellaneous, Hits, or Driving Tunes.

11. **Test the CD Writing process, if necessary.**

   If your CD-R drive hasn't created an audio disc, click the Perform the test button. It simulates the writing process, making sure your computer is fast enough to handle the writing process. After creating a few successful audio CDs, don't bother with the test anymore.

12. **Choose the Create CD later option.**

   Choosing the Create CD later option lets you rearrange the order the songs appear on the CD; it also lets you create a label for the case.

13. **Drag and drop the songs into the order you want them played.**

14. **Create a label for your CD's case.**

   Adaptec's Easy CD Creator lets you print a label for your CD's case, showing its contents, as shown in Figure 11-11.

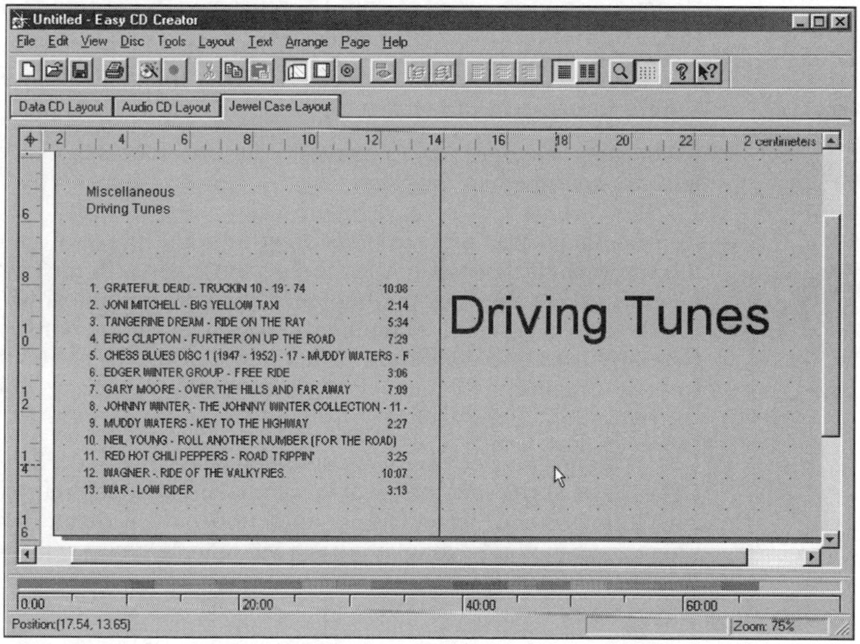

Figure 11-11: Create a label for your new CD's case with Adaptec Easy CD Creator.

15. Choose Create CD from the File menu.

This step puts the CD into motion. The software tells the drive what to do, and it begins burning your songs onto the disc in the correct order, as shown in Figure 11-12.

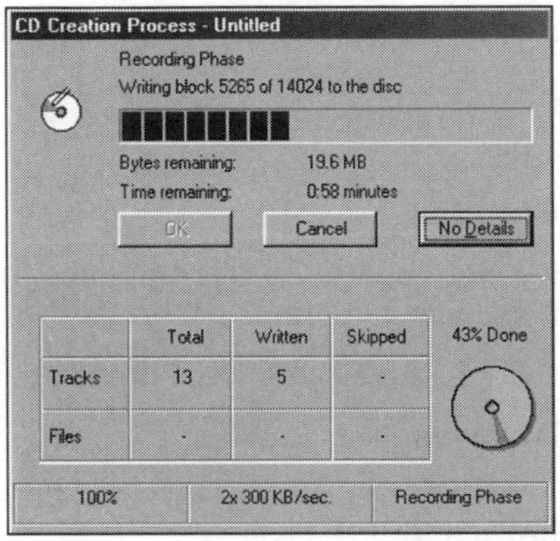

Figure 11-12:
Create a label for your new CD's case with Adaptec Easy CD Creator.

Depending on the speed of your CD burner, your CD could take an hour to create. Yawn.

When you're done creating the CD, print out the label for your CD case. Trim it to size, and slide it into the case's grooves.

CD burning is a great way to convert your old albums to CDs. Doing so lets you hear them in the car.

✔ Here's another way to hear MP3s on your home stereo: Connect your Rio or other MP3 player to the stereo's amplifier with the same Y-adapter cable described in Chapter 5. Turn the volume down on both the Rio and the stereo, then plug the ⅛-inch jack into your Rio, and the two RCA jacks into your stereo amplifier's Aux plugs. Switch the stereo to Aux, turn on the Rio, and slowly turn up the volume on both until you hear your Rio's songs.

✔ Don't care for MusicMatch? Winamp can also convert MP3s to WAV files. Click in the upper-left corner of Winamp, and choose Preferences from the Options menu. Select Output and choose the Nullsoft Disk Writer plug-in. When you begin playing the MP3 file, Winamp will save the WAV in a file of your choosing.

✔ You can find everything you need to know about CDs at Andy McFadden's highly regarded CD-Recordable FAQ. It's at www.fadden.com/cdrfaq.

Part IV
MP3s for the Musician

The 5th Wave By Rich Tennant

"It's not great fidelity, but I'm surprised you can download an MP3 file into an electric pencil sharpener at all."

In this part . . .

Most people love MP3 because they can hear free music. But that's exactly why some musicians fear MP3. If it's free, how can I make a buck?

This part of the book is aimed at the musicians in the crowd — the people creating the music that's being tossed around on the Internet.

After sweating for months to create a CD, why just give it away to people who probably won't even buy it? Why go through the hassles of creating CDs, boxes, and artwork?

In short, why bother?

This part of the book not only tells why, it tells exactly how. It interviews four musicians, from Broadway show players to back-porch pickers trying to learn a Macintosh. You'll hear how a musician with a synthesizer and a Sound Blaster recorded a CD that ended up on Amazon.

Finally, you'll discover exactly how to record your CD, package, and put it in the right retail channels to sell after the MP3-listening audience realizes how good your songs really are.

Chapter 12

Why Bother with MP3s?

*Y*ou've heard the songs, you've seen the names. Now, here are the stories behind some musicians with MP3 songs on the Internet. Some have made money, received radio play, and been featured on television; others have sold three CDs.

But whether they're selling three hundred CDs or three, they're all happy that they've embraced MP3 technology. This chapter tells why.

Cobain Morrisson and The Remedy

Site: www.mp3.com/artists/3/cobain_morrisson.html

As an 11-year-old kid in New Jersey, Cobain Morrisson started his first band. Six years later, his band "The Weevils" landed an East Coast hit with its single, "Space Girl." Morrisson took his British Invasion sound on the road, eventually winding up on the West Coast for a one-CD deal with a small independent label, Red Raven.

"About a month after I signed," he remembered, "someone at the label said there's a new technology out called MP3." Morrisson converted a few songs to MP3 and uploaded them to MP3.com (see Figure 12-1). His decision came quickly.

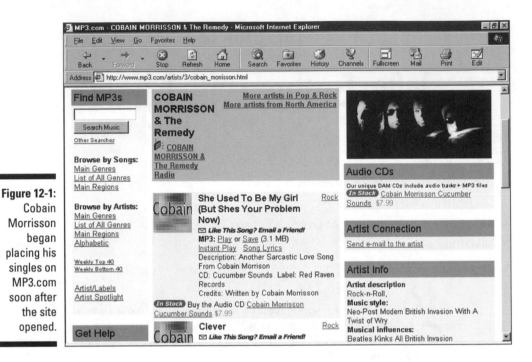

Figure 12-1:
Cobain
Morrisson
began
placing his
singles on
MP3.com
soon after
the site
opened.

"Everybody's thinking that their music's going to get robbed," he said. "I wanted to get the CD out there; start getting some comments on it. If you're into music for the art, then it's not always about making a buck. I just wanted to get the music out there."

Being one of MP3.com's first offerings, Morrisson quickly got attention with his snappy, British Invasion pop songs. Morrisson's singles drew 44,000 downloads in November, 1998, making him one of the most successful acts up to that time. When Dan Rather's staff contacted MP3.com about their company, MP3.com used Morrisson as an example on the CBS evening news.

"Being on MP3.com led to the CBS appearance," Morrisson said, and the exposure was phenomenal. "Being on TV brought people up to me in restaurants, saying 'I know you.'"

He has since become something of an MP3 spokesman. He has sold several hundred CDs through the site, and MP3.com sells a "Cobain Morrisson and the Remedy" DAM CD (covered in Chapter 11) for $7.99.

"I didn't make a ton of money off the site, but I love the exposure I got," he said. "You can't make a ton of money from MP3s, but you can get a good fan base. I love the fact that some kid somewhere in the world is listening to one of my songs right now."

Morrisson says uploading the songs is only the beginning. Musicians must create a complete product to sell. "You need merchandising — T-shirts, bumper stickers — that's the stuff that you're going to be able to sell. The shirts will probably sell more than your CDs will. Set up a Web site where you can sell your merchandise."

Les Fradkin's "Get Wet"

Site: `www.mp3.com/artists/15/get_wet.htm` and `www.getwetpage.com`

An original member of the Broadway show "Beatlemania," Les Fradkin heard of MP3 through "industry buzz" — the Internet and talking with other musicians.

At first, Fradkin was hesitant about the new medium, having reservations about MP3's sound quality and lack of copyright protection compared to other sites. "Liquid Audio offers great encryption protection but clearly doesn't enjoy the widespread popularity of the MP3 format," Fradkin said. After checking out the MP3.com site, he decided to use it as a test market for his latest recordings (see Figure 12-2). Called "Get Wet," the CD features classic surf guitar using tones created from Roland's VG-8 guitar system.

Figure 12-2: An original member of the Broadway show "Beatle-mania," Les Fradkin test-marketed his new surf guitar recordings at MP3.com.

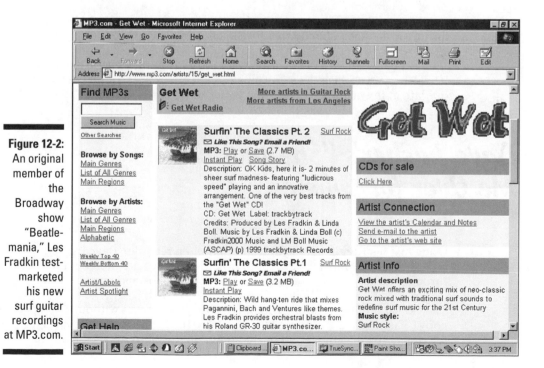

But when his "Get Wet" began racking up downloads, sales, and interviews, the work began. Although he had escaped a record label's clutches, he found himself doing the chores normally performed by the label: manufacturing, packaging, distribution, and more.

He knew a Web site would be a necessity to promote and sell his work, but his first quote from a Web designer came in at $900. Like many other musicians, he decided to create his own.

Touring created another problem. "There wasn't a 'Get Wet' band," Fradkin said. He'd recorded the songs with only one person, Linda Boll, who helped with songs and arrangements. Hiring a band for a new show isn't easy.

"How do you get musicians to commit to something when it's just starting to happen?" he asked. "And how do you afford to perform if no one will pay to hire you until you have a hit?"

Fradkin has received good reviews, sold CDs, and seen plenty of downloads from both MP3.com and AMP3.com, so he's happy with his MP3 dealings so far.

"How else can you reach so many people so inexpensively?" he said. "My recent 'Get Wet' concert in Los Altos Hills, California, was wonderful. How else could that have been possible without MP3 and the Internet?"

Fradkin certainly isn't partying with the Rolling Stones yet. But MP3 has given his music enough publicity that he can afford to play more.

"Financial rewards are much lower than I would see if I were on a major label," he said. "Still, at least my music is uncompromised, and I'm able to operate in the marketplace without being constrained too much."

Dave Lasher's "She Invited Me Over for Lobster"

Site: http://www.mp3.com/artists/10/dave_lasher.html

Using just his Korg Trinity synthesizer's built-in recorder, Dave Lasher recorded a CD's worth of "Psychobilly Satire" music and offered it for sale through Amazon (www.amazon.com), the online book and music retailer.

The CD sat on the vendor's cybershelves for "six months without selling one copy," Lasher said. Taking a chance on MP3, the Maine resident converted a few songs to MP3 format and posted them on the Internet (see Figure 12-3).

Figure 12-3:
A few months after posting his MP3s on the Internet, Amazon reordered Dave Lasher's CD twice.

"In the first month after I posted my MP3s on the Internet, Amazon.com reordered CDs from me twice," Lasher exclaimed. "I had over 1,500 downloads of my MP3s within the first two months!"

Lasher recorded his CD, "She Invited Me Over for Lobster," entirely on his Korg Trinity, singing into a Shure BG 5.1 microphone. After spotting an ad in Musician's Magazine, he sent his recording to be professionally manufactured by EuropaDisk in New York. He added a cover, complete with barcodes, to make it more attractive to stores and distributors.

Lasher has learned several things about the MP3 business, and he is applying them to his second CD. First, he traded in the Korg Trinity for a fast PC with a "huge hard drive." He also bought an inexpensive Kaysound MIDI keyboard to control computer software: Cakewalk Pro and Band-in-a-Box software (discussed in Chapter 13). Vocals come in through Creative Labs' Soundblaster Live sound card.

By composing on a PC instead of a synthesizer, Lasher figures he will save time and money when it's time to upgrade his sound.

Second, Lasher plans to route his second CD straight through MP3.com's DAM program instead of pressing 500 advance copies. "They only manufacture CDs as fast as orders come in," Lasher said, "and then they split the proceeds of each sale with the artist. This way the artist does not have to lay down a ton of money to have a professional-looking product."

Lasher has plenty of advice for other musicians interested in MP3. "Get into it as soon as possible," he said. "Get your music out there where people all over the world can hear it. Don't be intimidated. It's very easy to convert even a basement cassette tape into an MP3 and post it on the Internet.

"The exposure is priceless," he said.

Bill Furner "Mr. Tile"

Site: http://www.mp3.com/artists/10/mrtile.html

Tiling contractor Bill Furner, called simply "Mr. Tile," says he feels different from most musicians posting MP3 files. First, he's older than the crowd, having played acoustic and slide guitar for several decades. "It seems most of the groups featured are younger — teens, 20s, or 30s," Furner said.

"I don't play real loud," he said. "It might be too 'laid back' to be really popular."

He differs from the majority in his choice of computer, too. And, while most MP3 users own IBM compatible PCs, Furner plugs his Takamine acoustic/electric guitar directly into his Macintosh G3. He then mixes the tunes with Cubase VST software.

After suffering from a lack of MP3 encoders for a Macintosh, he finally found a free one: Mpecker. Soon after Furner figured out Mpecker's controls, his tunes quickly began appearing on MP3.com.

Furner has had plenty of downloads, but only sold three CDs so far. Still, he obviously enjoys the process: MP3.com offers nearly 40 of his compositions for download.

"The thrill of knowing that thousands of people are going to hear and download my tunes is very compelling to me," Furner said.

"I have recorded many times at studios," he said, "but one of the neatest things for musicians on the Internet today is being able to compose on your instruments, then upload to www.mp3.com.

"You can you do all that at your own home, then get instant recognition the next week if you have a tune that is climbing the charts."

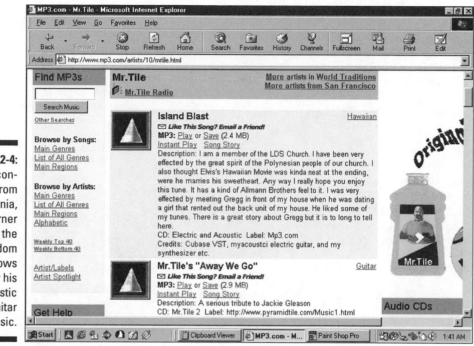

Figure 12-4:
A tile contractor from California, Bill Furner likes the freedom MP3 allows over his acoustic slide guitar music.

Chapter 13

Composing Songs for MP3

· ·

In This Chapter

▶ Using analog recorders

▶ Using digital recorders

▶ Using MIDI recording

▶ Using digital studio workstations

▶ Choosing your sound card

▶ Choosing your software

· ·

A few years back, there weren't many options for recording songs. Everybody used tape.

Today, just about everybody's switched to computers in one way or another. Computers record the sound, enhance it, and burn it onto a compact disc, ready to be played on the stereo.

This chapter examines the options available to musicians trying to release their tunes in MP3 format. It explains the most popular hardware and software options.

Whether you're considering a four-track tape deck, a sexy Roland VS-1680, or some of the latest computer music software, check out this chapter for some general-purpose information about the format, plus its suitability for creating the best MP3 recordings.

Using Analog Recording

For years, musicians recorded their music onto an *analog* tape recorder, ranging from a cheap cassette deck to a more expensive four-track or reel-to-reel machine.

To understand the word *analog,* you need some theory about sound waves, and because this involves physics, it gets boring fast. So here's the abbreviated version:

Sound travels through the air in waves of pressure. When somebody bangs a drum, the drumhead vibrates back and forth. This pushes the air back and forth in waves of pressure. The pressure bounces against our ears, vibrates our eardrum, and our brain translates the poundings into what we hear.

The air pressure bounces against microphones, too, which translate the waves of sound into waves of electricity. The tape recorder then stores a "picture" of the incoming waves as magnetic information on the tape's coating.

When playing back an analog recording, the recorder uses the magnetic information to recreate the actual sound waves being played.

Analog's MP3 Rating: Good. Although cheap, portable, and relatively easy to use, analog quality suffers from occasional background hiss. Plus, the sound is recorded twice: once into your recorder, and then again into your computer. Each recording allows noise to creep in.

First, the good stuff:

✔ Analog tape recorders are inexpensive, starting at around $150 for a beginner's 4-track model. Four tracks leave room for the drummer on one track, bass on the next, guitar or keyboard on the next, and vocals on the last one.

✔ Analog tapes don't cost much, either. Most recorders use the same cassettes found in a boom box or record store.

✔ Use a 30-minute tape when recording on an analog tape recorder. Longer-capacity tapes use thinner material, which doesn't record as well. Also, fast forward and rewind the tape once before recording.

✔ Want more than four tracks out of a four-track tape recorder? Try *bouncing.* Record three tracks, then mix them all down to the fourth track. That leaves all the sounds on one track, and three more tracks to play with.

Now the bad news:

✔ Analog tape recorders tend to pick up a hiss in the background. The hiss increases as you bounce tracks. While analog tape recorders work great for recording song ideas and recording live shows, they're not the best audio workstations for professional-quality material.

✔ There's one last drawback to using analog tape recorders to create MP3s: To move the sound into your computer, you must route the sound through your sound card, adding even more hiss. That's why more people are turning to digital tape recorders (described next) or creating their songs directly on the computer (described later in this chapter).

Um, what's a *track*?

Musicians rarely record songs live in the studio anymore. Instead, everything's recorded in layers. The drummer records the drum track, for instance. Then the bass player plays the bass line while listening to the drummer. The guitar player lays down the rhythm or leads, followed by the vocalist, who sings over the completed instrumental version.

Every time a musician plays a part, it's recorded as a *track*. When all the musicians have their own track, it's easier to mix the layers into the finished product. The drum's volume can be lowered, and the bass can be punched up — all without interfering with anybody else's track.

The more tracks available, the better the final sound. For instance, everybody needs at least two tracks to record in stereo: The left track and the right track. Drummers are sound hogs; they sound best when each separate drum is recorded separately on its own track: Increasing the snare's volume, for example, doesn't affect the rest of the drum sounds, allowing more versatility in the final mix.

Using Digital Recording

Analog tape recorders, as described earlier, take a "picture" of incoming sound waves and store the image onto magnetic tape. To play back the sound, they read the picture, and recreate the sounds from the image.

Digital audio works much differently. As sound waves enter the digital audio recorder, they're converted to a stream of numbers that represent the waves, as shown in Figure 13-1.

The recorder stores the numbers on Digital Audio Tape (DAT), a compact disc, a MiniDisc, a hard drive, or any other computer-savvy medium. When it's time to recreate the sound, the recorder reads the numbers and creates sound waves based on the digits.

Because digital sound is really just numbers, it's a natural for computers. In fact, everything is recorded onto a computer.

Digital's MP3 Rating: Good. It's expensive, but high quality. Plus, digital recorders come in a wide variety of formats, each tailored to a different need.

- ✔ The compact discs sold in the stores have always used digital audio; they contain numbers, which a CD player uses to recreate sounds.

- ✔ When sounds become numbers, they're much easier to edit. They can be cut and pasted, just like words in a word processor. Best yet, different tracks can be moved around, mixed together and bounced without adding any hum to the mix.

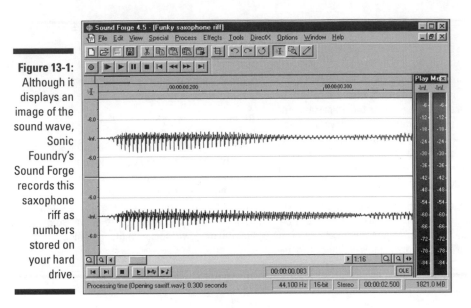

Figure 13-1:
Although it displays an image of the sound wave, Sonic Foundry's Sound Forge records this saxophone riff as numbers stored on your hard drive.

✔ The more numbers used to store a song, the higher its sampling rate. The MP3 standard sampling rate of 44kHz, for example — means the recorder splits up the incoming sound into more numbers than a low sampling rate — 22kHz, for instance.

✔ Don't use laptops for digital sound. Although some play back songs okay, they're simply not up to the task of recording music smoothly.

Using MIDI Recording

Sooner or later, you'll encounter the term MIDI when recording sound. Unlike analog and digital recording, however, MIDI doesn't contain any sounds or representations of sound waves. Instead, MIDI is a computerized instruction set that tells instruments how they should play.

MIDI works in two different ways. With the first, called *real-time sequencing,* the MIDI device listens to a musician play on an instrument. For example, somebody sits at a synthesizer's keyboard, turns on the synthesizer's piano sound, and plays a song. The MIDI device listens to the person play, and makes notes of which notes are played, when, and for how long. The resulting file is called a MIDI *sequence.*

Figure 13-2 shows a MIDI sequence of a bass line recorded in Cakewalk Pro. By changing the shape and location of the little lines, you change the placement and length of the notes. The software also translates the MIDI file into sheet music or notation.

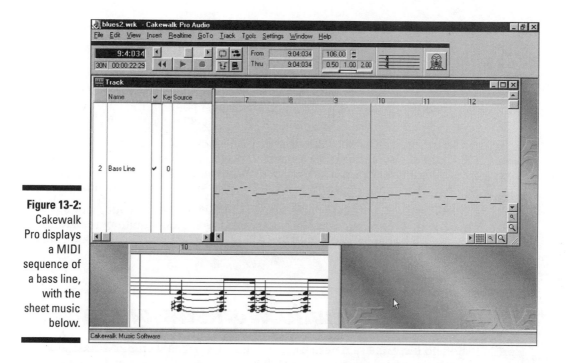

Figure 13-2:
Cakewalk
Pro displays
a MIDI
sequence of
a bass line,
with the
sheet music
below.

When the MIDI file is played back, it recreates the same sounds of the person playing a piano — mistakes and all. (Luckily, MIDI files can be edited to remove the mistakes.)

In fact, that's where the second method of recording comes in. Called *step-time sequencing,* it's a laborious method of calling up an empty MIDI file and entering notes, one by one. Not only must the notes be entered, but the duration of the notes must be entered, as well.

But MIDI does much more. Because it keeps track of what instrument created what notes, the type of instrument can also be edited. Edit the MIDI file and assign the recorded instrument to a flute instead of a piano, for instance, and the MIDI file tells the synthesizer to sound like a flute when playing the file.

MIDI's MP3 Rating: Very good. You can use MIDI inexpensively on a home computer using an existing sound card or linked to any MIDI-compatible synthesizer.

 ✔ MIDI files are very transportable, and the quality of the sound depends on the quality of the instrument they're played back on. A computer's cheap sound card can play a MIDI file created by a $1,000 synthesizer. It won't sound as good, but you'll hear the melody.

 ✔ Likewise, songs recorded using MIDI on a cheap sound card can sound extraordinarily realistic when played back on an extraordinarily expensive synthesizer.

✔ Think of MIDI as sheet music. It contains instructions for which instruments to play, and at what times. By editing the sheet music, you change the sound of song. Likewise, the same sheet music can sound completely different when played by different instruments.

✔ Most people edit MIDI files using computers and special MIDI editing software. Cakewalk Pro is one of the most popular; the latest version not only handles MIDI, but can insert to 128 audio tracks, as well.

✔ You can chain MIDI files together. The *master* instrument — a keyboard on one synthesizer, for example — could be connected to a different synthesizer known as the *slave*. Whatever is played on the master instrument's keyboard is played back using the slave's sounds.

✔ For years, only keyboards could use MIDI; today, MIDI adapters work with guitars and other instruments, as well. Now a guitar with a Roland GK-2A adapter can sound like a flute, too. (Just don't bend your strings, or the flute will sound damaged.)

Using Digital Studio Workstations

Roland blew open a new market with its VS-880 digital studio workstation. Basically a hard drive in a box with input jacks, built-in software, mixing capabilities and special effects, the VS-880 worked like a word processor of music.

Musicians could record their pieces straight onto the hard drive, and then move them around into the right locations, adding effects where needed. Made a mistake? Hit the Undo button. Digital recording eliminated background noises found in analog machines.

Today, Roland markets several digital workstations at varying prices. The top-of-the-line VS-1680, shown in Figure 13-3, features 16 tracks, a 2.1 gigabyte hard drive, and an attachment for adding a CD burner for completing songs.

Digital Studio's MP3 Rating: Very Good. Fantastic quality, but expensive and a very steep learning curve limits use by beginners.

✔ Although several other companies now market digital studio workstations, Roland still has a firm grasp on the market, outselling the others by a wide margin.

✔ Built from the ground up to record music, digital studios come with special shielding to keep any electrical noise from creeping into the mix. Computers, on the other hand, come with whirling fans, noisy power supplies, and other components. They're not particularly well shielded to protect sound.

✔ Now for the bad news. The least-expensive Roland VS-840EX workstation starts at around $1,000 — and it substitutes a 250MB Iomega Zip drive instead of a hard drive. The VS-1680 costs around $2,500. Plus, the learning curve is very steep. Be sure to buy the instruction video and plan on attending all possible "how-to" classes at music stores.

Figure 13-3:
Roland's
VS-1680
records
songs
directly onto
its own hard
drive,
allowing for
cut-and-
paste
editing and
effects.

Composing and Recording on a Computer

Chapter 2 explained how to beef up your computer to create MP3s. To use that computer for actually composing your music, you need a few more items. Make sure you're using the largest and fastest hard drive you can afford. You also want a CD-ROM drive that can write to CDs as well as read from them.

And then comes the big decision — the sound card and the software, both discussed in the next section.

Choosing a sound card

Sound cards come in a wide variety of models and prices, each designed to fit a particular niche. Any sound card can work for creating MP3s. In fact, you don't even need a sound card to rip MP3s off an audio CD — the music flows onto your hard drive directly from the CD.

However, better sound cards translate to either better sound, better effects, easier use, or all three. Here are some features to look for when shopping for sound cards, as well as a few recommendations. I define the terms you'll encounter when shopping, and how important they are to your work.

✔ **Digital Capable:** The best sound cards offer three types of digital sound, and you need all three. First, a *Digital to Analog Converter* (DAC) plays digital audio, like a recorded sneeze. An *Analog to Digital Converter* (ADC) records sounds from the card's Line-In or Microphone jacks. Finally, *Digital I/O* routes the card's digital output straight to a DAT recorder or CD burner, which keeps the sound digital as it moves from your computer to its storage area, bypassing any analog conversion where it can pick up noise.

✔ **Effects:** Most software can add effects like reverb. It's not especially important for the card itself to have these built in.

✔ **Environmental Audio (EQ Presets):** Most software usually handles this feature, so it's not very important. These options shape your sound as if it were recorded in different places: a stadium versus a jazz club versus a church, for example. A band playing in each location sounds very different; Environmental Audio or EQ Presets mimic those locations by tweaking the sound.

✔ **Full-Duplex:** Everybody knows that a sound card plays sounds. But a Full-Duplex card can play sounds at the same time as it records them, which is essential for musicians. You need to hear the drums and bass when recording the guitar or keyboard parts, for instance. A half-duplex card, by contrast, can either record or play, but not both simultaneously.

✔ **Gold-plated connectors:** The best cards plate their connectors with gold. Gold conducts electricity exceptionally well, and it's resistant to corrosion.

✔ **MIDI:** Described earlier in this chapter, MIDI is another essential. MIDI IN and OUT ports let you control other MIDI compatible devices — even the ones you haven't purchased yet. Almost all cards have it, so make sure yours does. Some cards come with built-in MIDI-controlled synthesizers that create sound. Chances are, however, you'll be connecting your own higher-quality MIDI instruments to the ports and letting the sound card send them instructions.

✔ **Music Synthesis:** Here's where the sound card creates musical tones, which can be played through its MIDI capabilities. When playing MIDI files on your computer, you hear these tones. The more sounds available, the better. (Chords grab more than one tone, quickly diminishing your sound reservoir.) A wide variety of built-in sounds is important for computer game players, but not very important for musicians. Musicians use MIDI to control the sounds of their keyboards, synthesizers, guitars and other instruments; they don't use the sound card's built-in tones.

✔ **PCI:** Sound cards plug into slots inside your computer. (Chapter 2 describes how to install a sound card.) PCI cards are much faster than ISA cards; make sure yours is a PCI card, and make sure you have an available PCI slot inside your computer. (You may have to shift some existing cards around.)

✔ **Samplers:** Instead of making a synthesizer create synthesized tones for playback, other sound cards use *real* sounds — actual recorded sound waves. People store *samples* of these recorded sounds into the card's memory, and the card uses those as a basis for creating music. By adjusting a few samples, the card plays them in different keys. Creative Labs calls its samples "Sound Fonts"; Turtle Beach cards calls them a "sample store."

✔ When installing a sound card, keep it as isolated as possible from other cards. If you can, keep an empty slot on both sides of it, or connect it on an end slot, as far away from the others (especially TV and video cards because they're the noisiest).

✔ Just as musicians argue over the best guitar amplifier, computer composers argue over the best sound card. Ask your musician friends, and listen to as many cards as possible.

✔ Most computers come with a Soundblaster card or clone. These cards work fine for most computing chores, but they're not musician-quality. Look for something with multiple input and output jacks.

Choosing software

Just like sound cards, audio software comes with its own variety of bells and whistles. They help you create the music by recording what you play. Then it's time to edit out the mistakes, add in extra layers of sound, and sprinkle in some effects for aural interest. Finally, they save the completed work in a format other people can listen to on different machines, be it a CD player, cassette, or minidisc.

Here's a look at some of the features listed on the boxes of the software on today's shelves, and what all the words mean.

✔ **Accompaniment:** Need a back-up band? Pick up some accompaniment software to play your backing tracks. The most famous, Band-in-a-Box, lets you type in chords, choose a style, and press Play. The software creates a MIDI backing band based on your chord progressions. The latest version even tosses in a few solos.

✔ **Editing:** Editing packages often come with composing packages, ready to fix the mistakes. Did the vocalist's accidental blast of air leave a huge puff sound on the recording? Find the blast on the sound wave, isolate it, and trim it down to size so it's not as noticeable.

✔ **Effects:** Just like guitar toys can add wah, flange, phase, echo, reverb, and other sounds to a guitar, software adds effects to the sound. The garage gospel band can sound as if it performed in a huge hall.

✔ **Notation:** After creating a magnificent MIDI musical piece, it's time for everybody to learn it. But the bass player went to music school and she reads music. The solution? Buy a notation package. The software reads the MIDI file, and prints out standard music notation (the little musical notes on charts) for each instrument. Yep, it's a real time saver. (Figure 13-4 shows a glimpse of Cakewalk Pro's notation software.)

✔ **Recording:** Some software is dedicated to only certain parts of music; notation packages only create sheet music, for instance. Composing software writes down notes as you play them, so that you can edit them later. The more tracks of digital audio your software can handle, the better. Beware, however — your computer's processing power is often the limit, not the software.

Cakewalk Software (www.cakewalk.com)

An industry veteran, Cakewalk puts out a large collection of music software to meet a wide variety of needs. The beginning package, Cakewalk Home Studio 8, records four tracks of audio with MIDI, prints notation, and tosses in effects like chorus and reverb. The top-of-the-line, Cakewalk Pro Audio Deluxe, handles 128 tracks, 256 effects, and just about everything else you can think of.

Figure 13-4 shows Cakewalk Pro Audio displaying a MIDI track, four layers of digital audio tracks, and music notation down below.

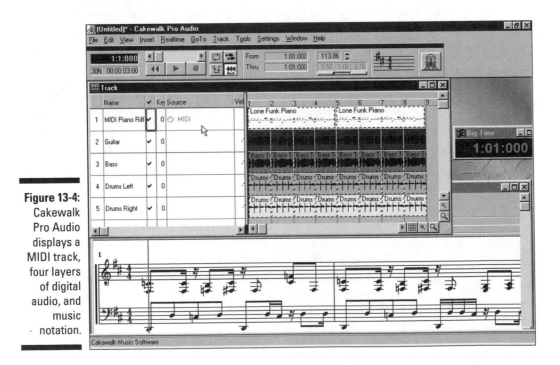

Figure 13-4: Cakewalk Pro Audio displays a MIDI track, four layers of digital audio, and music notation.

Acid Software (www.soundforge.com)

Sound Forge creates several popular packages. Acid Pro, shown in Figure 13-5, comes with precreated musical loops, ready to be arranged into your own, royalty-free creations. After you've set down a base, add your own loops, instruments, or vocals to create original tunes.

The company's sound editor, Sound Forge (shown earlier in Figure 13-1), records and processes sounds, as well as creates loops for Acid Pro.

Band-in-a-Box (www.pgmusic.com)

Band-in-a-Box, shown in Figure 13-6, serves as a creative inspiration and backup band. Select the type of music you're interested in, and the software creates a complete song in that style, with its own chords, melody, and solos. Click the Play button, and it creates a different song.

Or, if you prefer a little more input into your songs, add your own chords, and Band-in-a-Box creates your backing track by adding bass, drums, and whatever other instruments you want to toss in. It works in MIDI, so it'll play on your computer's sound card. Or connect it to a professional synthesizer for professional-sounding tunes.

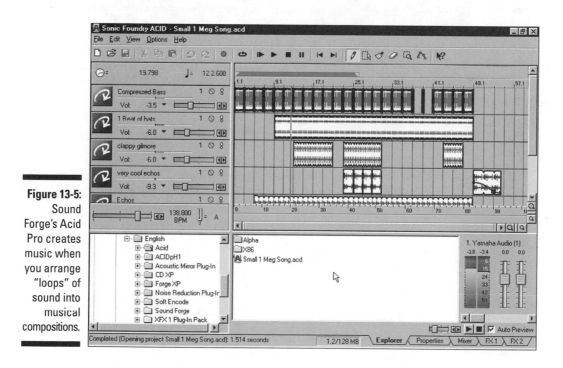

Figure 13-5:
Sound Forge's Acid Pro creates music when you arrange "loops" of sound into musical compositions.

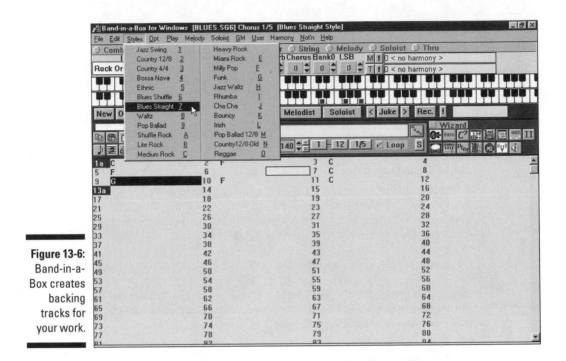

Figure 13-6:
Band-in-a-
Box creates
backing
tracks for
your work.

Chapter 14

Musician's Guide to Turning Songs into MP3s

*N*ow that MP3 has grabbed the public's curiosity, MP3 files are pouring into virtual record bins. Listeners won't have time to listen to them all, reminded MP3 guitarist Les Fradkin — even when the songs are free.

"Get your music right and in shape before putting anything on the Internet," Fradkin warned. "Just because it's out there doesn't mean folks will want to hear it."

Following MP3's "road to riches" may bypass the evils of a record company, but it eliminates a record label's conveniences, too. In addition to practice time, musicians now handle recording, mixing, packaging, distribution, sales, and promotion.

This chapter shows you how to make a song sound the best when issued as an MP3, giving you that much more of an edge over the competition.

Doing Everything Yourself

In order to make money from your MP3 files, you need to sell a CD — it's as simple as that.

That leaves two options. You can handle all the chores of creating, packaging, and manufacturing your own CDs, or you can pay somebody to handle everything for you.

Each side has its advantages. You save money by doing it yourself, but it takes time away from your music. Lacking experience, you're never sure if you're giving your music its best shot.

If you pay a CD packager to handle everything, you're assured of a reasonably good final product. Plus, digital music is growing in popularity, so CD packagers are lowering prices to attract customers.

This section shows you how to create a professional-looking CD yourself. And don't worry if it gets too difficult. Do all the work you can, and let an all-in-one packager pick up where you leave off.

Preparing the computer

Here's a secret: Computers don't store your files neatly onto your hard drive. They break them into little pieces and stuff them into any available empty nook. After a few months, your hard drive becomes cluttered with stray file pieces, slowing it down as it retrieves files.

To combat the problem, Windows includes a defragmenter program, shown in Figure 14-1. It realigns the little file pieces until they sit next to each other. When they lie together in neatly aligned rows, plenty of empty, uncluttered space on your hard drive becomes available for laying down new material.

Empty, uncluttered space is just what you need to create MP3s and record audio. Uncompressed audio grabs about 10MB of space each minute. If your computer can work uninterrupted as it lays down the incoming audio in one long strip, the recording sounds that much better.

To defragment a drive, right-click its icon from either My Computer or Explorer. Choose Properties from the menu and then choose the Tools tab. Click the curt Defragment Now button and then follow the instructions.

Figure 14-1:
Open My
Computer
and right-
click your
hard drive;
choose
Tools, and
click
Defragment
Now to
speed up
your hard
drive before
recording.

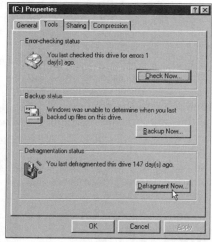

✔ While the hard drive churns away at its lengthy defragmentation ritual, take the time to clean the heads of your tape recorder. Some folks use rubbing alcohol and a Q-Tip. Others buy high-quality tape-head cleaner at music stores. Either way, rub a little of the liquid where the recorder's protruding silver bulges rub against the tape, and let it dry completely before use.

✔ Finally, forget about the thin audio cables that came with your computer or Soundblaster card. Although many types of patch cords dangle from the music store's walls, head for the thick-and-durable ones with "Monster Cable" (www.monstercable.com) printed along one side. Monster Cables might not be the very best, but they're a very good step in that direction.

Routing the cables into the computer

Did you create your song on your PC? Then your song is already inside the PC, ready for conversion. Take your nice clean sound to the next section and start setting recording levels.

Everybody else, whether you recorded in a studio, on a 4-track player, or with a DAT recorder, must route the sound into the computer.

Analog tape recorders plug into the sound card's Line-In jack. Use your sound recording program to save it as a WAV file. (A Macintosh stores sound as an AIFF or SDII sound format.)

DAT recorders might get lucky. A sound card with digital inputs (the Soundblaster Live offers inexpensive digital inputs) allows recording of the song while staying digital.

Chapter 8 explains the connection process; the next section explains how to set the levels before you finally push the record button.

Don't plug anything but a microphone into the sound card's Mic input jack. That jack's meant for more sensitive sound levels than the ones from a tape player.

For the best sound from a Digital Audio Tape (DAT) player, plug its output into a professional-level sound card featuring DAT input jacks.

Setting the recording levels

Nosy sound recorders want to know the *sampling* rate to use when converting the incoming sound to numbers. The higher the sampling rate, the more the computer pays attention to the incoming sound, resulting in higher sound quality. However, the higher the sampling rate, the more disk space is taken up.

There's something else to consider. Divide a sampling rate by two to see its *cycles*. The human ear can only detect about 20,000 cycles. That leaves little reason to sample at a rate higher than the MP3 standard of 44.1kHz — most people wouldn't be able to hear the difference anyway. (Besides, MP3 eliminates most of those frequencies during compression.)

Cables connected? Levels set correctly? Push the record button on your recording software, and then push the play button on your tape player, in that order. (You can edit out any blank spots later.)

The idea here is to get as clear of a representation of your work stored into your computer. You can add the effects later.

Processing the sound

Rev up your sound editing software's package and start editing. Start by trimming the empty spots at the beginning or end, as described in Chapter 8. Next, your amount of work depends on your budget, and how happy you were when you recorded the sound.

If you have the cash, burn a CD and take it to a mastering specialist. These folks work with the best equipment, and give your work a fresh ear. They adjust the levels, fix mistakes, and generally make your songs sound more alive.

But I *like* being abnormal!

Normalizing is necessary for even antiestablishment musicians. To *normalize* sound means to adjust its peak values to a certain level. That cuts down the screams, boosts the whispers, and makes everything audible.

When normalizing a song, set the software for –0.5 dB. Normalizing means something a little different when preparing a set of songs for a CD. In this case, normalizing adjusts the average volume of all the songs so they don't differ wildly.

One caveat, however: When ripping a song from a CD and creating an MP3 file, don't bother with the normalizing option. Keep the song at the same levels as it was originally recorded. (The record company paid somebody a lot of money to set those recording levels. Don't mess with them.)

If you're a working-class musician, or simply want to learn about home recording, try some subtle tweaks. Would the song sound better fading out in different places, for instance? Use your software's Fade effect in several different spots, using different rates. Does the song sound better? Or just different?

You may want to leave your song alone, especially if you've recorded it in a professional studio. But if your computer *is* your studio, experiment with different effects in different parts of your song. (If there's no Undo button, be sure to save a copy of your clean WAV file as a backup.)

When you're finished editing, it's time to punch your software's Normalize button — especially if you're uploading several pieces from the same CD. Normalizing makes your file play as loud as possible without distortion. By normalizing all your MP3s to the same value, listeners won't have to reach for the volume knob when moving switching between songs.

Duplicating and packaging your CD

Today, burning your own CD is relatively easy. Chapter 11 covers the finer points. But selling your own CDs creates additional problems.

The CD itself needs artwork (and barcodes on the packaging, if you're planning sales through larger retail outlets like record chains). You need a plastic CD case (known as a *jewel case*) or sleeve. The CD case needs to be wrapped in tooth-shattering plastic wrap. Some companies handle these chores for you. Just mail them the disc, and they mail back your professional-looking copies.

Other companies do bits and pieces of the work, forcing you to make more decisions. No matter which method you choose, here's a look at the chores necessary to professionally package your CD.

Mastering

After recording and mixing the songs, you're not finished. Which order will they play on the CD? Is there a natural progression between them? Do the songs have the right amount of delay between them? Should some songs fade into each other?

Should the bass, treble, or midrange be adjusted on some tracks? Did you put too much reverb on the vocalist?

And most important, are you too involved in your own composition to predict what will sound best to somebody else?

That's where mastering comes in. A sound engineer listens to your work using a different studio environment, different speakers, and different equipment. The mastering engineer tweaks your mix until it sounds the best according to his or her professionally tuned ear.

When the mastering is complete, you have a CD that's ready to be duplicated.

If you don't have your CD mastered, the folks at the pressing plant will master it. Though they might be great at duplicating thousands of CDs in a hurry, they may not be the best ones to add fine finishing touches to your music.

Designing the cover

First impressions count. And your audience's first impression won't come from your music, it will come from your CD's cover artwork.

So start thinking about your cover as soon as you begin songwriting. Take pictures of jam sessions, band members, or early morning reflections in pools of water on terra cotta tiles. Try to find something stating the mood of your music.

Draw up a rough picture of what you want, and then spend time trying to add in the details. Then hire a graphic artist.

- ✔ That doesn't necessarily mean you have to pay somebody. Check the local schools for beginning graphic artists. Some may exchange work for credit on the CD.

- ✔ Some CD packagers recommend graphic artists in your area, but you still save money by creating as much of the cover yourself. Graphic designers charge less for smoothing out an idea than for creating something themselves.

✔ When hiring any graphics artist, make a contract stating who is responsible for artwork, layout, typesetting and film (if applicable), and
printing.

Manufacturing

A computer's CD-ROM drive burns numbers into a compact disc when creating a music CD. Mass-produced CDs come to life through a different process
known as *injection molding*.

Also known as replication, the second method is less expensive in bulk, and
more reliable.

When looking for a company to replicate your CDs, make sure that it's rated
with an ISO-9002 certification.

If you tour a lot, make a few cassettes, as well. Some people still don't like
CDs. Plus, plenty of people have cassette players in their cars, and they'll
want to hear your tunes on the drive home.

Letting Somebody Else
Package Your Music

If you'd rather make music than manufacture CDs, hire an all-in-one CD packager to handle the details. They'll take care of the artwork, mastering, and
manufacturing of your masterwork.

Check out the Information Database on www.musicianassist.com for a list
of CD packagers; here are some to start with.

✔ **Oasis Recording, Inc.** (www.oasiscd.com), shown in Figure 14-2, offers
one of the most comprehensive CD creation packages.

Oasis offers its services in stages, picking up where you left off. No cover
design? It helps you find a designer. It creates both CDs and cassettes
from your work. Finally, it offers advice and programs to promote your
music. Be sure to check out the Web site's great links section for more
information.

✔ **Global Express Media** (www.globalexpressmedia.com) offers design,
film, proofs, all printed materials, and polywrap packaging in one price
(see Figure 14-3). (Check the competition's prices to see whether these
services are "extras.") Get everybody in the band to chip in for 1,000 full-
color posters at $1,500.

Figure 14-2:
Oasis Recording offers mastering, duplication, promotion, and sales through CDnow, Borders, Amazon, and other retail outlets.

Figure 14-3:
Global Express Media offers everything in one price with no extras (except for full-color posters).

✔ **CD-Lab** (www.cd-lab.com) hails from Glendale, Arizona. As shown in Figure 14-4, the company offers anything from a quickie 24-hour turn-around to complete mastering, duplication, and machine-inserted covers. Be prepared to turn in your own artwork according to their specifications and pay a film charge.

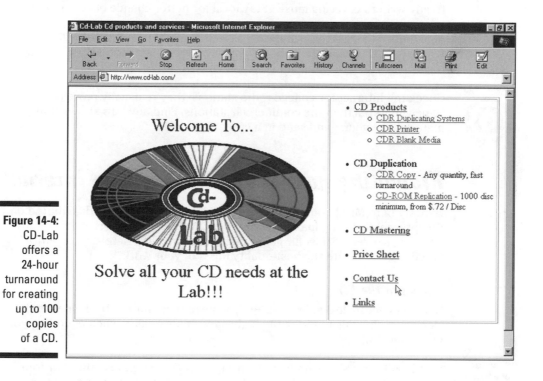

Figure 14-4:
CD-Lab offers a 24-hour turnaround for creating up to 100 copies of a CD.

Selling Your Music

At this point, you've created a product to sell — music has moved from inside your head onto stacks of CDs. It's time to convince the public to buy your music, and the first step is to convince them to listen to it. This section shows several ways to put your music into the public's ears through the Internet.

There's no such thing as too much marketing and promotion. Marketing doesn't always cost money. It can be as simple as wearing a band T-shirt during the day and carrying a stack of promotional CDs in the trunk.

Writing press releases

Don't forget the simple, traditional channels of promotion. Write up a press release — a single-page letter describing your band, your music, and when/if you'll be playing live. Send the press release — and a free copy of your CD — to any writers covering music. Stay local for better chance of coverage.

Mail copies to local radio stations, as well. It might hurt inside to give away your precious CDs, but if nobody's talking about them, nobody will know to buy them. The best publicity is word of mouth.

Check the Internet for college radio stations; they're usually more receptive to new material than the commercial stations. Find any DJ's shows that play material like yours, and send in a copy of your CD.

Promoting your songs through the Internet

Here's where MP3s come in; they're easily and inexpensively distributed on the Internet, bringing maximum coverage. Although Chapters 8 and 9 show you how to create MP3s for general-purpose listening, here are some tips you'll need to create the best-quality MP3s of your work.

Encoding the CD

Encoders get their due in Chapter 9, so head there for the basic mechanics. Here are some tips to wring the highest possible quality when encoding your own compositions:

- ✔ Don't offer MP3 versions of your entire CD. Just choose three or four of the strongest songs. You need to leave the listener wanting to hear more.

- ✔ If your encoder program offers an HQ option, use it. HQ stands for High Quality, and it means that the encoder reads the entire file before choosing the best encoding scheme. When HQ is turned off, the encoder only tests part of the file.

- ✔ Don't use Variable Bit Rate (VBR) encoding. Most encoders grab files at the Constant Bit Rate (CBR) of 128Kbps. VBR gives the encoder more leeway when converting files. A pause within a song doesn't need much encoding. A finger-bleeding guitar solo that breaks the silence could need more than average encoding to maintain CD quality. But although VBR can create better sounds with less file size, it occasionally increases file size, too. The clincher? Winamp and RealPlayer's RealJukebox can handle VBR, but Creative Labs' Nomad and other MP3 players can't.

- ✔ A sure sign of professionalism is to fill out the MP3 file's tag immediately after encoding. Enter the title, artist, album, year, genre, and comment. Stick your band's Web site in the comments area to allow for instant feedback and, hopefully, CD sales.

> ✔ When naming the completed MP3 file, use the band or artist's name followed by the song title. If the Red Cabbages create "Shredder" for the Cole Slaw CD, entitle the song "Red Cabbages – Shredder.mp3."

Choosing an MP3 site

Today, lots of Internet sites beg musicians for uploads. But make sure you upload to MP3.com first. Being one of the first and certainly the largest source of MP3 songs and information, listeners usually visit there first.

It works like this: You upload your MP3s to the site. Or if you don't have an MP3, mail them your CD plus $20; the techies at MP3.com will convert the songs for you.

MP3.com puts the music on their site, www.mp3.com, cataloged by both location and genre. By sifting the MP3 databases, visitors find bands in their hometown, for example, or just hear tango music from Brazil.

After you've won the hearts of the public with your music, they buy your CDs by mailing you a check. Most artists price their CDs at well under $10.

Want to track downloads of your music? As shown in Figure 14-5, log into MP3.com with your artist's password to see a tracking sheet of your downloads. You can tell your bar buddies you've had 2,561 downloads in the past two weeks.

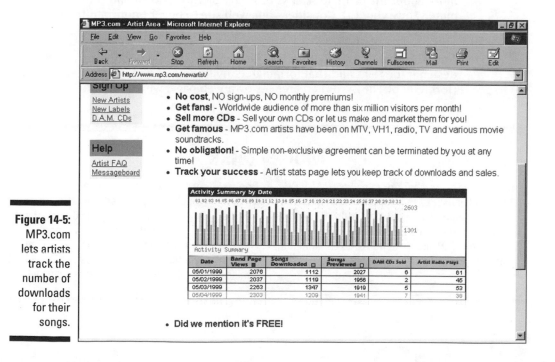

Figure 14-5: MP3.com lets artists track the number of downloads for their songs.

- ✔ Several other popular sites offer MP3 downloads. Check out `www.amp3.com` and `www.rollingstone.com`.

- ✔ Too busy jamming to create, package, distribute, and sell your work? Make MP3.com handle the chores. Send them a CD with less than 57 minutes of music, and MP3.com creates a *DAM* CD. As described in Chapter 11, a DAM CD plays MP3 versions of songs on your computer and normal songs in a regular CD player. Your fans purchase the DAM CD directly from MP3.com, and MP3.com sends you 50 percent of the proceeds.

Appearing on sampler CDs

Right now, the industry's hot for sampler CDs featuring MP3 songs. MP3.com frequently gives away CDs with 100 or more songs; Diamond's Rio and Creative Labs' Nomad come with 100 songs, as well. You'll even find 100 songs on the CD in the back of this book.

Be sure to sign agreements with Web sites, allowing them to include your songs on any upcoming sampler CDs.

You're in charge of promoting your band. If that means giving away some of your music for free, try to smile while gritting your teeth. You need exposure.

Creating a Web site

You definitely need a Web site; it's the place where listeners head to read more about the band, look at your pretty pictures, download songs, and, ultimately, buy your CD. Consider your Web site to be a 24-hour multimedia press release.

Not a computer buff? Neither was Les Fradkin. "I got a quote from one Web designer for $900, and that formulated my decision," he said. "Roger McGuinn [formerly of The Byrds] creates his own Web page, why not me?"

Money talks

The band sets the price on its DAM CDs, although it usually sells for under ten dollars. For each sale, MP3.com pays the artist 50 percent of the net revenue. (Net revenue is what's leftover after MP3.com subtracts taxes, shipping, and returns from any incoming cash.)

Don't expect checks coming in every week. MP3.com tabulates proceeds every three months; if they owe you more than $50, expect a check within two months. If it's less than $50, wait three more months. That means you're paid about five months after your sales reach $50 (which is better than the book business, actually).

With a Web site, you can not only sell CDs, but T-shirts and posters. (Those often make more money than the CDs.) Most MP3 sites offer links to the posting band's Web pages, providing quick access for curious listeners.

Put your Buy This CD! link on every page of your Web site, so it shows up easily. This isn't the time to be modest. The easier you make it for people to buy your CD, the more copies you will sell.

Distribution

Carry a batch of CDs in your trunk and drop by music stores or chains. When you drop by, ask the manager to carry your stuff on *consignment*. That means you drop off the CDs; if they sell some, they send you part of the money. If they don't sell any, they return the CDs after a given period of time.

Your music gains more legitimacy when in the bins; many chains in larger stores carry a "local artists" section.

Instead of driving from store to store with a box of CDs in the trunk, consider some online consignment. One popular online consignment store for independent music is CD Baby (www.cdbaby.com), shown in Figure 14-6.

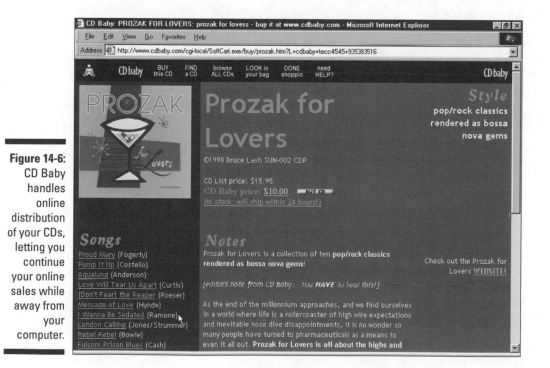

Figure 14-6:
CD Baby handles online distribution of your CDs, letting you continue your online sales while away from your computer.

Send CD Baby a box of your band's CDs, and they'll accept all credit card payments for it through their Web site or 800 number. Fans listen to the tunes using Real Audio; if they like the CD, they buy it, and CD Baby ships it to them within 24 hours.

Attracting 30,000 visits each day, CD Baby sells 100 CDs each day from independent artists like the ones featured in this section.

This concept lets you keep your own Web site sales active while you're on the road or in the studio. (And, unlike MP3.com, CD Baby sends checks each week.)

Oasis, one of the full-service CD packagers covered earlier, handles distribution in several national retail chain stores through Valley Media, the largest full-line distributor in the nation.

You'll find more information at IndieCentre (www.indiecentre.com), a site devoted to helping people create their own labels to help sell records.

Part V

The Part of Tens

The 5th Wave   By Rich Tennant

The Tubmans successfully download an entire multimedia MP3 file of Gustav Holst's composition, "The Planets."

In this part . . .

Sometimes chapters simply turn into lists. When that happens, they're shuttled off to a special part of the book: The Part of Tens.

It's full of lists: The Ten Best MP3 Song Sites, for instance, details exactly where to go for MP3 songs and information. Musicians enjoy the "Ten Ways MP3 Helps Musicians." (It's full of tricks like how the Rio MP3 player helps you learn Steve Vai riffs.)

Looking for more practical stuff? Check out the Ten Best MP3 Utilities, along with how to grab them. Or, when searching for tunes, check out the "Ten Clues for a Web Site's Location." It shows how to identify a site's country by its name.

If you're interested in the Recording Industry's take on MP3, check out the "Ten Online Piracy Myths by the RIAA." (Remember, that's not the law you're reading; it's the group's interpretation of the law.)

Finally, MP3 technology is new enough to spawn rumors. Can the Rio really dial long distance calls — and for free? This section reveals the truth to the MP3 oddities you read on the Web sites.

Chapter 15

Ten Best MP3 Sites

. . . .

. . . .

New MP3 site pop up daily; some list MP3 files, others carry utilities, and still others carry news about the latest MP3 happenings. For the current day's list of sites, head for www.dogpile.com and search on the term MP3. Believe me, you'll be flooded with thousands of sites to explore.

But for a quicker way to fish for sites, start with the ones listed here. No, there aren't exactly ten. But we're looking for quality here, not quantity. Besides, many of the sites here list other sites, which list other sites, which list, well, you get the idea.

MP3

Site: www.mp3.com

As you can tell by the way they snagged the rights to the MP3 domain name, MP3.com grabbed hold of the MP3 explosion before most people even heard the boom.

And, as you can tell by Figure 15-1, the site has reached 27 million downloads and holds 100,000 MP3 songs.

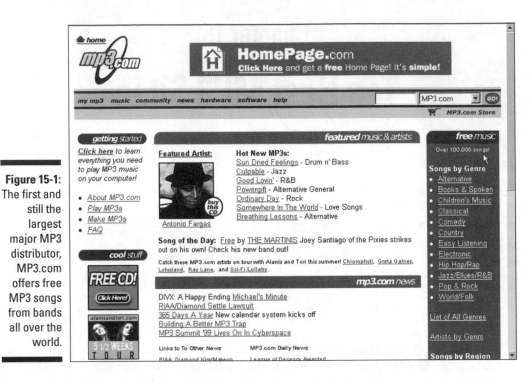

Figure 15-1:
The first and
still the
largest
major MP3
distributor,
MP3.com
offers free
MP3 songs
from bands
all over the
world.

You won't find illegally traded MP3s here; there's no room for them. Instead, you'll find surprisingly professionally produced songs by bands around the world. Less than one percent of all bands make it onto the charts. MP3.com lets you hear what the other 99 percent sound like.

If you're a musician, upload your songs to MP3.com for maximum exposure.

RollingStone

Site: www.rollingstone.com

RollingStone magazine has been around since before most MP3 fans were born. There's no denying the magazine holds a strong grip on the music industry.

The magazine waited cautiously before extending its Web site to include MP3s. Now, it not only embraces the MP3 concept, but nearly every other flavor of audio: MP3, Liquid Audio, a2b (a proprietary format like Liquid Audio), and Microsoft's Windows Audio.

The site is picking up momentum, as artists rapidly upload their songs to take advantage of the site's strong name recognition. Viewers rate songs and upload their comments.

Don't know anything about a band that's vaguely familiar? Head for RollingStone's site and click the band name's first letter in the ARTISTS A to Z box, shown in the upper-left corner of Figure 15-2. The site displays a history of the band. A similar box on the site's MP3 page displays information about MP3 bands, as well.

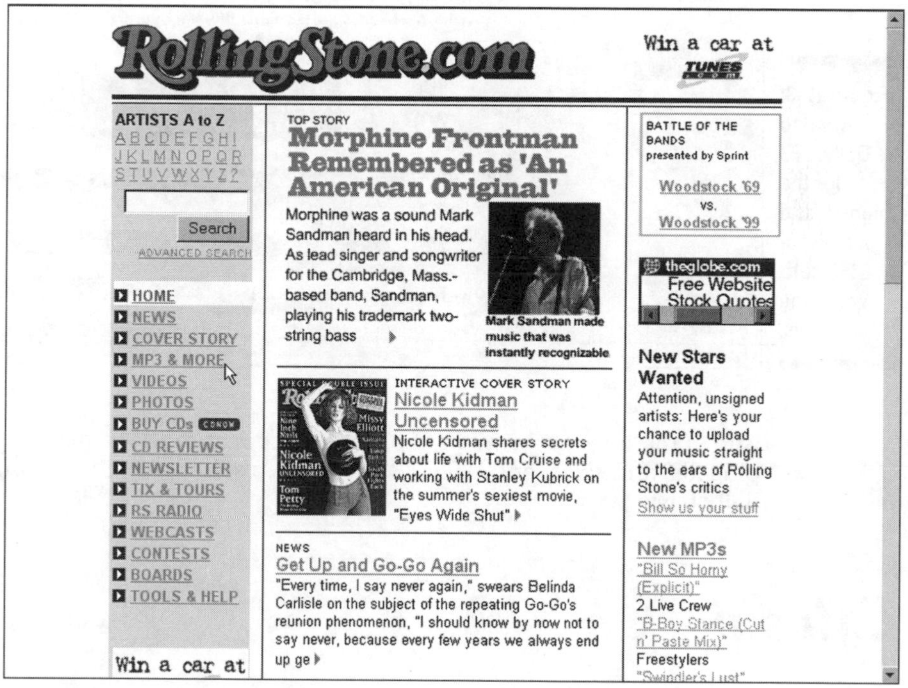

Figure 15-2:
Rolling Stone magazine's big name makes for a rapidly growing MP3 section.

DailyMP3

Site: www.dailymp3.com

As the name says, Daily MP3 updates its massive list of MP3 software daily to reflect new entries. Last look showed eight different entries for Rio MP3 player software, for example, as well as bunches of MP3 searchers, renaming utilities, screen savers that play MP3s, lyric grabbers, MP3 alarm clocks, "pop" removers, and programming utilities (see Figure 15-3).

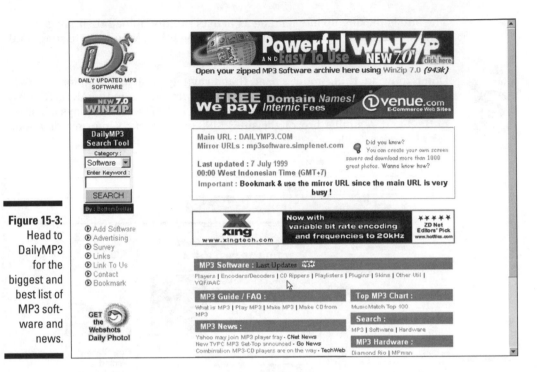

Figure 15-3: Head to DailyMP3 for the biggest and best list of MP3 software and news.

Add in the huge assortment of players, encoders, rippers, playlist makers, plug-ins, and skins, and DailyMP3 becomes a site worthy of visiting on an, er, daily basis.

EMusic

Site: www.emusic.com

While the recording industry twiddled its thumbs in secret sessions over how to control online music distribution, other sites simply branched out on their own. The LiquidAudio and a2b sites came up with their own proprietary distribution system, forcing people to download a proprietary player before the music could be heard.

EMusic, (formerly Goodnoise.com), sells downloadable music online, but it stuck with the MP3 format (see Figure 15-4). They've added another twist, too.

Most MP3 sites give away a few of an artist's MP3 songs to entice listeners to purchase the entire CD. EMusic, however, sells MP3 singles for about 99 cents a piece, with an entire downloadable album averaging about $9. Instead of downloading promotional singles, EMusic lets visitors download samples of songs to get a feel for their content.

Figure 15-4:
EMusic sells
MP3 singles
online from
big-name
artists for
about a
dollar a
piece.

Because the site uses the MP3 format, users retain the most control over playback, letting them choose their favorite players and use any of the hundreds of MP3 utilities already floating around the Internet.

Rioport

Site: www.rioport.com

With its third portable MP3 player already on the market, Diamond Multimedia keeps dropping the price of its original Rio, making the low-cost device a standard tool in the arsenal of many MP3 fans.

The Rio's support site matures along with the technology of its players. With more than one hundred links to independent labels and MP3 sites, Rioport.com is a great starting point for discovering legitimate distributors of MP3s (see Figure 15-5).

The site also carries the usual lists of MP3 players and utilities. Plus, it's the spot of spots to find out when the next Rio version will appear, and what features the device promises.

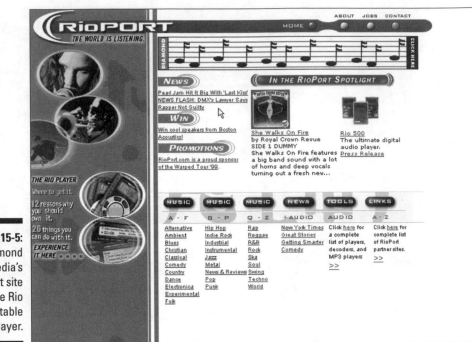

Figure 15-5:
Diamond
Multimedia's
support site
for the Rio
portable
MP3 player.

MPEG

Site: www.mpeg.org/MPEG/mp3.html

You'll find oodles of information for the newbie and the techie at Mpeg.org's site, shown in Figure 15-6. Although the site deals with all types of media compression, including video, DVD, audio, and streaming, click the MP3 section from the top menu.

The site claims to have the best MP3 resources, and it's not kidding. It lets you search for the latest in MP3 news at the top MP3 sites; it gives history and background on the MP3 format, it answers Frequently Asked Questions (known as a FAQ in the trade), it searches for MP3 songs, locates search engines and newsgroups, and lists both portable and software players.

If that's not enough, it details MP3 technical resources and test sites, and discusses patents and licensing details.

In short, if you have a question about MP3, you'll either find the answer here, or a pointer to the answer.

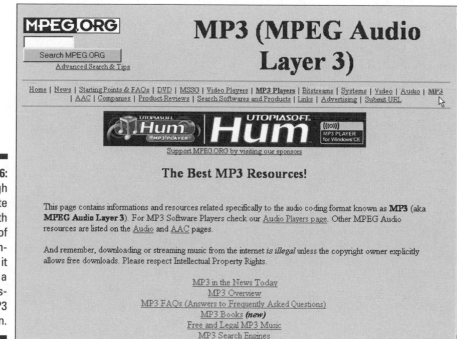

Chapter 16

Ten Ways MP3 Helps Musicians

MP3s bring a "get-rich-quick" promise to musicians, as they post their songs on sites like MP3 and wait for the talent agents to knock on their door.

But while waiting for that to happen, musicians can use these practical MP3 tips.

Practicing with a Portable MP3 Player

Like many musicians, guitar player Sean Cusiter of San Jose, California, doesn't read music. While listening to a song, he grabs a guitar and plays along until he's figured out the sound. This works fine for some songs, but others aren't as easy to pick up on the fly.

For years, musicians taped songs they needed to learn. Then, their fingers moved rapidly between the fretboard and the Rewind button until they either learned the guitar parts or wore out the tape.

When Sean bought his Rio portable MP3 player, he found a new way of learning songs.

"I discovered by accident that the Rio can record and loop sections — or entire songs — that have been recorded to MP3 format," Sean said. "I found that by pushing the Rio's 'A-B' button once, and then pushing it again after a few seconds, that the Rio would replay the section of music over and over."

He picked up an acoustic guitar, pressed the Rio's A-B button, shown in Figure 16-1, and within about five minutes he had nailed down two simple songs: Everlast's "What It's Like" and Sugar Ray's "Every Morning."

Figure 16-1: By pressing the Rio's A-B button at the beginning of a passage and again at the passage's end, music sections can be looped indefinitely for easier learning.

"I've probably added 30 or more songs to my list of songs that I can play," he said, "and have definitely improved on some of the ones that I already knew."

- ✔ Although Creative Labs Nomad will repeat entire songs, it doesn't repeat snippets of songs, like the Rio. Unlike the Rio, however, the Nomad fast-forwards and rewinds through songs.

- ✔ To sneak in some extra listening, Sean also bought a CD-to-cassette-player adapter (covered in Chapter 5) for listening to his Rio's songs while driving.

Recording Quick Music Ideas on the Nomad

It's happened to every musician. You're strumming a guitar at the beach or playing saxophone at a friend's house. One thing leads to another, and you stumble across a great riff or a catchy phrase to start a new song.

But how can you possibly remember it the next day? If you're near a telephone, you can play it onto your answering machine – but that's kind of awkward and draws stares in public places.

Instead, try turning on the Voice Record mode of your Creative Labs' Nomad or other portable MP3 player. Record your tune, and save it onto the machine.

Later, when you play it back, see if your musical idea still sounds workable or it just sounded great at the time. . . .

Swapping Song Ideas with Band Members

A Hong Kong musician who calls himself "Gemini" plays part-time in a rock band, but the members are scattered through the city, working in different office locations. Before MP3, band members swapped their song ideas and tunes by mailing each other tape recordings or burned CDs.

Now, with MP3, they send each other song ideas instantly through e-mail.

"Band members can swap songs for our next gig," Gemini said. "We exchange guitar riffs for upcoming songs."

The band members store a list of songs on their Rios for practice, adding new songs to its memory as soon as they're received through e-mail. They play along with the Rio for quick practice sessions — even though the band members are miles apart.

Removing Vocal Tracks

The DeFX program, covered in Chapter 18, removes vocal tracks from MP3 files. Guitar players can tune out David Lee Roth when trying to pick up some of Eddy's more manic shreds.

Shown in Figure 16-2, the sound editor performs its magic by cutting out the "middle" track, which is where the vocals usually lie. Usually is a key word, however. Although the software completely erases the vocals from some songs, other times it merely turns down the volume on everything.

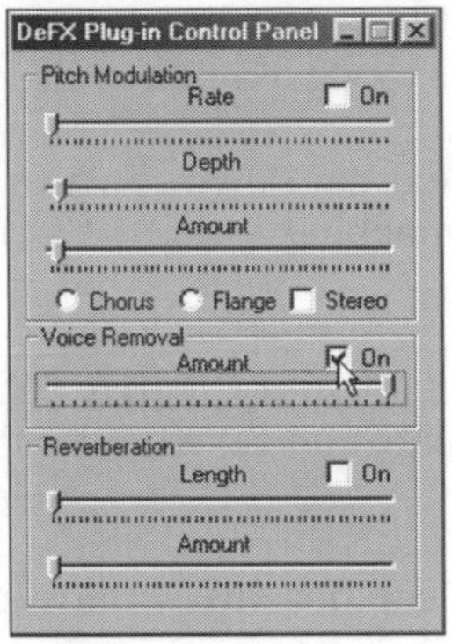

Figure 16-2: By removing vocals from a song, singers gain a backing band, and musicians can hear their parts better.

Still, it's a valuable tool when it works. Lead singers can also use it to practice singing with a backing band.

Adding Sounds to Live Shows

The Spice Girls give it a bad rap. But plenty of other bands perform live to prerecorded backing tracks. Got a bar gig playing a single guitar? Adding some sound effects to the show? For years, bands used prerecorded sounds to synchronize with the real live performance. This was either expensive and delicate (DAT tape) or unreliable (the all-too-skippable CD-Rs).

MP3 brings a reliable, skip-proof format to bring on tour for live concerts. Plug a laptop into the sound board, and make sure the sound guy isn't reading e-mail instead of playing back the required explosions.

Exchanging Rough Production Tracks

Derek Sivers, this book's technical editor, sometimes works for Nike and VH1 to compose and record music for commercials. Since commission projects like this need several rounds of approval, Sivers used to FedEx his Digital Audio Tapes of his work to their office.

With MP3, he creates a rough mix of the music as he goes, encoding it into MP3 and e-mailing it to the company for feedback on the composition or even the balance of the final mix.

For Sivers and many other freelance musicians, MP3 has reduced a week-long process into a day-long process, impressing the deadline-driven corporations along the way.

Chapter 17

Ten Most Useful MP3 Utilities

Soon after MP3 flooded the Internet, thousands of MP3-struck program-mers began churning out MP3 utilities. (Chapter 5 covers the MP3 players; Chapter 8 handles the CD rippers, and Chapter 9 covers the encoders.)

This chapter describes some of useful MP3 utilities you see listed under Miscellaneous at sites like www.dailymp3.com or www.mp3.com.

Diamond Rio Enhancers

The Rio's customers were computer-savvy folk who wanted *more* from their expensive new toy. Most wrote Rio software from necessity, curiosity, or laziness.

Here's a look at some of the best programs available for wringing the most out of your Rio, as well as where to find them.

  ✔ Dreaming of Brazil, shown in Figure 17-1, earns top name accolades, as well as top feature list for Rio programs. Brazil uploads or downloads *any* file to the Rio, adding file transporter to the Rio's musical workload. The program reformats SmartMedia cards to original specifications so they'll work again in digital cameras. The program is at www.parkverbot. org/harald/download/. (And it works with Windows NT.)

  ✔ Somebody claims the Rio can dial phones, something the phone com-pany frowns upon. (That's because the Rio, uh, doesn't put in a quarter before dialing.)

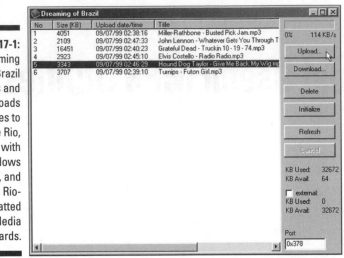

Figure 17-1:
Dreaming of Brazil uploads and downloads files to the Rio, works with Windows NT, and fixes Rio-formatted SmartMedia cards.

✔ RioPump (`http://publish.uwo.ca/~mhogan/`) began when "laziness prevailed" over programmer Mike Hogan, and he tired of handpicking songs for the Rio to play. He created RioPump, a quick playlist generator that randomly selects MP3s until reaching the Rio's memory limit. When you drag the Pump's newly chosen playlist into RioManager (or Dreaming of Brazil, mentioned earlier), it sends your new list of tunes into the Rio.

Winamp Plug-ins

The popular MP3-player Winamp enthusiastically embraces modifications. The program creates a folder for user-created plug-ins — software tidbits that customize Winamp to give it more power. To use a plug-in from the Internet, download the file, unzip it (a process described in this book's appendix), and copy the plug-in into Winamp's plug-ins folder. (Chapter 5 describes Winamp and its plug-ins.)

Here are a few favorite Winamp plug-ins to start playing with; most are free or shareware.

✔ **MusicTicker:** Running a SHOUTcast radio station, as described in Chapter 7? Check out this freebie: It posts the name of your currently playing song to an HTML file, ready for publication on your ration station's Web page. It also keeps a list of currently played songs, letting listeners discover what songs you're playing.

✔ **Nullsoft Crossfading output plug-in:** Written by Justin Frankel, the driving force behind Winamp, this fades one song into the next when playing from a list. Smooth stuff.

WARNING!

Don't mix a Rio with a digital camera

Digital camera users began posting frantic messages soon after the Rio hit the market. The camera owners, hoping to share their camera's expensive SmartMedia cards with their Rio, found out Diamond Multimedia's dirty little secret: The Rio deviated from the standard SmartMedia format. After being used in a Rio, the cards no longer worked in the cameras.

Unless the camera had a built-in card-formatting function, the camera no longer recognized the cards. Rio had reformatted the cards to its own special format, and it wouldn't let go.

A few angry programmer/photogs wrote their own "SmartMedia-afy" programs to reformat Rio-altered cards back to normal specifications, and eventually Diamond wrote its own reformatting program, cautiously offered at www.diamondmm.com/products/drivers/rio.html.

The Rio's not the only portable MP3 player that antagonizes digital camera owners. Almost all of the players have the same problem. Be sure your camera has the ability to reformat SmartMedia cards to its own specification before swapping cards with your new brand of portable MP3 player.

- ✔ **Realizer:** An outstanding equalizer for Winamp that brings MP3s closer to CD-quality sound by boosting the bass, enhancing the stereo, and recreating missing frequencies on the fly.

- ✔ **Winamp Alarm:** Here's the perfect way to wake up to your favorite song playing on the home stereo. (Chapter 5 explains this much-needed process.) Give the program your wake-up time, and leave your computer and stereo turned on. Choose a song to set the mood you'll need that day.

ID Taggers and Renamers

MP3 files include more than music. They contain the artist's name, the song's title and album, the recording date, and other interesting tidbits. Known as the ID tag, this information comes lodged inside every MP3 file — *if* the MP3's creator took the time to fill out the form when making the file.

Unfortunately, many don't bother with this descriptive information. But there's a second problem. File names for the same song often differ drastically. The same Grateful Dead show might be stored as dead110673.mp3 by one person and Grateful_Dead_-_11_6_73.mp3 by another.

To solve these problems, programmers wrote two sets of programs — *renamers*, and *ID taggers*. Renamers, like the one in Figure 17-2, let you choose a standard setting for your filename: Artist — Song, for instance. When you select your MP3 filenames, the program renames each file according to your own standards. (Or, it can grab information from the file's tag and use that for the filename.)

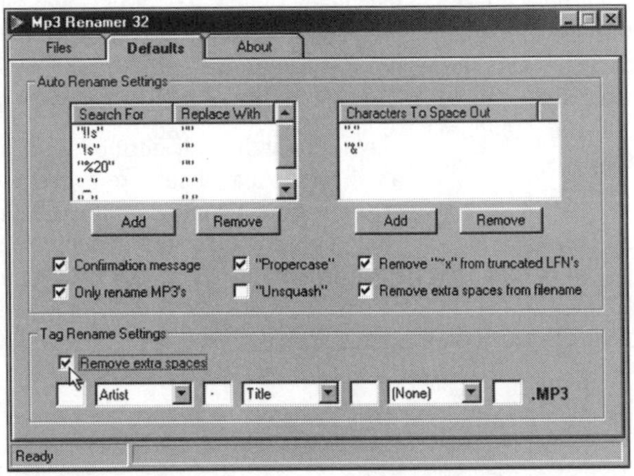

Figure 17-2:
Renamer
utilities
create
uniform
filenames by
removing
underlines,
adding
spaces,
changing
capitaliza-
tion, and
performing
other
tweaks.

ID taggers, like the one in Figure 17-3, also examine your selected files, and compare the tag, if any, with the filename. It fills in any empty tags, grabbing the artist and song title from the filename. Or, if you've created the MP3s, you can fill in the tag yourself. By using renamers and ID taggers together (or waiting until somebody writes an all-in-one renamer/tagger), your MP3s stay neatly tagged and named.

Dozens of these programs exist; head for www.mp3.com or www.dailymp3 to find a current version of one you like.

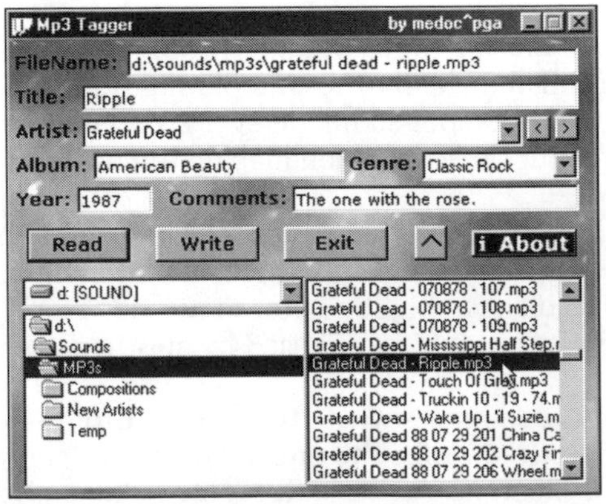

Figure 17-3:
ID taggers
allow
viewing,
editing, and
automatic
changing of
an MP3's
ID tag.

Sound Enhancers

Many utilities help wring as much sound as possible from your MP3s. Sometimes sound-fixing is as easy as copying Winamp's Realizer plug-in to your hard drive. Described earlier in this chapter, it picks up where Winamp's built-in equalizer stops.

✔ **DeFX:** Another program for Winamp, DeFX (shown in Figure 17-4), does basic pitch and reverb alterations, but it also does a pretty good job of removing a song's vocals for karaoke or musicians interested in the instrumental parts.

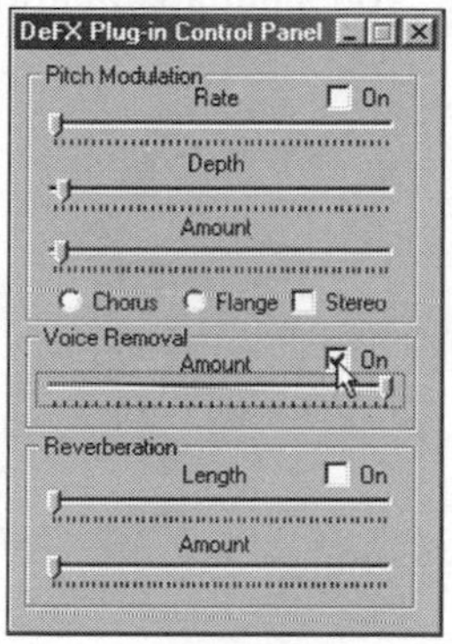

Figure 17-4:
DeFX not
only
changes
pitch and
adds reverb,
it removes
an MP3
song's
vocals for
karaoke.

✔ **Normalizers:** Different CDs play back at different volumes — whatever sounded good to the record producers at that point. When you hear lots of MP3 songs shuffled around on a hard drive, the volume difference stands out. *Normalizing* software fixes the problem by maximizing your MP3 file's volume to a certain rate without distorting it. By normalizing the WAV files, as shown in Figure 17-5, before burning them onto a CD, each song on the CD will play back at a constant volume.

✔ **Pop Removers:** These programs repair the aural oddities left in WAV files ripped from CDs. To remove the pop or tick sounds from a WAV file, look for a Pop Remover program; some also clean up scratchy records. (Pop Removers are different than the Pop-Up Remover programs that remove annoying pop-up advertisements that appear on Web sites.)

WinZip

One of these days, you'll download a file that doesn't seem to do anything — it's a zip file. Think of a zip file as a box; it's usually a collection of files that have been compressed and stuck together with a program called WinZip, shown in Figure 17-5.

WinZip can zip files into a single convenient file, and unzip the files back into their normal state.

People zip files for two reasons. First, if a program consists of several files, it's easier to download a single file and unzip it than to download each file separately. Second, zipped files are compressed, making them faster to download. Zipping MP3 files rarely saves space, however, because they're already compressed in the first place. Instead, programs usually find themselves zipped before distribution.

WinZip is included on this book's bundled CD; you'll find installation instructions in Appendix A.

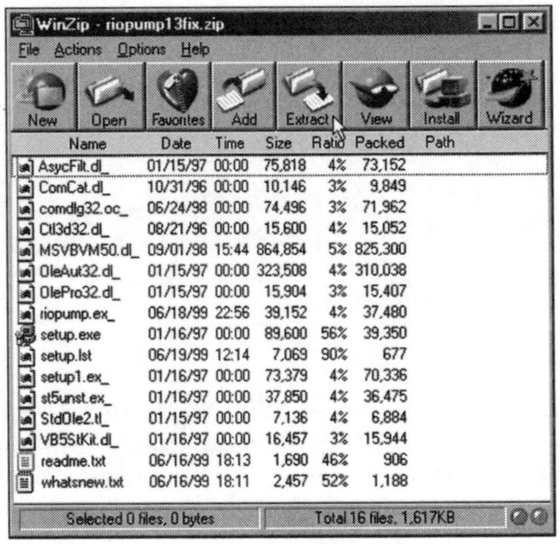
WinZip - riopump13fix.zip
File Actions Options Help
New Open Favorites Add Extract View Install Wizard
Name Date Time Size Ratio Packed Path
AsycFilt.dl_ 01/15/97 00:00 75,818 4% 73,152
ComCat.dl_ 10/31/96 00:00 10,146 3% 9,849
comdlg32.oc_ 06/24/98 00:00 74,496 3% 71,962
Ctl3d32.dl_ 08/21/96 00:00 15,600 4% 15,052
MSVBVM50.dl_ 09/01/98 15:44 864,854 5% 825,300
OleAut32.dl_ 01/15/97 00:00 323,508 4% 310,038
OlePro32.dl_ 01/15/97 00:00 15,904 3% 15,407
riopump.ex_ 06/18/99 22:56 39,152 4% 37,480
setup.exe 01/16/97 00:00 89,600 56% 39,350
setup.lst 06/19/99 12:14 7,069 90% 677
setup1.ex_ 01/16/97 00:00 73,379 4% 70,336
st5unst.ex_ 01/16/97 00:00 37,850 4% 36,475
StdOle2.tl_ 01/15/97 00:00 7,136 4% 6,884
VB5StKit.dl_ 01/16/97 00:00 16,457 3% 15,944
readme.txt 06/16/99 18:13 1,690 46% 906
whatsnew.txt 06/16/99 18:11 2,457 52% 1,188
Selected 0 files, 0 bytes
Total 16 files, 1,617KB

Figure 17-5: WinZip displays the contents of the zipped RioPump file, ready to be unzipped onto the hard drive.

Chapter 18

Ten Piracy Myths from the RIAA

In This Chapter

▶ Top ten myths (and a few more) by the RIAA about online piracy

*T*he Recording Industry Association of America (the RIAA at www.riaa .com) represents companies and people in the recording industry. Based on its own interpretation of copyright laws, the RIAA considers these to be the top myths regarding online piracy.

You can find this list and more information at the RIAA's Soundbyting Web site (www.soundbyting.com).

If I upload music from a CD that I own, I'm not violating copyright law.

Just because you own the CD does not mean you own the music. You cannot upload music to the Internet without permission of the copyright owners of the sound recording and the musical composition.

If I do not charge people for downloading music from my site, it is not a violation of the law.

If you do not hold the copyright, you can not authorize downloads of sound recordings even if you do not charge a fee. The No Electronic Theft Act (NET), which amended Section 506 of the Copyright Act, clarified that even if a site barters or trades infringing materials or does not charge or otherwise make a profit there still may be criminal liability.

If I just download sound recordings, it's not a violation.

It is a violation if you upload or download full-length sound recordings without permission of the copyright owners. You should assume other people's works are copyrighted and can't be copied unless you know otherwise.

The "fair use" exemption protects me.

Some uses may be "fair," but uploading and downloading full-length recordings without permission almost certainly is not "fair use."

If a Web site does not display a copyright notice for the music, the music is not copyrighted.

In the U.S., almost every work created privately and originally after March 1, 1989, is copyrighted and protected whether or not it has a notice.

If I upload or download a sound recording and leave it on my server or hard drive for less than 24 hours, then I am not liable for copyright infringement.

Whether you upload or download a sound recording for 24 hours, 24 minutes or less, you are still likely to be violating copyright law.

Posting sound files to an Internet site is legal as long as you put a disclaimer on it such as:

- ✔ If you download a sound file, you must delete it from your hard drive in 24 hours.

- ✔ You must already own these CDs to legally download the sound files.

- ✔ This site is for promotional purposes only.

- ✔ Please support the artist and buy the CD.

It does not matter how many disclaimers you put on a site. If you operate a site that posts unauthorized copies of copyrighted recordings, you are violating copyright law.

Uploading music on the Internet does not hurt anybody. In fact, it's promotional and free advertising.

It's up to the artist and copyright owner to decide how their music will be heard, distributed and promoted. Though most people do not realize it, approximately 85 percent of the records released do not recover production costs. Record companies rely on income from the 15 percent of recordings that are successful to subsidize less profitable types of music (classical, jazz), new performers and composers.

The Recording Industry Association of America (RIAA) is a government law enforcement agency associated with the CIA and FBI.

The RIAA is not a government agency, nor is it affiliated with any government agency. The RIAA is a nonprofit trade association whose member companies create, manufacture and/or distribute approximately 90 percent of all sound recordings produced and sold in the United States. A key mission of the RIAA is to protect the intellectual property rights of artists and record companies.

The RIAA wants to make MP3s — a popular compression format — illegal.

The RIAA does not select the technologies that its members use to promote and distribute their recordings. In fact, several of its members have used different formats — including MP3 — to electronically distribute their music. However, the RIAA does not support unlicensed music sites whether they are in MP3 format or not. Unauthorized music sites violate copyright law or other artists' rights.

It is within my First Amendment rights to post recordings to my site.

The First Amendment does not include the right to infringe copyrighted works. If you are interested in learning about First Amendment issues that are currently facing recording artists, you should check out RIAA's web site (www.riaa.com). The RIAA devotes a great deal of its resources to protecting free speech.

The RIAA wants to censor the Internet.

The RIAA wants to ensure that music fans and artists reap the benefits of the Internet. Record companies are excited about, and are actively pursuing, the vast promotional opportunities of the Internet. Protecting the copyrights of artists and record companies on the Internet is not censorship.

A site hosting unauthorized sound recordings is legal if the server is physically outside the U.S. because U.S. copyright law does not apply.

First, U.S. law may well apply when the uploading and downloading takes place in the United States, even if the server is physically located in another country. Second, the copyright laws of foreign countries are, in many cases, similar to those in the United States. In addition, U.S. trade law allows the Office of the United States Trade Representative (USTR) to take action against those countries that fail to provide adequate and effective copyright protection and market access.

It is okay to have a site which links to a number of unauthorized files. As long as the actual files are not on my server, it is legal.

Liability for copyright infringement is not necessarily limited to the persons or entities who created (or encoded) the infringing sound files. In addition to being directly liable for infringing conduct occurring via the site, a linking site may be contributorily or vicariously liable for facilitating copyright infringement occurring at the sites to which it links.

Contributory liability may be imposed where an entity knowingly and materially contributes to the infringing activity. In the case of a linking site, the RIAA believes that providing direct access to an infringing file would constitute material contribution to infringing activity.

Vicarious liability may be imposed where an entity has the right and ability to control the activities of the direct infringer and also receives a financial benefit from the infringing activities. Liability may be imposed even if the entity is unaware of the infringing activities. In the case of a linking site, the RIAA believes that providing direct access to infringing works may show a right and ability to control the activities of the direct infringer and that receiving revenue from banner ads may be evidence of a financial benefit.

Chapter 19

Ten Clues to a Web Site's Location

In This Chapter

▶ Figuring out which country's Web you're viewing

MP3 is a worldwide phenomenon, which becomes especially apparent when noticing how your Web browser travels the world to find Web pages.

It's fairly easy to tell which country a Web site hails from — if you know what secret codes to look for.

For example, look at the names of the following sites: www.mp3.gr, www.iis.fhg .de, and www.mp3.com.pl.

Notice the two letter codes at the end of each Web address? The first is .gr, the second is .de, and the third is .pl. Now, look up those codes in Table 19-1.

The .gr stands for Greece, the .de stands for Germany, and the .pl stands for Portugal.

So what? Well, by examining a Web page site's country codes, you often predict the type of music you'll find on the page — and be wary if the Web site uses a language you don't understand.

Table 19-1	Codes for Countries
Domain	**Country**
.ad	Andorra
.ae	United Arab Emirates
.ag	Antigua and Barbuda
.al	Albania

(continued)

Table 19-1 *(continued)*

Domain	Country
.am	Armenia
.ar	Argentina
.at	Austria
.au	Australia
.aw	Aruba
.ba	Bosnia-Herzegovina
.be	Belgium
.bg	Bulgaria
.bh	Bahrain
.bm	Bermuda
.bn	Brunei Darussalam
.bo	Bolivia
.br	Brazil
.bs	Bahamas
.bw	Botswana
.by	Belarus
.bz	Belize
.ca	Canada
.ch	Switzerland
.ci	Cote D'Ivoire (Ivory Coast)
.cl	Chile
.cn	China
.co	Colombia
.cr	Costa Rica
.cy	Cyprus
.cz	Czech Republic
.de	Germany
.dk	Denmark

Domain	*Country*
.dm	Dominica
.do	Dominican Republic
.ec	Ecuador
.ee	Estonia
.eg	Egypt
.es	Spain
.et	Ethiopia
.fi	Finland
.fo	Faroe Islands
.fr	France
.gb	Great Britain
.ge	Georgia
.gl	Greenland
.gr	Greece
.gt	Guatemala
.gu	Guam
.gy	Guyana
.hk	Hong Kong
.hn	Honduras
.hr	Croatia
.hu	Hungary
.id	Indonesia
.ie	Ireland
.il	Israel
.in	India
.ir	Iran
.is	Iceland
.it	Italy

(continued)

Table 19-1 (continued)

Domain	Country
.jm	Jamaica
.jo	Jordan
.jp	Japan
.ke	Kenya
.kg	Kyrgyzstan
.kr	Korea (South)
.kw	Kuwait
.kz	Kazakhstan
.lb	Lebanon
.lc	Saint Lucia
.li	Liechtenstein
.lk	Sri Lanka
.lt	Lithuania
.lu	Luxembourg
.lv	Latvia
.ma	Morocco
.mc	Monaco
.md	Moldova
.mk	Macedonia
.mn	Mongolia
.mo	Macau
.mt	Malta
.mu	Mauritius
.my	Malaysia
.mx	Mexico
.na	Namibia
.nc	New Caledonia (French)
.ng	Nigeria

Domain	Country
.ni	Nicaragua
.nl	Netherlands
.no	Norway
.np	Nepal
.nu	Niue
.nz	New Zealand
.om	Oman
.pa	Panama
.pe	Peru
.pf	Polynesia (French)
.pg	Papua New Guinea
.ph	Philippines
.pk	Pakistan
.pl	Poland
.pt	Portugal
.py	Paraguay
.qa	Qatar
.ro	Romania
.ru	Russian Federation
.se	Sweden
.sg	Singapore
.si	Slovenia
.sk	Slovak Republic
.su	USSR (former)
.sv	El Salvador
.th	Thailand
.tn	Tunisia
.tr	Turkey

(continued)

Table 19-1 *(continued)*

Domain	Country
.tt	Trinidad and Tobago
.tw	Taiwan
.ug	Uganda
.uk	United Kingdom
.us	United States
.uy	Uruguay
.uz	Uzbekistan
.ve	Venezuela
.vi	Virgin Islands (USA)
.vn	Vietnam
.ye	Yemen
.yu	Yugoslavia
.za	South Africa
.zm	Zambia
.zw	Zimbabwe

Chapter 20

Ten Rumors About MP3

In This Chapter

▶ You can dial phones for free with a Rio

▶ The record industry's new digital watermark renders all existing MP3s useless

▶ Some mainstream artists let you record their concerts and trade MP3s

▶ Winamp has two hidden Easter Eggs

▶ MP3 files contain CD quality sound

▶ Proprietary audio files from SDMI, Microsoft, and Liquid Audio are secure

For all practical purposes, MP3 lives on the Internet. That's where you find MP3 players, file search engines, MP3 utilities, and the songs themselves.

Because rumors always spread along the Internet like ants after cheeseballs, MP3 technology is rife with rumors. What's true and what's false? This chapter holds the answers.

The Rio Makes Free Long-Distance Calls

It's true — you can make long distance phone calls from the Rio, and they're free. By playing back the sound of coins dropping into public telephones, the Rio fools the phone into thinking you really paid for the call. A device that does this is called a "redbox" in the hacker's trade.

This Rio rumor is nowhere near unconditionally true, however, and here's why:

✔ It's illegal. Possession of a red box is a felony in the United States.

✔ Any portable MP3 player can do it, not just the Rio.

✔ The trick only works on older public phones. The newer phones recognize the trickery and aren't fooled.

✔ You need to fiddle with a sound editor to create the precise "beep beep" tones heard when coins slide down the chute.

✔ Headphones aren't up to the task. You need to attach a speaker to the Rio or other MP3 player, making your acts pretty obvious in a public place.

✔ Finally, when you're caught holding a Rio with a speaker and the contraband tones, it's difficult to deny your intentions to the FBI.

The Record Industry's New Digital Watermark Renders All Existing MP3s Useless

False. The recording industry, upset over the growing power of MP3, joined with several technology companies to create the secret "Secure Digital Music Initiative" (SDMI). The SDMI Web site (`www.sdmi.org`) remained closed to the public while the group held its first batch of meetings, and only recently opened its cyberdoors to the public.

The SDMI adopted an "ARIS Technologies" digital watermark to be embedded in all newly recorded music. Most portable MP3 players released by the end of the year will be SDMI compliant in order to recognize the digital watermark.

So, what does all this stuff mean? Well, it means the record industry will be embedding secret, inaudible codes into its recorded music. By examining the digital codes in any piece of music, the record industry can tell which master the CD was made from, making it easier to catch the counterfeits.

MP3 lovers should take note of the code's "Copy Prohibit" tag. When the coding turns on that tag, SDMI-compliant devices (usually portable MP3 players) won't be able to play the song.

The SDMI's work comes in two phases. The first phase requires SDMI-compliant devices (including portable MP3 players) to be able to read the watermarks in digital music files. Many new portable MP3 players released at the end of 1999 will be SDMI compliant.

It's the *second* phase of the plan that affects consumers. When "Phase II" goes into effect, all digital music will begin to contain the watermarks. Then, when SDMI-compliant players come across any music marked with a "Copy Prohibit" tag, they won't play them.

However, SDMI-compliant players will still be able to play MP3 files — even illegally copied ones — created from songs without a digital watermark. And that includes just about every song released before the year 2000.

Rumors floated around that the SDMI's code contained a "time bomb" — a special date when the Copy Prohibit flag would become active on *all* SDMI-compliant MP3 players, making it impossible for them to play any MP3 songs that weren't digitally watermarked.

Although that's currently not true, the SDMI Initiative is still being formed. Keep your ears open; things could change.

Some Mainstream Artists Let You Record Their Concerts and Trade MP3s

True. Although many artists forbid the taping of their live shows, many not only allow it, they help the fans place the microphones. They let fans trade tapes or MP3s of their live shows, and they don't mind if the MP3s of the live shows are posted on the Internet.

For the best list of the MP3-friendly bands, check out the mammoth Bands That Allow Taping Web site (`www.enteract.com/~wagner/btat/`), maintained by Kurt Kemp and Mike Wagner.

The site lists dozens of bands and their policies. Some allow audio taping, others allow videotaping, and some invite fans to plug into the soundboard to make copies. In some cases, the site lists the name of the soundman for on-site information.

Some of the bands listed as allowing taping of concerts include the Allman Brothers Band, Arlo Guthric, The Black Crowes, The Dave Matthews Band, Dire Straits, Henry Rollins, Jefferson Starship, Little Feat, Los Lobos, Mike Keneally, and dozens of other bands that are too young and hip for me to recognize.

Before lugging your gear to the show, however, keep these things in mind:

✔ Just because a band allows fans to tape and trade their concerts doesn't mean they allow people to make MP3s of their released MP3s and trade them. These guys have to make a living somehow.

✔ Don't try to bring a microphone stand unless the list says they're acceptable. And even then, try to check with the venue beforehand to see whether they're allowed.

✔ Finally, even though a band may allow taping, their venue may not be as friendly. When you tell the security guard you're allowed to bring in your reel-to-reel, you may be greeted with a blank stare. Your best bet is to buy a portable DAT recorder and sneak it in.

> ✔ A friend of mine hid her DAT recorder under her belt, ran the microphone wires beneath her shirt above her back, and hid the tiny microphones in her hair, one microphone above each ear. Then, to keep the background crowd noise to a minimum, she glared at anybody who came within five feet.

Winamp Has Two Hidden "Easter Eggs"

True. By clicking certain areas in the program, you can make the programmer's face appear, as well as his current age. Turn to Chapter 5 to see which keys to press, and in which order.

MP3 Files Records in CD Quality

False. MP3 files are compressed versions of audio files. To compress the files, MP3 technology removes some of the information from the file — the upper and lower frequencies.

It filters out other sounds found in "CD-quality" audio. Although many of these sounds aren't audible to the human ear, they're still missing from the MP3 version of the song.

So, when you see MP3 touted as "CD-quality" sound, you know they're wrong. It should always be described as "near CD-quality" sound.

Proprietary Audio Files from SDMI, Microsoft, and Liquid Audio Are Secure

False. The proprietary systems proposed by the SDMI and currently used by Microsoft and Liquid Audio are meant to keep users from copying the files. Although designed to keep people from making illegal copies of songs, these formats also keep people from making legal copies of their songs.

Frustrated programmers quickly put their keys to the keyboards, and all the proprietary formats released so far have been defeated by programmers. For instance, on the same day Microsoft released its copy-protected MS Audio 4 technology, an anonymous programmer announced a release of another program: One that removes the security from MS Audio files.

The program takes Microsoft's registered WMA files and outputs them as a WAV files. The program then re-encodes the WAV files into an unprotected WMA file.

Two other programs, AudioJacker and Total Recorder, work similarly to defeat copy protection schemes from Liquid Audio, the SDMI, and a2B music. Both programs work similarly, recording any sound generated by another computer program and saving it in a WAV file, which can be converted to an MP3 file.

The point? The battle will be left up to the courts as to whether these programs can legally convert protected MP3s, as long as the conversion is for noncommercial and personal use. After all, the major movie studios tried to declare VCRs as illegal because they could be used to make illegal copies of tapes. But in 1984, the U.S. Supreme Court legalized VCRs because the devices had legitimate, legal uses.

Actually, the movie industry is now pleased at the court's decision: They're now making huge profits by releasing their movies on videotape.

Chapter 21

Ten MP3 Players for Windows CE

*T*he first portable MP3 players simply played MP3 files. But then the programmers got to work, creating software to convert the Rio into a file transporter. Music fans could also carry 32MB of files back and forth to work.

More features crept into subsequent models. Like the other players, Sensory Science's rave MP2000 plays MP3s and transports files. It also records voice messages and stores thousands of telephone numbers, memos, and text files. The unit even comes with a makeshift Korean phrase translator for travelers.

As portable MP3 players slowly become pocket organizers, pocket organizers turning into MP3 players is only natural. MP3 player software now exists for most Windows CE palmtops and handheld computers. (Sanyo even announced a cell phone that plays MP3 files, but I'll wait for this book's second edition for that one.)

This chapter provides some background on Windows CE, rates the available MP3 players, and describes their features.

What Is Windows CE?

In the mid-1990s, tiny computers became the rage; dozens of manufacturers created their own little computer. However, each machine used different software. Microsoft, eager to expand Windows into yet another area, created the tiny Windows CE operating system for the new breed of palmtop and handheld PCs.

Windows CE looks and acts a lot like Windows. The Start button and Start menu haven't strayed, as shown in Figure 21-1, and the familiar folders and files still wait for your touch. Wallpaper waits when you're bored.

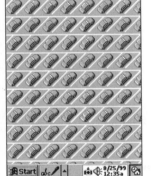

Figure 21-1: Running on a palmtop, Microsoft's Windows CE looks just like Windows, but smaller.

But beneath the surface, Windows CE is a lot different than its parent. Because it's only a tiny subset of Windows, it can't run regular Windows programs. In fact, you can't even move some of your data files from your desktop PC to the palmtop or handheld PC without first running them through a special conversion program.

All these differences mean Windows CE calls for some special considerations when playing MP3 files:

- ✔ For instance, the standard Winamp won't run on Windows CE, nor do its programmers have a Windows CE version available. You need an MP3 player written specifically for your particular palmtop.

- ✔ Not only that, Windows CE palmtops use one of several CPUs: MIPS, SH3, or ARM. You usually need an MP3 player written for your particular model of palmtop or handheld.

- ✔ Palmtops and handhelds don't have much storage space, usually maxing out at 16MB. Most portable MP3 players come with 32MB of RAM or more.

✔ In fact, a lack of storage space is why Casio's Cassiopeia E-100 and E-105 Windows CE palmtops automatically convert MP3 files into Microsoft's WMA files. At less than half the space, WMA files fit more easily into small palmtops. (Casio's machines can still play MP3 files, however, after you install a Windows CE MP3 player.)

✔ To copy MP3 files to a Cassiopeia palmtop, bypass the Mobile Audio Player Manager. That keeps them from being converted to WMA files. Instead, drag and drop the MP3 files straight into the palmtop's My Documents folder using the Explore option of Microsoft's ActiveSync.

✔ Stuck with a PalmPilot? They sell much better than Windows CE palmtops or laptops, but they're not powerful enough to play MP3 files. (In fact, many models come with just 2MB of memory — not enough to store an Alice Cooper MP3, much less the software to play it.)

Should you feel guilty for using Microsoft's WMA format?

MP3 inspires a loyalty among its fans. It sounds great, the songs are everywhere, and MP3 players and utilities abound. MP3 aficionados often view other formats, like Liquid Audio or Microsoft's Windows Media Audio (WMA), with suspicion. After all, these products are trying to curtail MP3's lack of copy protection.

However, Microsoft says that a song converted into WMA format will be half the size of that song's MP3 file, while sounding just as good or better. And it's that small size that makes WMA attractive to space-starved palmtops and hand-held computers.

How do they do it? First, here's how they *don't* do it. The default bit-rate for WMA is 64K, whereas you must encode MP3 files at 128K to retain near-CD quality. But Microsoft doesn't cut a file half in size simply by slicing the bit-rate in half. Instead, they've found a mechanism for grabbing higher sound quality from a lower bit rate.

WMA has its pros and cons. First, many people simply hate Microsoft. Second, MP3 is the default standard; people don't like using two different formats to store their files.

So, what do you do? Well, if your palmtop or handheld has the storage space to hold your complete MP3 collection of Monster Heavy Metal Ballads, stick with MP3. But if you're looking to stuff twice as much music onto your computer, go with WMA.

And even if WMA doesn't sound as good, a palmtop — or even an MP3 player — isn't exactly a high-fidelity listening environment. When you're listening to "Wildfire" while horseback riding, you're not going to hear any subtle audio nuances, anyway.

Which Windows CE Palmtops Play MP3s the Best?

This one's easy: Casio's Cassiopiean E-100 series, shown in Figure 21-2, wins the hi-fi contest. It is the only Windows CE device with stereo, near-CD quality sound. Plug a pair of headphones into the stereo headphone jack, and start listening to your favorite tunes.

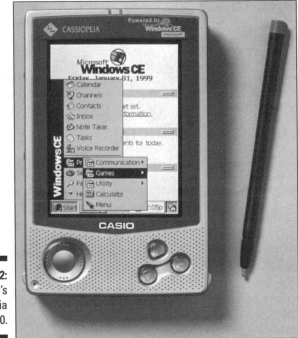

Figure 21-2:
Casio's
Cassiopeia
E-100.

As for the competition, well, Microsoft designed Windows CE to organize data, not play music. So most palmtops and handhelds cost more and sound worse than a portable MP3 player like the Rio or Nomad.

But regardless of Windows CE's audio limitations, palmtops are taking big steps into the MP3 arena with Casio's Cassiopeia E-100 series. Billed as "multimedia" palmtops, they even play color movies.

Utopiasoft, creators of the first Windows CE MP3 players, rates Windows CE palmtops and handhelds as shown in Table 21-1:

Table 21-1	Utopiasoft's MP3 Quality Ratings for Windows CE Palmtops and Handhelds	
Performance Rating	*Brand and Model Number*
5-Star (the only stereo units)	Casio Cassiopeia E-100/105/500
4-Star	Casio Cassiopeia E-10/11/55
	Vadem Clio
	Compaq Aero 2100 series
	Compaq 2010 series
	Everex Freestyle series
	IBM WorkPad z55
	NEC MobilePro 770
	Philips Nino 300 series
	Sharp Tripad PV6000
3-Star	HP 620LX
	HP Jornada 820
	Sharp HC-4500, 4600
2-Star	HP Jornada 420
	Philips Velo 500

Which Windows CE MP3 Players Are the Best?

Owners of Windows CE palmtop or handheld computers can pluck five different audio players from the Internet. Most sound pretty much the same; the quality of the palmtop or handheld makes the difference.

However, each player has its own character and set of features. You won't find any free MP3 players for Windows CE, unless you're living in Japan, where all the cool toys show up first.

But none of the players cost more than $20, and as more programmers get into action, the price will probably drop. Here's a look at how to listen to tunes as you enter lunch appointments in your Windows CE palmtop.

Microsoft's Mobile Audio Player

Web site: www.casio.com

Price: Free with Casio E-105; $69 for Casio E-100

Trial Version: None

Supports: WMA only

Requires: Casio E-100 or E-105

Display: Color

Microsoft's Mobile Audio Player, shown in Figure 21-3, doesn't play MP3 songs. So why list it here? Because it comes free with Casio's Cassiopeia E-105. With 32MB of RAM, it's the most powerful Windows CE palmtop.

Figure 21-3: Microsoft's Mobile Audio Player comes free with the E-105, but only plays WMA files.

Owners of Casio's E-100 (which costs $100 less for only 16MB RAM) must purchase the software for, gulp, $69.

But because the program's free with the E-105, it's definitely worth checking out. The program comes with an MP3 conversion program; click your MP3 file, and the converter changes it to WMA format (cutting its size in half), and copies it to your E-105.

It lets you assign your Casio's buttons to different functions like Play, Next, and other bits of handiness. It supports playlists, allows skins, and cuts the backlighting to conserve energy. If only it played MP3 files as well. . . .

Don't confuse Microsoft's Mobile Audio Player with Casio's Mobile Audio Player, described later in this chapter. Microsoft's player, distributed in the United States, plays only WMA files. Casio's player, distributed everywhere but the United States, plays both WMA and MP3 files.

The latest released version of Windows Media Audio (version 4.0 non-beta) wasn't working correctly on the Mobile Audio Player bundled with the Cassiopeia at the time this book went to press. Casio and Microsoft were still working on a fix. Microsoft will likely post the fix at www.casio.com as well as at www.microsoft.com/Windowsmedia.

Utopiasoft's Hum

Web site: www.utopiasoft.com

Price: $19.95

Trial Version: Plays only five minutes (usually one song)

Supports: MP3

Requires: Palm-size/Handheld PC running Windows CE 2.0 operating system or later

Display: Color or grayscale

Utopiasoft's Hum, the world's first commercial MP3 player for Windows CE, uses Xaudio's MP3 decoder engine. Hum, shown in Figure 21-4, works on nearly every palmtop or handheld PC with a speaker or an earphone jack. (Check out Table 21-1 for a list.)

Figure 21-4:
Utopiasoft's Hum works with a wide variety of Windows CE devices.

Hum offers easy playlist editing, and the big buttons make them easy to stab while riding the bus. It also supports skins, offering several for download at its Web site. Best yet, customer support people respond quickly.

Although it's a bit pricey at $19.95, registered owners can upgrade their software to future versions for free. (And an upcoming version promises to turn off the display to save power during playback.)

Conduit Technologies' PalmPlayer

Web site: www.conduits.com

Price: $14.95

Trial Version: Works only 15 days

Supports: MP3

Requires: Palm-size/Handheld PC running Windows CE v2.0 operating system or later

Display: Color or grayscale

Shown in Figure 21-5, PalmPlayer also uses XAudio MPEG Audio engine to play MP3s on many machines; like the competition, it brings stereo sound to Casio's E-100 series.

Figure 21-5:
Conduit Technologies' PalmPlayer offers fully customizable skins and playlists.

It offers playlists and customizable skins, letting skin creators define everything from backgrounds to button location.

Xaudio Classic

Web site: www.xaudio.com/wince

Price: $19.95

Trial Version: Works only 15 days

Supports: MP3

Requires: Palm-size/Handheld PC running Windows CE v2.0 operating system or later

Display: Grayscale

While developing its Windows CE MP3 decoder engine, Xaudio released its MP3 player for free. Now that other players are using its engine, Xaudio's charging $19.95 for its early "Classic" program, shown in Figure 21-6. After all, if it gave the program away, nobody would buy the competition, and Xaudio wouldn't make any licensing fees.

Figure 21-6:
Xaudio, the
creators of
the MP3
engine for
most
Windows
CE players,
now sells its
beta version
that was
once free-
ware.

The public isn't missing much, however. The program lacks most of the features found in other programs. It just plays MP3s and playlists. No color, no skins, nada. Just tunes. Buy one of the others.

Casio Mobile Audio Player

Web site: www.casio.co.jp

Price: Varies according to country

Trial Version: None

Supports: MP3, WMA

Requires: Casio E-100 or E-105 (E-500 or E-507 in Japan)

Display: Color

The Japanese get all the cool gadgetry first. They got to play with Casio's E-100 series way before the machine made it overseas. Now, their version of the E-100, the E-500, comes with a camera for taking pictures and movies. The camera arrived in the United States months later.

Also, the free multimedia package bundled with the Japanese version of the E-105 contains a Mobile Audio Player similar to Microsoft's. Although they're both named "Mobile Audio Player," the Japanese version plays WMA *and* MP3 files. Unfortunately, Japan's Casio Mobile Audio Player, shown in Figure 21-7, isn't sold in the states. Pick up a copy on your next vacation.

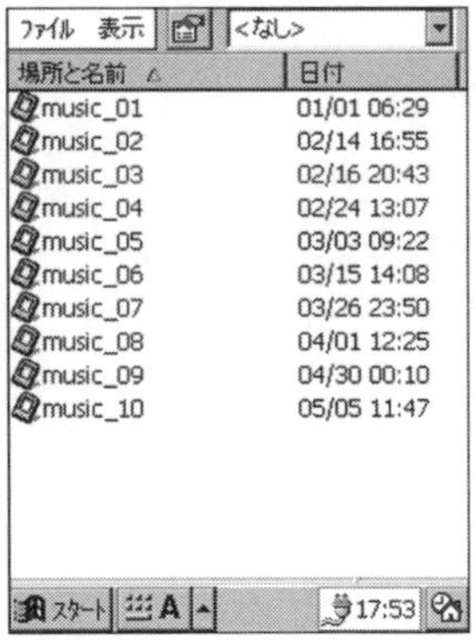

Figure 21-7: The Japanese version of the Mobile Audio Player plays both WMA and MP3 files.

```
ファイル  表示  [⌂] <なし>         ▼
場所と名前  △      日付
🎵music_01       01/01 06:29
🎵music_02       02/14 16:55
🎵music_03       02/16 20:43
🎵music_04       02/24 13:07
🎵music_05       03/03 09:22
🎵music_06       03/15 14:08
🎵music_07       03/26 23:50
🎵music_08       04/01 12:25
🎵music_09       04/30 00:10
🎵music_10       05/05 11:47



🗾スタート ⌨A ▲       🎤17:53 🔧
```

Lucky listeners say it's the best sounding player of them all. Plus, it allows users to turn off the display to save the battery. However, you won't find support for playlists or skins. Nor will it play in the background while running other applications. You can't play solitaire while listening to "Only the Lonely."

Tips and Tricks for Playing MP3s on Windows CE

Windows CE palmtops and handhelds weren't designed to play music, so a certain amount of tweaking is involved to make them work the best. In keeping with The Parts of Tens, here are five tips and tricks for squeezing the best audio out of your Windows CE computer.

Buy a CompactFlash card

Face it — there's never enough storage space for MP3s. No Windows CE devices currently come with more than 16MB of built-in storage space. And some devices make you share that with your programs, leaving precious little space for songs.

The solution is to buy a CompactFlash card. They range in size from 4 to 128MB. Just pop them in, and begin storing your songs on them.

Unfortunately, they're frightfully expensive. Chapter 6 has the lowdown on CompactFlash cards.

Make a My Documents folder on the CompactFlash card

There's a problem with CompactFlash cards. You can't simply copy all your songs onto the card because Windows CE won't find them. Windows CE only looks for data in a folder named My Documents. The solution? Create a folder named My Documents on your CompactFlash card, and store your MP3 files in there.

Windows CE is very picky about its My Documents folder. Make sure you capitalize the first "M" and "D" in My Documents, or your computer might not find your CompactFlash card's new folder.

Use WMA if your E-100 is starved for space

CompactFlash cards are expensive. A 128MB card costs around $300. To jam as many tunes as possible onto your Cassiopiea E-100 or E-105, consider converting them to WMA and playing them with Microsoft's Mobile Audio Player. Although it's an inconvenience, you may not notice a difference in sound.

Buy converters to play MP3s in the car

Just like portable MP3 players, you can't hear Windows CE palmtops in traffic while driving around town. Check out Chapter 5 to see how to connect the palmtop to your car's radio or tape player.

You can also find cigarette lighter adapters to keep your palmtop's batteries from draining while you're driving.

Watch out for design flaws

Different machines come with different problems. For example, if the Casio E-100's Screen Tap Sounds or Hardware Button Sounds are turned on, some MP3 players freak out in the middle of a song. Unfortunately, a bug in Casio's sound driver causes the problem. To fix it, disable the sounds by clicking the Start button, select Settings, and choose Volume & Sounds from the menu.

On the Hewlett Packard Jornada 420 and 620LX, the Velo 1, and the BCom MARS, the sound plays back slower than normal or breaks up, no matter which sound quality is chosen. This, too, seems to be a sound driver problem.

Part VI
Appendixes

The 5th Wave — By Rich Tennant

"Get the cannon ready kids! Your Mom's almost got the '1812 Overture' downloaded!"

In this part . . .

By now, you've probably digested most of this book. Therefore it's time for a little tidbit added to the end of the digestive tract: the appendixes.

By now, you've probably noticed the CD bound to the back of this book. Appendix A, dubbed the special "CD Appendix," describes all the cool MP3 players, encoders and other programs included on the CD (as well as installation instructions, where appropriate). Mac user? Linux user? You're not left out; the disc includes programs for both those platforms.

The CD Appendix also contains bunches of freebie MP3 songs for listening, as well as information about the bands creating them. Finally, you'll find copies of the latest versions of Web browsers Netscape and Internet Explorer.

And if any technical terms left you burping, head for Appendix B, "Glossary." There, you'll find explanations for all the book's multi-syllablic terms and anacronyms.

Appendix A

About the CD

Here's what you can find on the *MP3 For Dummies* CD-ROM:

- ✔ Internet Explorer 5.0, for browsing the Web
- ✔ Netscape Communicator 4.5, for browsing the Web
- ✔ MindScape Internet service provider
- ✔ WinZip, for unzipping files ending in the letters ZIP
- ✔ Windows MP3 players
- ✔ Linux MP3 players
- ✔ Macintosh MP3 players
- ✔ Windows CE MP3 player
- ✔ Sample MP3 songs

System Requirements

Make sure that your computer meets the minimum system requirements described in the following list. If your computer doesn't match up to most of these requirements, you may have problems using the contents of the CD.

- ✔ A PC with a 486 or faster processor, a Mac OS computer with a 68030 or faster processor, or a palm-size/handheld PC running Windows CE v2.0 operating system or later.
- ✔ Microsoft Windows 95 or later, or Mac OS system software 7.55 or later.
- ✔ At least 16MB of total RAM installed on your computer. For best performance, I recommend that Windows 95-equipped PCs and Mac OS computers with PowerPC processors have at least 32MB of RAM installed.
- ✔ Approximately 5MB of hard drive space to install an MP3 player onto your computer and 210MB additional space to copy all the MP3 songs. (The songs can be played straight from the CD, if you prefer, saving hard disk space.)

> ✔ A CD-ROM drive — double-speed (2x) or faster.
>
> ✔ A sound card for PCs. (Mac OS computers have built-in sound support.)
>
> ✔ A monitor capable of displaying at least 256 colors or grayscale.
>
> ✔ A modem with a speed of at least 14,400 bps.

If you need more information on the basics, check out *PCs For Dummies,* 7th Edition, by Dan Gookin; *Macs For Dummies,* 6th Edition, by David Pogue; *Windows 98 For Dummies,* or *Windows 95 For Dummies,* 2nd Edition, both by Andy Rathbone. (They're all published by IDG Books Worldwide, Inc.)

Using the CD with Microsoft Windows

To install the items from the CD to your hard drive, follow these steps:

1. **Insert the CD into your computer's CD-ROM drive.**

2. **Windows 95/98 users: Click Run from the Start menu.**

3. **In the dialog box that appears, type** D:\SETUP.EXE.

   Replace *D* with the proper drive letter if your CD-ROM drive uses a different letter. (If you don't know the letter, see how your CD-ROM drive is listed under My Computer in Windows 95/98.)

4. **Click OK.**

   A License Agreement window appears.

5. **Read through the license agreement, nod your head, and then click the Agree button if you want to use the CD — after you click Agree, you'll never be bothered by the License Agreement window again.**

   The CD interface Welcome screen appears. The interface is a little program that shows you what's on the CD and coordinates installing the programs and running the demos. The interface basically enables you to click a button or two to make things happen.

6. **Click anywhere on the Welcome screen to enter the interface.**

   Now you are getting to the action. This next screen lists categories for the software on the CD.

7. **To view the items within a category, just click the category's name.**

   A list of programs in the category appears.

8. **For more information about a program, click the program's name.**

   Be sure to read the information that appears. Sometimes a program has its own system requirements or requires you to do a few tricks on your computer before you can install or run the program, and this screen tells you what you may need to do, if necessary.

9. **If you don't want to install the program, click the Back button to return to the previous screen.**

   You can always return to the previous screen by clicking the Back button. This feature allows you to browse the different categories and products and decide what you want to install.

10. **To install a program, click the appropriate Install button.**

    The CD interface drops to the background while the CD installs the program you chose.

11. **To install other items, repeat Steps 7 through 10.**

12. **After you finish installing programs, click the Quit button to close the interface.**

    You can eject the CD now. Carefully place it back in the plastic jacket of the book for safekeeping.

Using the CD with Mac OS

To install the items from the CD to your hard drive, follow these steps:

1. **Insert the CD into your computer's CD-ROM drive.**

   In a moment, an icon representing the CD you just inserted appears on your Mac desktop. Chances are, the icon looks like a CD-ROM.

2. **Double-click the CD icon to show the CD's contents.**

3. **Double-click the Read Me First icon.**

   The Read Me First text file contains information about the CD's programs and any last-minute instructions you may need in order to correctly install them.

4. **To install most programs, just drag the program's folder from the CD window and drop it on your hard drive icon.**

5. **Other programs come with installer programs — with these, you simply open the program's folder on the CD, and then double-click the icon with the words *Install* or *Installer*.**

   Sometimes the installers are actually self-extracting archives, which just means that the program files have been bundled up into an archive, and this self extractor unbundles the files and places them on your hard drive. This kind of program is often called a .sea. Double-click anything with .sea in the title, and it will run just like an installer.

   After you have installed the programs you want, you can eject the CD. Carefully place it back in the plastic jacket of the book for safekeeping.

Using the CD with Linux

The following sections show how to read the CD's directory in Linux.

Reading the directory with Linux

Before grabbing the programs off the CD, you need to see them on the disc. Follow these steps to read the disc's directory.

1. **Insert the CD into your computer's CD-ROM drive.**

   Give your computer a moment to take a look at the CD.

2. **When the light on your CD-ROM drive goes out, go to the command prompt and type:**

   ```
   mount -t iso9660 /dev/cdrom /mnt/cdrom
   ```

   Then type:

   ```
   cd /mnt/cdrom.
   ```

3. **Type 'ls' to list the files in the CD's contents.**

   The 'ls' command will list the contents of the CD for you.

Viewing the disc's information and using the files

Here's how to view the disc's information and use the files.

1. **To view the licenses in their respective directories, type vi and the file name of the license (either gpl.txt or IDG_EULA.txt).**

   This file contains the end-user license that you agree to by using the CD.

   In Linux, the most convenient way to read this file is to use the vi editor.

   When you are done reading the license, exit the program by typing 'Esc', then typing :q!.

2. **Use the 'cp' command to copy the program you want to run from the /cdrom directory to where you want to store it.**

   For example, if you want to copy 'mon' from /cdrom to your /etc directory, do the following:

```
cp mon /etc
```

3. Use the 'cd' command to change directories to the directory you placed the program.

For example, if 'mon' is in the /etc directory, you should type the following to get to the /etc directory:

```
cd /etc
```

4. Type the name of the program you want to run and press Enter if you want to run it.

Note: On some systems, Linux may claim that it can't find the program. If it acts this way, it's just being fussy. Type a period and a slash in front of the program you wish to start and press Enter. This tells Linux that you want this specific program, right in the current directory.

What You'll Find

Here's a summary of the software on this CD arranged by category. If you use Windows, the CD interface helps you install software easily. (If you have no idea what I'm talking about when I say "CD interface," flip back a few pages to find the section, "Using the CD with Microsoft Windows.")

If you use a Mac OS computer, you can take advantage of the easy Mac interface to quickly install the programs.

Shareware programs are fully functional, free trial versions of copyrighted programs. If you like any particular programs, register with their authors for a nominal fee. Usually, this involves mailing a check to an address listed in the program, although some programmers take credit card numbers. Upon registering, you receive a license, an enhanced version, and technical support.

Freeware programs are free, copyrighted games, applications, or utilities. You can copy them to as many PCs as you like — free — but you they don't come with any technical support.

GNU software (GNU stands for *GNU's Not Unix*, if that's any help) is governed by its own special license, which is included inside the folder of the GNU software. Basically, it's a distribution system where programmers create free enhancements to a chunk of software that's compatible with the UNIX operating system. Linux is the best-known program of this type. There are no restrictions on distribution on this software.

Internet browsers

Both Internet Explorer 5.0 and Netscape Communicator Suite 4.5 are included if, for some reason, you don't have an Internet browser:

- ✔ **Microsoft Internet Explorer:** *For Windows and Mac. Commercial version.* Microsoft Internet Explorer is one of two major players in the Web browser market. However, just in case you don't have the latest version (at the time of publication), we include a copy of Microsoft Internet Explorer 5.0 for Windows and Internet Explorer 4.0 for Mac on this CD-ROM. You can always find the latest information about Internet Explorer at the Microsoft support site: www.microsoft.com/ie.

- ✔ **Netscape Navigator:** *For Windows and Mac.* From Netscape Communications, this is the other major Web browser and comes as part of the Netscape Communicator suite (Version 4.5 for Windows, 4.04 for Mac) that we include on this CD-ROM. Whether you use the Netscape or Microsoft Web browser is largely a matter of personal preference. Check out both. You can find the latest versions and important updates on the Netscape support site: www.netscape.com/browsers/index.html.

An Internet service provider for Windows and the Macintosh

In case you don't have an Internet connection, the CD-ROM includes sign-on software for MindSpring, an Internet service provider. For more information and for updates of MindSpring, visit the MindSpring Web site: www.mindspring.com/.

Note: You need a credit card to sign up with MindSpring Internet Access.

If you already have an Internet service provider, please note that MindSpring Internet Access software makes changes to your computer's current Internet configuration and may replace your current settings. These changes may stop you from being able to access the Internet through your current provider.

WinZip — A handy tool for Windows

WinZip 7, from Nico Mak Computing, is a shareware version of an invaluable file compression and decompression Windows shareware utility. Many files you find on the Internet are compressed, or shrunken, in size via special programming tricks, both to save storage space and to cut down on the amount of time they require to be downloaded. You may also occasionally receive compressed files (ZIP files) as e-mail attachments. After you have a compressed file on your hard disk, you can use WinZip to decompress it and make it useable again. For more information, check out www.winzip.com.

MP3 Players and Tools

This CD includes MP3 players for several types of computers and operating systems. Make sure to use the correct one for your particular computer setup, or the player won't work.

Windows

MusicMatch Jukebox v4 by MusicMatch (Shareware)

MusicMatch gets complete coverage in Chapter 10: It's an "everything" system that creates, plays, and categorizes your MP3s. To create MP3s, put a music CD into your CD-ROM drive, select the tracks you want to record, and click Start.

Tracks are recorded (*ripped* or *encoded*) at up to 5 times faster than normal play time — with no intermediate WAV file eating up your hard drive. Create MP3s and WMAs from vinyl, cassette, or microphone sources as well, with the Line-In recording capability.

As you download digital audio from the Internet, it's automatically added to your Music Library, which contains tracks from your personal CD, vinyl, and cassette collections, or music downloaded or streamed over the Internet. Sort your MP3 collection by Artist, Title, Album, Genre, Preference, or other criteria, or use the Find Music feature to locate a specific track quickly. Drag and drop songs from your Music Library into custom playlists, or let the MusicMatch AutoDJ create personalized playlists per your criteria.

The program lets you view cover art, lyrics, track information, personal notes or artist bios while you listen to songs on your jukebox. Play your customized playlists on your PC, either through your PC sound system, your portable MP3 player, or through your stereo amplifier using plug-and-go specialized audio cables offered by MusicMatch.

This trial version only encodes MP3s up to 96K rather than the MP3 standard of 128K. Register the program for $29 to receive the full working copy.

Check out www.musicmatch.com for more information.

Winamp v2.5 by Nullsoft, Inc (Shareware)

If you haven't installed Winamp on your Windows computer, install this copy, and quickly. One of the first high-fidelity MP3 players, Winamp is fast, highly configurable, and supports MP3, CD, WMA, Audiosoft, Mjuice, MOD, WAV, and other audio formats.

If you're an arty type, slip some decorative software called "skins" onto Winamp to change its appearance. Special software called plug-ins change Winamp's audio and visual effects.

Check out `www.winamp.com` for more information.

Windows and Linux

BladeENC v0.82 (GNU)

This is an encoder — not a player — for creating MP3 files. It's GNU software governed by the GPL license included on the CD. The use of this program is subject to the terms of the GNU General Public License contained on the CD.

For information about MP3 players for this encoder, head for `http://bladeenc.cjb.net`. There, you'll find Windows and Linux graphical front ends that make this product easier to use.

Linux

Xaudio v1.0 (Shareware)

Xaudio creates MP3 decoders for a wide variety of platforms. When a decoder is properly installed, it plays MP3 files.

This particular decoder runs on Linux; registration costs $9.95. For more information, head to `www.xaudio.com/downloads/#linux`.

For more basic Linux information, you can also check out *LINUX For Dummies,* 2nd Edition, by Jon 'Maddog' Hall.

Windows CE

Hum v1.6 (Shareware)

Take a Windows CE palmtop or handheld out of its box, and the little gadget can't play MP3 files. Add this copy of Hum, however, plug in your earphones, and you can listen to your favorite tunes.

Like Nullsoft's WinAmp, Hum supports skins. (Windows CE players get complete coverage in Chapter 21.) Hum sounds best on Casio's Cassiopeia E-100 series. (It's currently the only Windows CE machine with a stereo headphone jack.)

For the latest information, head to `www.utopiasoft.com`.

Macintosh
SoundJam MP V1.01 by Casady & Greene (Trial version)

SoundJam MP is the first full-featured, all-in-one, MP3 player and encoder for the Macintosh. SoundJam MP converts music quickly into high quality MP3s from CD, AIFF, QuickTime, and WAV formats. SoundJam MP takes full advantage of the 10:1 compression of the MP3 format, allowing you to compress your music collection to a fraction of its size while maintaining near-CD quality. With MP3 compression, you can put all your music into a jukebox collection on your Mac.

SoundJam requires Mac OS 7.6.1 or later or Power Macintosh with a 603 processor at 100 MHz or faster; a G3 is recommended.

This copy is a seven-day trial; for more information or to update to the full version, check out www.soundjam.com/.

SoundApp Version 2.6.1 by Norman Franke (Freeware)

It requires at least System 7.0, Apple's Sound Manager 3.1 or greater, the Drag Manager (also known as Macintosh Drag and Drop, part of System 7.5) and at least a Macintosh with a 68020 or a Power Macintosh.

For more information, head to www-cs-students.stanford.edu/~franke/ SoundApp/.

Songs category

What fun is having all these MP3 players if you don't have some music to listen to? The CD also includes 30 sample MP3 files contributed by artists throughout the U.S. and Canada. Table A-1 lists the artists, their songs, and the musical style of each track. Please use these files to try out any of the MP3 players included on this CD.

Some artists list their own Web sites and e-mail addresses. If you find a song you particularly like, visit the artist's site or send them an e-mail message. You might find more MP3 files from that artist, buy one of their CDs, or find out where you can see the artist perform live. Artist Web sites and other cool links are included on the CD. Check out links.htm at the root of the CD.

Table A-1		MP3s on the CD	
Artist	**Song Title**	**Music Style**	**Web Site / Other Info**
Bergers with Mayo	Saw the Lights Go Down from the album "In Real Time"	Up Tempo Blues	Credit Lines/Trademarks: Berger Platters ©1997, Mayo, Held, Berger Platters Writers: Bob Mayo, Little L Music (ASCAP) & Bob Held, Hit List Music (ASCAP) misteral@aol.com; (914) 793-8206
Dead Sexy	Paid off, baby	Electronic Instrumental	Jkiempisty@ earthlink.net; © Dead Sexy
*dream*STATE	Between Realities	Ambient Electronic	www.dreamstate.to; Between Realities on e-SPACE Recordings. Between Realities is a live recording of the 'wave forms' ambient electronic sound-scape installation at the H5 Project in Toronto, Canada. Music and system design by Scott McGregor Moore & Jamie Todd. © *dream*STATE™ 1998. Rapic Eye Music SOCAN. Produced by Scott McGregor Moore.
Dual Eden	Underside	Pop	www.dualeden.com
Fiksate	Eyeball Eclipse	Heavy Rock	jkiempisty@earthlink.net; © Fiksate
Fiksate	Squeeze	Heavy Rock	jkiempisty@earthlink.net; © Fiksate
Harbor Lights	Never Looking Back	Jazz Instrumental	©1996 Harbor Lights Music. All rights reserved.
Harbor Lights	Tonight's Inspiration	Jazz Instrumental	©1996 Harbor Lights Music. All rights reserved.
Harbor Lights	Forever	Jazz Instrumental	©1996 Harbor Lights Music. All rights reserved.
HIT ME	Ready To Live	Pop	www.hitme.net; ©1999 Hit Media.
JOBOJ	The Twiddle	Rock guitar instrumental	www.gtrbque.com; © (P) JOBOJ Music / 1999. JOBOJ: All instruments.
eleven2go	Looks Like Rain	Pop	©1998 Joshua D. Schachterle & eleven2go

Artist	Song Title	Music Style	Web Site / Other Info
eleven2go	Believe	Modern Folk	©1998 Joshua D. Schachterle & eleven2go.
Nate Mahler & Adam Fazio	November	Electronic Instrumental	©Nate Mahler & Adam Fazio
One Trick Pony	Blue Memory	Pop	©1999 Rinda's Rhythm & Rhyme Shop.
One Trick Pony	These Tired Bones	Pop	©1999 Rinda's Rhythm & Rhyme Shop.
Rachael Sage	Sistersong	Pop	spiritwe@aol.com; ©1998 Rachael Sage / Flying Dybbuk Music, BMI.
Robert Guess	Asanka	Avant Garde Electronic	www.rue.org
Robert Guess	Somatron: hamsadhvani	Electronic Instrumental	www.rue.org
Ron Sunshine & Soul Drug	Plant the Seeds	Soul	www.goldenbug.com; © Sunshine (Sjoholm), Golden Bug Publishing, BMI.
Someday	My Generation	Electronic Instrumental	© Adam Fazio
Spac Epod	Marqtty	Avant Garde Electronic	www.rue.org
Splendid	Obscured	Pop	© Tim Artz
Stru Tural	In the Trials	Pop	www.strutural.com; © Stru Tural
Stru Tural	Lancelot of Sorts	Heavy Rock	www.strutural.com; © Stru Tural
The Common	Tuesday	Pop	www.thecommonoline.com; ©1996 The Common
The Hitmen	San Francisco Acid Wave	Techno Dance	© Adam Fazio & Patrick Vigil
the magical attraction of BOOTY	Find a Million Reasons	Pop	www.magicbooty.com; ©1999 Steak Sauce Publishing

(continued)

Table A-1 *(continued)*			
Artist	**Song Title**	**Music Style**	**Web Site / Other Info**
The Painted iD	Home On Moon	Modern Folk	www.thepaintedid.com
Vito Alvaro	Closer Now	Country	www.alvaromusic.com

If You Have Problems (Of the CD Kind)

I tried my best to include MP3 player programs that work on most computers with the minimum system requirements. Alas, your computer may differ, and some programs may not work properly for some reason.

You won't be able to play MP3 files without a fast computer. For the PC world, that usually means a fast 486 or, best yet, a fast Pentium running Windows 95, 98, 2000, or NT 4.

The two likeliest problems are that you don't have enough memory (RAM) for the programs you want to use, or you have other programs running that are affecting installation or running of a program. If you get error messages like `Not enough memory` or `Setup cannot continue`, try one or more of these methods and then try using the software again:

- ✓ **Turn off any antivirus software that you have on your computer.** Installers sometimes mimic virus activity and may make your computer incorrectly believe that it is being infected by a virus.

- ✓ **Close all running programs.** The more programs you're running, the less memory is available to other programs. Installers also typically update files and programs; if you keep other programs running, installation may not work properly.

- ✓ **In Windows, close the CD interface and run demos or installations directly from Windows Explorer.** The interface itself can tie up system memory, or even conflict with certain kinds of interactive demos. Use Windows Explorer to browse the files on the CD and launch installers or demos.

- ✓ **Have your local computer store add more RAM to your computer.** This is, admittedly, a drastic and somewhat expensive step. However, if you have a Windows 95 PC or a Mac OS computer with a PowerPC chip, adding more memory can really help the speed of your computer and enable more programs to run at the same time.

If you still have trouble installing the items from the CD, please call the IDG Books Worldwide Customer Service phone number: 800-762-2974 (outside the U.S.: 317-596-5430).

Appendix B
Glossary

● ●

Access time: The number of milliseconds a drive takes to find and grab a piece of information. Buy a low access time for the best recording.

ADC (Analog-to-Digital Converter): A sound card that's able to record sound.

AIFF: Short for Audio Interchange File Format, it's the Macintosh format for digital sounds.

Analog: Naturally moving things, like waves, sounds, and motion — things that computers turn into numbers for storage. (See also *Digital*.)

Analog-to-Digital Converter (ADC): A device that records sounds and converts them into numbers.

Bootleg: Another word for an illegally traded or recorded file. Bootleggers are also known as pirates.

Burning: The process of writing files onto a CD with a CD-R.

Cardioid microphone: Microphones that pick up sound mostly from in front of them. (See also *Omnidirectional microphone*.)

CD Digital Audio (CD-DA): A CD-ROM is in this mode when it's playing a musical CD. (Also called *Red Book*, for some corporate reason.)

CD-DA (Compact Disc Digital Audio): Also known as Red Book or CD-Audio, this is simply a music CD.

CD-Quality sound: A phrase describing sound recorded at 16 bits, 44.1 kHz. (That's the rate used to record your musical CDs.)

CD-R: Short for "CD Recordable," these discs can be written to as well as read from. Because they can't be erased and reused, they're also called WORM discs, short for Write Once, Read Many.

CD-ROM: Compact Disc Read-Only Memory. A fancy name for a CD.

CD-RW: Short for CD Rewritable, you can erase and reuse these discs. Although all CD-RW drives work with both CD-R and CD-RW discs, not all CD-R drives work with CD-RW discs.

Codec: A way to compress sound or video into a file and then decompress it when playing it back. MP3 files use different codecs to compress files to the MP3 standard.

Compression: A way of making files take up less space.

Condenser microphone: These battery-powered guys work best when recording sensitive sounds like pianos and whispers.

Copyright: A legal term establishing ownership rights of a created work. In the case of a song, a copyright can be established for the tune's composer, the lyrics, and the band's performance of the song.

DAC (Digital-to-Analog Converter): A sound card that can play sounds stored in a file.

DAM CD: Short for Digital Automatic Music, DAM CDs are used by the MP3.com Web site to stuff both MP3 songs and standard CD audio format songs onto the same CD. As a result, the CDs play on your regular stereo, and you can easily copy MP3 files to your hard drive or into MP3 players.

Data buffer: A way to temporarily store information, leading to smoother transfers. Streaming sound often uses a buffer; increase the buffer size if the sound breaks up upon arrival.

Daughterboard: A small card that pops onto a sound card to give it new capabilities. For example, plugging a digital daughterboard onto a Sound Blaster Live adds digital in/out capabilities.

Decibel: A way to measure sound.

Decoder: A program that reads an encoded file and decompresses it for use. Winamp, for instance, contains a decoder for playing MP3 songs.

Digital: Computerized things; collections of numbers to represent pictures, sounds, text, or video. (See also *Analog*.)

Distortion: Although electric guitarists spend hundreds of dollars trying to create it, most sound card owners consider it unwanted noise.

DSP (Digital Signal Processor): A bit of computer mechanics for adding echoes, reverb, and other effects to sound.

Dubbing: Touching up recorded material by adding new pieces of audio.

Dynamic microphone: The best mike for recording loud, powerful stuff, such as heavy metal bands or arguments on Larry King's show.

Encoding: Compressing a file. (When you create an MP3, you're encoding the sound.)

Equalization: The art of changing a song's recorded frequencies to enhance its sound.

Filter: To remove an undesirable quality, such as removing a hiss from a recording.

Freeware: Programs given away to the general public.

Frequency: Without getting complicated, an annoying mosquito whines at a *high* frequency; a foghorn rumbles at a *low* frequency.

FTP: Short for File Transfer Protocol, it's a simple way to transfer files online.

GM (General MIDI): A MIDI numbering sequence with all the instrument sounds lined up in a designated order, starting with pianos and ending with sound effects.

High Sierra: A format for placing files and directories on CD-ROM so that DOS can read them. Also known as *ISO 9660.*

ID3 tag: A space at the end of a sound file for adding information about the song: the artist, title, band name, genre, year, and other information. Constantly in flux, the ID3 tag has undergone several changes to include lyrics and artwork.

IRQ (Interrupt Request): A computerized "tap on the shoulder" used by sound cards when they need the CPU's attention. Your computer has only a few of these "shoulders," and cards trying to use the same IRQ usually won't work right.

ISO-9660: A format for placing files and directories on CD-ROM so that DOS can read them. Also known as *High Sierra.*

Jewel box: The cheap little plastic box that CDs come packaged in.

Jukebox: Large CD-ROM drives that hold several CDs, thereby letting you switch among discs easily and expensively. Not to be confused with RealAudio's *Jukebox* — software for creating and playing MP3s.

Leech: A semi-derogatory description for people who log on to a Web site and download all the available MP3 files without posting any in return. Mostly used by pirate sites.

Lossy compression: Compressed files like MP3, which cut out some of the sound in order to save space.

MIDI (Musical Instrument Digital Interface): A way to store music as a series of computerized instructions; the resulting file can be played back on a wide variety of computers and electronic instruments.

MP3: A method of compressing audio files into one-tenth of their normal size while still keeping near CD-quality sound. MP3 stores about one minute of audio in 1MB of space. (See also *MPEG 3, Layer 1*.)

MPEG: The abbreviation for the Moving Picture Expert Group. Pronounced M-peg, it's a group of standards used for coding sound and video compressed digital format.

MPEG 3, Layer 1: The official term the Moving Picture Expert Group chose for MP3.

Multisession: A multisession CD-R drive lets you add data to a disc on different occasions. (Older CD-R drives made you burn all your data onto the disc in one session.)

Multi-voice: Ability to mimic more than one instrument; found in most cards.

Newsgroups: International discussion areas based on a single topic. Outlook Express locates, reads, and downloads files posted on newsgroups. (The alt.binaries.sounds.mp3 is a large outlet for song piracy.)

Omnidirectional microphone: Microphones that pick up sound from all around them, not just in front. (See also *Cardioid microphone, Dynamic microphone*.)

Orange Book: Standard for WORM format, also known as *Write Once Read Many* CDs. (Big companies use them to back up their boring computerized paperwork.)

Philips: A huge company that developed CD technology with Sony.

Phono cable: Cable used mostly for connecting audio equipment and sound cards.

Playlist: A list of MP3 files and their location; Winamp reads the playlist and begins playing the songs.

Plug-in: A file that controls part of Winamp when placed in Winamp's plug-ins directory. One plug-in displays flashy graphics onscreen that twitch in time to the tunes. Another fades songs into each other as they play. Head for www.winamp.com to see them all.

Public domain: Works that may be freely copied and distributed. They enter the public domain when the copyright expires or the copyright holder gives his or her material to the public domain.

RCA audio cable: Commonly found on most home stereos, this cable ends with a little round metal "hat" that slides onto a little round metal "head."

RealAudio: Another popular sound format, but usually used for streaming — Webcasting — sounds over the Internet.

RIAA: Short for the Recording Industry Association of America, the RIAA is a trade group of record industry companies formed to foster "a business and legal climate that supports and promotes our members' creative and financial vitality around the world." Visit them at `www.riaa.com`.

Red Book: Nothing to do with the magazine, this term simply means a CD with music (like a Rolling Stones album) and no computer programs. Also means Compact Disc Digital Audio, or CD-DA.

Ripper: A program that digitally copies an audio CD's contents onto your hard drive where they can be encoded into MP3 files.

Sampling rates: When computers listen to a sound or watch a video to stick the information into a file, they're *sampling* the information. The *higher* the sampling rate, the better the quality, the closer the computer pays attention to the information, and the bigger the resulting file.

SCSI: Small Computer System Interface. A way to link several computer gadgets together.

SCSI port: A special connector required by some CD-ROM drives, it comes on a special SCSI card.

SCSI/2: Same as SCSI, but with a new and improved format.

Skins: Cosmetic enhancers for Winamp. Insert a skin file into Winamp's skins file and select it to give Winamp a woodgrain appearance, or cover it with pictures of rock stars.

Shareware: Programs given away under the condition that you'll buy it if you like it. Evaluation times differ, but the cost is usually under $40.

SHOUTcast: An Internet radio station Web site founded by the creators of Winamp. Listen to it at `www.shoutcast.com`.

Sound Blaster-compatible: This means the card works with any software written for the SoundBlaster card. (That's about 90 percent of the programs on the market.)

Synthesized: Sounds created by computer circuitry.

Tray-loading: A type of CD-ROM that sticks out a tray to accept CDs, like a tongue asking for a mint.

Tweaking: Fiddling with knobs until everything finally looks right.

VBR: Short for Variable Bit Rate, VBR encodes song at variable rate, using lots of encoding for sensitive parts and little encoding for pauses in songs. Not all MP3 players (including Creative Labs' Nomad) can handle VBR encoding.

VQF: Short for Vector Quantization Format, it's another freebie codec some claim works better than MP3. It's not compatible with MP3, however, and works a computer harder when encoding and decoding.

Voice: Another word for a musical instrument sound. A 20-voice synthesizer won't necessarily produce 20 instruments, however; many cards mix two or more voices when creating chords and complex instrument sounds.

Winamp: The most popular MP3 player by far, Winamp offers regular updates, easy customization, and great sound. Check it out at www.winamp.com.

Windows CE: A miniature version of Windows that runs on tiny computers. Utopiasoft's HUM software plays MP3 files on Windows CE; unfortunately, only the Casio Cassiopeia currently offers stereo sound.

Windows Media Audio: Abbreviated as WMA, it's the Microsoft response to MP3. Some say it sounds better, others say it sounds worse. Nevertheless, WMA files are smaller than MP3 files.

Yellow Book: A standard for compact discs containing computer programs and data.

Index

Notes

Notes

Notes

Notes

IDG Books Worldwide, Inc., End-User License Agreement

READ THIS. You should carefully read these terms and conditions before opening the software packet(s) included with this book ("Book"). This is a license agreement ("Agreement") between you and IDG Books Worldwide, Inc. ("IDGB"). By opening the accompanying software packet(s), you acknowledge that you have read and accept the following terms and conditions. If you do not agree and do not want to be bound by such terms and conditions, promptly return the Book and the unopened software packet(s) to the place you obtained them for a full refund.

1. **License Grant.** IDGB grants to you (either an individual or entity) a nonexclusive license to use one copy of the enclosed software program(s) (collectively, the "Software") solely for your own personal or business purposes on a single computer (whether a standard computer or a workstation component of a multiuser network). The Software is in use on a computer when it is loaded into temporary memory (RAM) or installed into permanent memory (hard disk, CD-ROM, or other storage device). IDGB reserves all rights not expressly granted herein.

2. **Ownership.** IDGB is the owner of all right, title, and interest, including copyright, in and to the compilation of the Software recorded on the disk(s) or CD-ROM ("Software Media"). Copyright to the individual programs recorded on the Software Media is owned by the author or other authorized copyright owner of each program. Ownership of the Software and all proprietary rights relating thereto remain with IDGB and its licensers.

3. **Restrictions on Use and Transfer.**

   (a) You may only (i) make one copy of the Software for backup or archival purposes, or (ii) transfer the Software to a single hard disk, provided that you keep the original for backup or archival purposes. You may not (i) rent or lease the Software, (ii) copy or reproduce the Software through a LAN or other network system or through any computer subscriber system or bulletin-board system, or (iii) modify, adapt, or create derivative works based on the Software.

   (b) You may not reverse engineer, decompile, or disassemble the Software. You may transfer the Software and user documentation on a permanent basis, provided that the transferee agrees to accept the terms and conditions of this Agreement and you retain no copies. If the Software is an update or has been updated, any transfer must include the most recent update and all prior versions.

4. **Restrictions on Use of Individual Programs.** You must follow the individual requirements and restrictions detailed for each individual program in Appendix A of this Book. These limitations are also contained in the individual license agreements recorded on the Software Media. These limitations may include a requirement that after using the program for a specified period of time, the user must pay a registration fee or discontinue use. By opening the Software packet(s), you will be agreeing to abide by the licenses and restrictions for these individual programs that are detailed in Appendix A and on the Software Media. None of the material on this Software Media or listed in this Book may ever be redistributed, in original or modified form, for commercial purposes.

5. **Limited Warranty.**

   (a) IDGB warrants that the Software and Software Media are free from defects in materials and workmanship under normal use for a period of sixty (60) days from the date of purchase of this Book. If IDGB receives notification within the warranty period of defects in materials or workmanship, IDGB will replace the defective Software Media.

   (b) **IDGB AND THE AUTHOR OF THE BOOK DISCLAIM ALL OTHER WARRANTIES, EXPRESS OR IMPLIED, INCLUDING WITHOUT LIMITATION IMPLIED WARRANTIES OF MERCHANTABILITY AND FITNESS FOR A PARTICULAR PURPOSE, WITH RESPECT TO THE SOFTWARE, THE PROGRAMS, THE SOURCE CODE CONTAINED THEREIN, AND/OR THE TECHNIQUES DESCRIBED IN THIS BOOK. IDGB DOES NOT WARRANT THAT THE FUNCTIONS CONTAINED IN THE SOFTWARE WILL MEET YOUR REQUIREMENTS OR THAT THE OPERATION OF THE SOFTWARE WILL BE ERROR FREE.**

   (c) This limited warranty gives you specific legal rights, and you may have other rights that vary from jurisdiction to jurisdiction.

6. **Remedies.**

   (a) IDGB's entire liability and your exclusive remedy for defects in materials and workmanship shall be limited to replacement of the Software Media, which may be returned to IDGB with a copy of your receipt at the following address: Software Media Fulfillment Department, Attn.: *MP3 For Dummies*, IDG Books Worldwide, Inc., 7260 Shadeland Station, Ste. 100, Indianapolis, IN 46256, or call 800-762-2974. Please allow three to four weeks for delivery. This Limited Warranty is void if failure of the Software Media has resulted from accident, abuse, or misapplication. Any replacement Software Media will be warranted for the remainder of the original warranty period or thirty (30) days, whichever is longer.

   (b) In no event shall IDGB or the author be liable for any damages whatsoever (including without limitation damages for loss of business profits, business interruption, loss of business information, or any other pecuniary loss) arising from the use of or inability to use the Book or the Software, even if IDGB has been advised of the possibility of such damages.

   (c) Because some jurisdictions do not allow the exclusion or limitation of liability for consequential or incidental damages, the above limitation or exclusion may not apply to you.

7. **U.S. Government Restricted Rights.** Use, duplication, or disclosure of the Software by the U.S. Government is subject to restrictions stated in paragraph (c)(1)(ii) of the Rights in Technical Data and Computer Software clause of DFARS 252.227-7013, and in subparagraphs (a) through (d) of the Commercial Computer–Restricted Rights clause at FAR 52.227-19, and in similar clauses in the NASA FAR supplement, when applicable.

8. **General.** This Agreement constitutes the entire understanding of the parties and revokes and supersedes all prior agreements, oral or written, between them and may not be modified or amended except in a writing signed by both parties hereto that specifically refers to this Agreement. This Agreement shall take precedence over any other documents that may be in conflict herewith. If any one or more provisions contained in this Agreement are held by any court or tribunal to be invalid, illegal, or otherwise unenforceable, each and every other provision shall remain in full force and effect.

GNU GENERAL PUBLIC LICENSE

Version 2, June 1991

Preamble

The licenses for most software are designed to take away your freedom to share and change it. By contrast, the GNU General Public License is intended to guarantee your freedom to share and change free software — to make sure the software is free for all its users. This General Public License applies to most of the Free Software Foundation's software and to any other program whose authors commit to using it. (Some other Free Software Foundation software is covered by the GNU Library General Public License instead.) You can apply it to your programs, too.

When we speak of free software, we are referring to freedom, not price. Our General Public Licenses are designed to make sure that you have the freedom to distribute copies of free software (and charge for this service if you wish), that you receive source code or can get it if you want it, that you can change the software or use pieces of it in new free programs; and that you know you can do these things.

To protect your rights, we need to make restrictions that forbid anyone to deny you these rights or to ask you to surrender the rights. These restrictions translate to certain responsibilities for you if you distribute copies of the software, or if you modify it.

For example, if you distribute copies of such a program, whether gratis or for a fee, you must give the recipients all the rights that you have. You must make sure that they, too, receive or can get the source code. And you must show them these terms so they know their rights.

We protect your rights with two steps: (1) copyright the software, and (2) offer you this license which gives you legal permission to copy, distribute and/or modify the software.

Also, for each author's protection and ours, we want to make certain that everyone understands that there is no warranty for this free software. If the software is modified by someone else and passed on, we want its recipients to know that what they have is not the original, so that any problems introduced by others will not reflect on the original authors' reputations.

Finally, any free program is threatened constantly by software patents. We wish to avoid the danger that redistributors of a free program will individually obtain patent licenses, in effect making the program proprietary. To prevent this, we have made it clear that any patent must be licensed for everyone's free use or not licensed at all.

The precise terms and conditions for copying, distribution and modification follow.

GNU GENERAL PUBLIC LICENSE

TERMS AND CONDITIONS FOR COPYING, DISTRIBUTION AND MODIFICATION

0. This License applies to any program or other work which contains a notice placed by the copyright holder saying it may be distributed under the terms of this General Public License. The "Program", below, refers to any such program or work, and a "work based on the Program" means either the Program or any derivative work under copyright law: that is to say, a work containing the Program or a portion of it, either verbatim or with modifications and/or translated into another language. (Hereinafter, translation is included without limitation in the term "modification".) Each licensee is addressed as "you".

    Activities other than copying, distribution and modification are not covered by this License; they are outside its scope. The act of running the Program is not restricted, and the output from the Program is covered only if its contents constitute a work based on the Program (independent of having been made by running the Program). Whether that is true depends on what the Program does.

1. You may copy and distribute verbatim copies of the Program's source code as you receive it, in any medium, provided that you conspicuously and appropriately publish on each copy an appropriate copyright notice and disclaimer of warranty; keep intact all the notices that refer to this License and to the absence of any warranty; and give any other recipients of the Program a copy of this License along with the Program.

    You may charge a fee for the physical act of transferring a copy, and you may at your option offer warranty protection in exchange for a fee.

2. You may modify your copy or copies of the Program or any portion of it, thus forming a work based on the Program, and copy and distribute such modifications or work under the terms of Section 1 above, provided that you also meet all of these conditions:

    a) You must cause the modified files to carry prominent notices stating that you changed the files and the date of any change.

    b) You must cause any work that you distribute or publish, that in whole or in part contains or is derived from the Program or any part thereof, to be licensed as a whole at no charge to all third parties under the terms of this License.

    c) If the modified program normally reads commands interactively when run, you must cause it, when started running for such interactive use in the most ordinary way, to print or display an announcement including an appropriate copyright notice and a notice that there is no warranty (or else, saying that you provide a warranty) and that users may redistribute the program under these conditions, and telling the user how to view a copy of this License. (Exception: if the Program itself is interactive but does not normally print such an announcement, your work based on the Program is not required to print an announcement.)

    These requirements apply to the modified work as a whole. If identifiable sections of that work are not derived from the Program, and can be reasonably considered independent and separate works in themselves, then this License, and its terms, do not apply to those sections when you distribute them as separate works. But when you distribute the same sections as part of a whole which is a work based on the Program, the distribution of the whole must be on the terms of this License, whose permissions for other licensees extend to the entire whole, and thus to each and every part regardless of who wrote it.

Thus, it is not the intent of this section to claim rights or contest your rights to work written entirely by you; rather, the intent is to exercise the right to control the distribution of derivative or collective works based on the Program.

In addition, mere aggregation of another work not based on the Program with the Program (or with a work based on the Program) on a volume of a storage or distribution medium does not bring the other work under the scope of this License.

3. You may copy and distribute the Program (or a work based on it, under Section 2) in object code or executable form under the terms of Sections 1 and 2 above provided that you also do one of the following:

a) Accompany it with the complete corresponding machine-readable source code, which must be distributed under the terms of Sections 1 and 2 above on a medium customarily used for software interchange; or,

b) Accompany it with a written offer, valid for at least three years, to give any third party, for a charge no more than your cost of physically performing source distribution, a complete machine-readable copy of the corresponding source code, to be distributed under the terms of Sections 1 and 2 above on a medium customarily used for software interchange; or,

c) Accompany it with the information you received as to the offer to distribute corresponding source code. (This alternative is allowed only for noncommercial distribution and only if you received the program in object code or executable form with such an offer, in accord with Subsection b above.)

The source code for a work means the preferred form of the work for making modifications to it. For an executable work, complete source code means all the source code for all modules it contains, plus any associated interface definition files, plus the scripts used to control compilation and installation of the executable. However, as a special exception, the source code distributed need not include anything that is normally distributed (in either source or binary form) with the major components (compiler, kernel, and so on) of the operating system on which the executable runs, unless that component itself accompanies the executable.

If distribution of executable or object code is made by offering access to copy from a designated place, then offering equivalent access to copy the source code from the same place counts as distribution of the source code, even though third parties are not compelled to copy the source along with the object code.

4. You may not copy, modify, sublicense, or distribute the Program except as expressly provided under this License. Any attempt otherwise to copy, modify, sublicense or distribute the Program is void, and will automatically terminate your rights under this License. However, parties who have received copies, or rights, from you under this License will not have their licenses terminated so long as such parties remain in full compliance.

5. You are not required to accept this License, since you have not signed it. However, nothing else grants you permission to modify or distribute the Program or its derivative works. These actions are prohibited by law if you do not accept this License. Therefore, by modifying or distributing the Program (or any work based on the Program), you indicate your acceptance of this License to do so, and all its terms and conditions for copying, distributing or modifying the Program or works based on it.

6. Each time you redistribute the Program (or any work based on the Program), the recipient automatically receives a license from the original licensor to copy, distribute or modify the Program subject to these terms and conditions. You may not impose any further restrictions on the recipients' exercise of the rights granted herein. You are not responsible for enforcing compliance by third parties to this License.

7. If, as a consequence of a court judgment or allegation of patent infringement or for any other reason (not limited to patent issues), conditions are imposed on you (whether by court order, agreement or otherwise) that contradict the conditions of this License, they do not excuse you from the conditions of this License. If you cannot distribute so as to satisfy simultaneously your obligations under this License and any other pertinent obligations, then as a consequence you may not distribute the Program at all. For example, if a patent license would not permit royalty-free redistribution of the Program by all those who receive copies directly or indirectly through you, then the only way you could satisfy both it and this License would be to refrain entirely from distribution of the Program.

   If any portion of this section is held invalid or unenforceable under any particular circumstance, the balance of the section is intended to apply and the section as a whole is intended to apply in other circumstances.

   It is not the purpose of this section to induce you to infringe any patents or other property right claims or to contest validity of any such claims; this section has the sole purpose of protecting the integrity of the free software distribution system, which is implemented by public license practices. Many people have made generous contributions to the wide range of software distributed through that system in reliance on consistent application of that system; it is up to the author/donor to decide if he or she is willing to distribute software through any other system and a licensee cannot impose that choice.

   This section is intended to make thoroughly clear what is believed to be a consequence of the rest of this License.

8. If the distribution and/or use of the Program is restricted in certain countries either by patents or by copyrighted interfaces, the original copyright holder who places the Program under this License may add an explicit geographical distribution limitation excluding those countries, so that distribution is permitted only in or among countries not thus excluded. In such case, this License incorporates the limitation as if written in the body of this License.

9. The Free Software Foundation may publish revised and/or new versions of the General Public License from time to time. Such new versions will be similar in spirit to the present version, but may differ in detail to address new problems or concerns.

   Each version is given a distinguishing version number. If the Program specifies a version number of this License which applies to it and "any later version", you have the option of following the terms and conditions either of that version or of any later version published by the Free Software Foundation. If the Program does not specify a version number of this License, you may choose any version ever published by the Free Software Foundation.

10. If you wish to incorporate parts of the Program into other free programs whose distribution conditions are different, write to the author to ask for permission. For software which is copyrighted by the Free Software Foundation, write to the Free Software Foundation; we sometimes make exceptions for this. Our decision will be guided by the two goals of preserving the free status of all derivatives of our free software and of promoting the sharing and reuse of software generally.

If the program is interactive, make it output a short notice like this when it starts in an interactive mode:

Gnomovision version 69, Copyright (C) 19yy name of author

Gnomovision comes with ABSOLUTELY NO WARRANTY; for details type `show w'.

This is free software, and you are welcome to redistribute it under certain conditions; type `show c' for details.

The hypothetical commands `show w' and `show c' should show the appropriate parts of the General Public License. Of course, the commands you use may be called something other than `show w' and `show c'; they could even be mouse-clicks or menu whatever suits your program.

You should also get your employer (if you work as a programmer) or your school, if any, to sign a "copyright disclaimer" for the program, if necessary. Here is a sample; alter the names:

Yoyodyne, Inc., hereby disclaims all copyright interest in the program

`Gnomovision' (which makes passes at compilers) written by James Hacker.

<signature of Ty Coon>, 1 April 1989

Ty Coon, President of Vice

This General Public License does not permit incorporating your program into proprietary programs. If your program is a subroutine library, you may consider it more useful to permit linking proprietary applications with the library. If this is what you want to do, use the GNU Library General Public License instead of this License.

Installation Instructions

To install the items from the CD to your hard drive, follow these steps:

1. **Insert the CD into your computer's CD-ROM drive.**

2. **Windows 95/98 users: Click Run from the Start menu.**

3. **In the dialog box that appears, type** D:\SETUP.EXE.

   Replace *D* with the proper drive letter if your CD-ROM drive uses a different letter. (If you don't know the letter, see how your CD-ROM drive is listed under My Computer in Windows 95/98.)

4. **Click OK.**

   A License Agreement window appears.

5. **Read through the license agreement, nod your head, and then click the Agree button if you want to use the CD — after you click Agree, you'll never be bothered by the License Agreement window again.**

   The CD interface Welcome screen appears. The interface is a little program that shows you what's on the CD and coordinates installing the programs and running the demos. The interface basically enables you to click a button or two to make things happen.

6. **Click anywhere on the Welcome screen to enter the interface.**

   Now you are getting to the action. This next screen lists categories for the software on the CD.

7. **To view the items within a category, just click the category's name.**

   A list of programs in the category appears.

8. **For more information about a program, click the program's name.**

   Be sure to read the information that appears. Sometimes a program has its own system requirements or requires you to do a few tricks on your computer before you can install or run the program, and this screen tells you what you may need to do, if necessary.

9. **If you don't want to install the program, click the Back button to return to the previous screen.**

   You can always return to the previous screen by clicking the Back button. This feature allows you to browse the different categories and products and decide what you want to install.

10. **To install a program, click the appropriate Install button.**

    The CD interface drops to the background while the CD installs the program you chose.

11. **To install other items, repeat Steps 7 through 10.**

12. **After you finish installing programs, click the Quit button to close the interface.**

    You can eject the CD now. Carefully place it back in the plastic jacket of the book for safekeeping.

For instructions on using the CD with a Macintosh, please see Appendix A.

IDG BOOKS WORLDWIDE BOOK REGISTRATION

We want to hear from you!

Visit **http://my2cents.dummies.com** to register this book and tell us how you liked it!

- ✔ Get entered in our monthly prize giveaway.

- ✔ Give us feedback about this book — tell us what you like best, what you like least, or maybe what you'd like to ask the author and us to change!

- ✔ Let us know any other *...For Dummies*® topics that interest you.

Your feedback helps us determine what books to publish, tells us what coverage to add as we revise our books, and lets us know whether we're meeting your needs as a *...For Dummies* reader. You're our most valuable resource, and what you have to say is important to us!

Not on the Web yet? It's easy to get started with *Dummies 101*®: *The Internet For Windows*® *98* or *The Internet For Dummies*®, 6th Edition, at local retailers everywhere.

Or let us know what you think by sending us a letter at the following address:

...For Dummies Book Registration
Dummies Press
7260 Shadeland Station, Suite 100
Indianapolis, IN 46256-3917
Fax 317-596-5498

™
...FOR DUMMIES

BESTSELLING BOOK SERIES